Bronze Age Settlement in the Welsh Marches

John Halstead

BAR British Series 384
2005

Published in 2016 by
BAR Publishing, Oxford

BAR British Series 384

Bronze Age Settlement in the Welsh Marches

© J Halstead and the Publisher 2005

ISBN 9781841716886 paperback
ISBN 9781407320311 e-format
DOI https://doi.org/10.30861/9781841716886
A catalogue record for this book is available from the British Library

BAR Publishing is the trading name of British Archaeological Reports (Oxford) Ltd.
British Archaeological Reports was first incorporated in 1974 to publish the BAR
Series, International and British. In 1992 Hadrian Books Ltd became part of the BAR
group. This volume was originally published by Archaeopress in conjunction with
British Archaeological Reports (Oxford) Ltd / Hadrian Books Ltd, the Series
principal publisher, in 2005. This present volume is published by BAR Publishing,
2016.

BAR

PUBLISHING

BAR titles are available from:

    BAR Publishing
    122 Banbury Rd, Oxford, OX2 7BP, UK
EMAIL   info@barpublishing.com
PHONE +44 (0)1865 310431
FAX   +44 (0)1865 316916
    www.barpublishing.com

Summary

This study examines Bronze Age settlement patterns between c.2500 and 750 BC in the Welsh Marches region of Britain. The context of Early Bronze Age settlement is examined closely as a response to a general lack of evidence for settlement in this period. The concept of residential mobility in the Early Bronze Age is examined by assessing the degree of longevity apparent in the occupation of specific locations and the relationship between settlement and other activities in the landscape. The extent of change in the form and pattern of settlement, apparent in other regions of Britain from the mid-second millennium BC, is also examined in order to assess the degree of continuity and discontinuity in settlement patterns in the Welsh Marches during the Bronze Age.

The study has highlighted the potential for continuity in settlement patterns during the Bronze Age and that changes in settlement form may not necessarily reflect widespread settlement dislocation. It has been suggested that residential mobility may have existed in the early to mid-second millennium BC, but that this does not necessarily reflect a wholly transient pattern of residency. The study has served to clarify the context of Bronze Age settlement in the region, but also emphasises the need for further research and debate upon the subject.

Acknowledgements

I would like to thank the following people for their significant contributions, help and advice towards producing this study. Paul Garwood, Institute of Archaeology and Antiquity, University of Birmingham, and Professor Chris Pare, (formerly University of Birmingham) for all their help and advice with the project in its original format as an MPhil. Dr. Peter Northover, Department of Materials, University of Oxford, for providing me with an additional database of Bronze Age metalwork finds for the study area. Mr Jamie Peart, Department of Geography, University of Birmingham, for all his assistance with relevant maps for the study. Dan Garner, formerly Gifford and Partners, Chester, for providing pre-publication information on excavation results at Manchester Airport Second Runway. Dr. Jan Harding, University of Newcastle Upon Tyne, for his comments on the original text.

Contents

List of illustrations……………..................……iv

1. Themes of Bronze Age settlement in Britain

Identifying Bronze Age settlement in Britain................ 1

The Bronze Age background.. 1

The study of Bronze Age settlement in Britain............. 3

Themes in Bronze Age settlement studies……………………………................... 4
.

The study area……………..................…………… 6

Principal Themes to be addressed…………................ 8

Data collection methods... 10

Agenda……………..................…………………11

2. The Physical Environment of the study area; past and present... 12

3. Settlement in the Early Bronze Age

Background: Early Bronze Age settlement in Britain.. 16

Settlement sites in the study area: location and longevity.. 19

The distribution of artefacts in the study area and their relationship with settlement locales................ 25

The relationship between monuments, artefact distributions and settlement..30

Interpreting the archaeological record: the context of Early Bronze Age settlement in the region...............30

4. Settlement in the Middle Bronze Age

Background: Middle Bronze Age settlement in Britain..33

Settlement evidence from the study area.......................33

Burnt mounds and Middle Bronze Age settlement..39

The distribution of Middle Bronze Age metalwork in the study area...41

Continuity during the mid-second millennium BC..45

5. Settlement in the Late Bronze Age

Background: the emergence of defended enclosures..47

The identification of Late Bronze Age enclosures in the Welsh Marches.................................... 47

The function of Late Bronze Age enclosures.................52

Production, exchange and deposition of metalwork in the Late Bronze Age....................................53

Late Bronze Age metalwork and enclosed settlement sites.. 54

Unenclosed settlements in the study area.....................56

The distribution of metal objects in the wider landscape of the study area...60

The emergence of centres of prestige within a settled landscape..63

6. Conclusions: interpreting Bronze Age settlement in the Welsh Marches................................65

Bibliography..71

Appendix: calibrated radiocarbon dates..................81

List of Illustrations

Fig.1   The extent of the study area............................7

Fig.2   General topography of the study area...........13

Fig.3   Drift geology and best quality agricultural land around Wrexham....................................14

Fig.4   Calibrated radiocarbon dates from burials at ring ditches and round barrows in the study area..18

Fig.5   The distribution of Early Bronze Age metalwork, settlement sites, funerary monuments and mines in the study area.......20

Fig.6   Early Bronze Age settlement sites, funerary monuments and possible copper mines in Cheshire..21

Fig.7   Radiocarbon dates from settlement sites in the study area and metalwork chronology....22

Fig.8   Location of detailed drift geology study.......24

Fig.9   Round barrows, Early Bronze Age metalwork and drift geology in north-west Shropshire, south-west Cheshire and north-east Wales..26

Fig.10   Examples of Early Bronze Age metalwork in river valley contexts..................................28

Fig.11   Numbers of Early Bronze Age metalwork finds in relation to increasing altitudes above OD..29

Fig.12   The distance between Early Bronze Age metal tools and funerary monuments in the study area..31

Fig.13   The distribution of Middle Bronze Age metalwork, settlement sites, burnt mounds and mines in the study area...........................34

Fig.14   Middle Bronze Age round-house, burnt mound and metal artefacts in the Upper Severn Valley, Powys...................................36

Fig.15   The location of Middle and Late Bronze Age settlement sites at Rhuddlan, Denbighshire and Thornwell Farm, Monmouthshire...38

Fig.16   The distribution of Middle Bronze Age metalwork, burnt mounds and drift geology in north-west Shropshire, south-west Cheshire and north-east Wales......................42

Fig.17   The altitude of Middle Bronze Age tools in the study area...43

Fig.18   Percentages of recorded hoards within Early Middle and Late Bronze Age metalwork assemblages in the study area......................48

Fig.19   The distribution of Late Bronze Age metalwork, hillfort enclosures, settlement sites and mines in the study area...................49

Fig.20   Late Bronze Age settlement sites and enclosures in the study area...........................50

Fig.21   Late Bronze Age metalwork, hillfort sites and drift geology in north-west Shropshire, south-west Cheshire and north-east Wales....57

Fig.22   The altitude of Bronze Age metal finds in the study area...60

1. Themes of Bronze Age settlement in Britain

Identifying Bronze Age settlement in Britain

The Bronze Age in Britain is considered to date between c.2500 and 750 BC (Needham 1996, 125-136). This period represents a break with earlier societies, which is characterised by the adoption of copper and bronze metallurgy and new modes of burial. Despite large numbers of monuments and artefacts having been recorded, the evidence for settlement during the period is comparatively rare. Where settlement has been identified for the late third and early second millennium BC it is often particularly ephemeral in nature. It is not until the mid-second millennium BC that more fixed nodes of occupation are recognisable in the archaeological record, although these show particular regional bias and are not widely recorded in Britain. Enclosures sited in defensive positions have been dated to the late second millennium BC and have been more extensively recorded, yet their function within wider patterns of settlement is not fully understood.

Greater archaeological attention has traditionally been paid to the excavation and interpretation of funerary and ceremonial monuments and the typological study of associated grave goods and metalwork. Investigation into Bronze Age settlement has largely been secondary to these studies as a result of its lack of definition in the landscape and has only been regularly identified when associated with clearly visible enclosures or monuments. Further areas of settlement have been identified through the excavation of more clearly defined settlement phases dating to later periods, or during large-scale landscape evaluations.

Evidence for Bronze Age settlement is limited for the early to mid-second millennium BC, particularly beyond southern England. Therefore it is important to establish the landscape context of known settlement sites if further examples are to be identified in the future. Examining the distribution of contemporary finds and monuments can be used to place a known settlement pattern into a wider social and economic context. The distribution of artefacts and monuments may also broaden the understanding of the use of contrasting landscape zones within patterns of settlement, and in turn be used to extrapolate limited evidence for nodes of residency.

It is necessary to establish the context of settlement, both through the location of domestic structures and the distribution of artefacts and monuments, in order to assess the extent of continuity and discontinuity during the Bronze Age period. Dislocation in the pattern of settlement and changing relationships with places in the landscape may reflect discontinuity in social and economic relations. Therefore it is important to assess the degree of change in the location and form of settlement during the Bronze Age.

The study of Bronze Age settlement is particularly relevant for regions where the subject has received limited archaeological attention. Therefore Bronze Age settlement has been examined in the Welsh Marches region, which has a profusion of monuments and artefacts datable to the period, but where evidence for Bronze Age settlement is limited and not fully understood. The evidence for Bronze Age settlement in the study area is measured against the principal arguments for change in residency patterns and forms which have largely been applied to southern England. The study of Bronze Age settlement in the Welsh Marches can widen the discussion of Bronze Age settlement beyond the core areas that have received the greatest archaeological attention on the subject and assess the applicability of perceived residency patterns to other regions.

The following overview of significant developments in funerary practices and the production, distribution and consumption of metalwork is intended to provide a background to the study of Bronze Age settlement within the context of monument and artefact distributions and highlight the potential for social and economic change in the period. The succeeding section introduces the main themes in Bronze Age settlement studies and their application to the Welsh Marches study area.

The Bronze Age Background

Single inhumations beneath round barrows or within ring-ditches may have been emerging during the Neolithic from c. 3000 BC (e.g. Warrilow et al. 1986), but become the dominant funerary rite during the Early Bronze Age. These monuments continue to act as a focus for funerary activity into the Middle Bronze Age. In the Late Bronze Age c. 1100-750 BC, the burial of individuals is rarely recorded in the archaeological record and this coincides with an apparent rise in the deposition of large hoards of metalwork and the construction of enclosures in defensive positions.

Early Bronze Age burials beneath round barrows or within ring-ditches appear to be intended as expressions of social status (Bradley 1990, 39). Inhumation burials could be accompanied by prestigious gold ornaments such as those recorded at Bush Barrow, Wiltshire (Megaw and Simpson 1988, 209-212) or the Bryn yr Ellyllon barrow, Mold, Flintshire (Powell 1953, 162-163). Such examples are exceptional, but inhumations are regularly accompanied not only by fine early Beaker vessels, but also barbed and tanged arrowheads and what have been interpreted as archer's wrist guards, suggesting status linked with hunting or warfare.

The Early Bronze Age witnesses a shift from inhumation burial to predominantly cremation rites in urns considered to occur c. 1700 BC (Needham 1996, 132). Earlier calibrated absolute dates have been recorded for Early Bronze Age cremation burials (e.g. Lynch 1993, 215), which may suggest regional variation, although where inhumation and cremation rites occur together, cremation is usually secondary (e.g. Warrilow et al. 1986, 64-68). Cremation burial does not appear to manifest status in the same way as inhumation. In contrast, where artefacts are recorded in association with cremations in urns, they are usually in the form of individual objects such as jet, amber or faience beads (e.g. Lynch 1991, 163-164), suggesting less overt expressions of status through material objects. It has been suggested that a greater temporal and spatial separation existed between status expressed in ceremonial acts and the interment of remains in the Middle Bronze Age (Barrett and Needham 1988, 130-133).

Despite changes in funerary rites, the location of burial does not appear to change, and cremations continue to be deposited at the same places as earlier inhumation burials (Warrilow et al. 1986, 64-68). Indeed, round barrows and ring-ditches continue to act as a focus of burial into the Middle Bronze Age (Barclay and Glass 1995, 31-37). Therefore the location of burial monuments appears to reflect an attachment to place and their fixed position in the landscape may have structured patterns of residency (Barnatt 2000, 5). However, Middle Bronze Age cremations at round barrow and ring-ditch sites are far less frequently recorded, particularly outside the south of England. With some exceptions (Stanford 1982, 316-317), burial at round barrows and ring ditches does not generally appear to extend into the late second millennium or Late Bronze Age, c. 1100-750 BC.

The production and distribution of metalwork in the Bronze Age may have been facilitated a number of economic and social interactions during the period. However, unlike the location of funerary monuments, the location of the production and exchange of metalwork is less easily identified in the landscape. Copper ores were exploited in south-west Ireland, north and mid-Wales during the Early and Middle Bronze Age (Brindley and Lanting 1990; Lewis 1990, 5-8; Timberlake 2001, 179-182). However, the relationship between ore extraction sites in Britain and Ireland and metal production and exchange, within the Bronze Age economy is still little understood (ibid.189-190).

Metalwork analysis has shown that a dependence upon European metal may have existed in the Late Bronze Age, at least for some regions of Britain (Northover 1982, 59-67), whilst continental metals were also in circulation in the Early Bronze Age (ibid. 51). Therefore metalwork may have been distributed over long distances and several processes of exchange must have taken place during an artefact's life cycle (Needham 1993a, 166). The social mechanisms of these exchange processes have been discussed by Rowlands (1980), who emphasised the potential use of objects in maintaining obligations or reinforcing status between individuals or groups, based upon historical analogy.

It is, however, the deposition rather than the exchange of objects that is represented in the archaeological record. The context of these depositions has been the focus of recent discussion (Bradley 1990; 1998). Objects can be seen to have been placed in non-utilitarian contexts from the Neolithic, with stone axes having been intentionally placed in wet places or at ceremonial monuments (Bradley 1990, 66). Such practices can also be suggested for the deposition of hoards of axes in the Early Bronze Age in significant locations such as mountain tops (e.g. Forde-Johnston 1964). Indeed, recent studies have emphasised the potential for natural places to be the focus of symbolic activities within a number of different historical contexts (Bradley 2000). The deposition of significant or symbolic objects can also be recognised within domestic contexts during the Middle Bronze Age (Brück 1999b, 152-155).

It is the Late Bronze Age that arguably witnesses the greatest intensity in the deposition of metalwork. This cannot necessarily be explained by a heightened production, since radiocarbon dates from native copper sources suggest that activity may have ceased at a number of mines by this period (Ambers 1990, 61-62). The quantity of fragmentary metal objects in Late Bronze Age hoards has frequently been interpreted as scrap for recycling (Needham 1986, 59-60), and it has been suggested that sources of copper were restricted (Northover 1982, 63). This is reinforced by metal analysis which records a reduction in the purity of copper in the period together with high additions of lead (Northover 1980, 234-235).

The hoarding of quantities of metalwork has traditionally

been seen as a response to threatening situations. This would be applicable to a period where raw materials were at a premium. However, metalwork hoards, particularly those from wet contexts, have been interpreted in terms of deliberate acts, whereby objects were never intended to be retrieved (Bradley 1990; 106-107). These have been seen as methods of enhancing prestige through the conspicuous consumption of valuable objects, which may have superseded the association of grave goods with inhumation burials (Barrett and Needham 1988, 133).

The fact that *weapons* are frequently recorded from wet contexts (Bradley 1990, 97) emphasises war and conflict in the Late Bronze Age and its association with acts of display. Rowlands (1980, 35) envisaged a period of "aggressive rivalry and status competition" in a British Late Bronze Age context. The fact that hoards of weapons and associated prestigious Late Bronze Age artefacts can also be associated with potential Late Bronze Age defended sites (Hall and Gingell 1974; Savory 1980, 119; Coles et al. 1999) allows for the possibility of an association between conflict, display and settlement in the period.

It is the relationship between settlement, the deposition of artefacts and funerary and ceremonial activity in the landscape that needs to be explored further for the Bronze Age period. The burial of the dead, the ostentatious display of prestige, the production and exchange of objects, has to be examined within the context of the communities involved. This cannot be fully realised without an understanding of the networks of domestic settlement and the degree to which areas of the landscape were intensively, repeatedly or infrequently occupied. However, far less discussion has been given over to the location of settlement in the Bronze Age than the study of metal objects, funerary monuments and grave goods. Therefore, it is important to look at the history of research into Bronze Age settlement in Britain, in order for the current interpretation of settlement patterns to be seen in context.

The study of Bronze Age settlement in Britain

The earliest investigations into the Bronze Age arose from early excavations into round barrows in the nineteenth century which constituted the predominant archaeological activity of the day. Recent studies into the archaeology of the Bronze Age have shown that barrow excavations formed 99 per cent of excavation activity in 1840, 79 per cent by 1900 and remained as high as 66 per cent in 1950 (Morris 1992, 420). The study of metalwork typology initiated in the late nineteenth century (e.g. Evans 1881) remained a significant specialist field during the twentieth century and an important means of establishing chronological developments in the Bronze Age (e.g. Smith 1959; Burgess

1968; 1979). The study of ceramic sequences arising from the excavation of barrows, began to be published in the early twentieth century (e.g. Ambercromby 1912). The study of ceramics associated with funerary contexts continued to remain a significant focus of study and an important means of establishing relative chronologies (e.g.Longworth 1961; Clarke 1970).

The study of Bronze Age settlement has largely remained secondary to that of funerary monuments and artefact chronologies. More recent studies focussing upon Bronze Age landscapes have continued to focus on monuments. The more ephemeral signs of domestic occupation detected in the form of flint scatters from ploughsoil contexts, have not been the subject of excavation (e.g. Gibson 1999). Debate upon the relative chronologies of artefacts continues (e.g. Needham 1990) and recent studies have begun to refine artefact dating by placing objects into absolute radiocarbon sequences (Needham et al. 1997).

However, the subject of Bronze Age settlement has not been entirely neglected during the twentieth century. The earliest discussions treat settlement in terms of the long-distance migration of peoples across Europe (Crawford 1912, 184-190). The known distribution of Bronze Age artefacts and sites are interpreted literally as representing movement of people between locations on regional (ibid. 196) and European levels (ibid. 190). The use of the physical remains from round barrows to represent distinctive races underpinned early interpretations that settlement represented waves of migrants (ibid. 188). The interpretation of Early Bronze Age settlement in terms of the long-distance migration of peoples, continued to dominate the limited discussions of the subject during much of the twentieth century (Childe 1930, 153; Piggott 1949, 110). However, such interpretations were beginning to be questioned by the 1970s, in favour of a Beaker cultural package transmitted through social or economic relations (Burgess and Shennan 1976, 309-312).

Childe's early references to Bronze Age settlement reflect the fact that the location and form of domestic sites in the period must have been the subject of contemporary discussion (Childe 1930, 160-1; 190; 226-227). He refers to the identification of round huts in upland and lowland contexts (ibid. 160) and suggests enclosures upon Dartmoor may belong to the period (ibid. 161). Despite the limited length of discussion on the subject, Childe essentially presages issues that are still relevant and current regarding settlement in the Bronze Age. He suggests for example that " hill camps" were being built in the Middle Bronze Age (ibid. 190). Also, he balances the apparent emergence of enclosed settlements in southern England in the Late Bronze Age by suggesting that they may not necessarily have been as fixed or permanent as more recent historical rural settlement patterns (ibid. 226-227).

The 1930s witnessed the first excavations of Bronze Age settlement sites in southern England (e.g. Holleyman and Curwen 1935; Stone 1941). These types of enclosure associated with groups of structures and evidence of cultivation in the form of lynchets, continued to provide a focus of research during the later twentieth century (e.g. Burstow and Holleyman 1957; Drewett 1982). Attempts were made in the 1970s to synthesise current evidence for excavated domestic sites in the British Early Bronze Age and these highlighted the ephemeral and piecemeal nature of the evidence (Simpson 1971, 131-135). A lack of recorded sites led to attempts to place the distribution of funerary monuments into the context of seasonal settlement (Fleming 1971, 159-164).

Some significant developments were made in the 1970s regarding the chronology of the period. Hillfort sites began to be recognised as belonging to the Late Bronze Age through radiocarbon dates obtained during excavations (e.g. Coombs 1971, 101-2; Musson 1976, 296-298). This had important implications upon the understanding of settlement in the period. Similarly the re-assessment of ceramic chronologies (Barrett 1976; Barrett 1980) were important in terms of the dating of middle and Late Bronze Age settlement phases, at least in southern England. The 1980s witnessed discussions on the location of settlement sites within systems of exchange (Ellison 1980) together with studies beyond the southern English counties (e.g. Jobey 1985). Influential theories on the social context of Bronze Age settlement were also discussed (Rowlands 1980). A significant contribution to the subject was also Burgess' debate over the implications of environmental change upon settlement patterns in the Late Bronze Age (Burgess 1985).

There has been a recent resurgence of interest in Bronze Age settlement (e.g. Brück 2001), which still largely concentrates upon the southern English counties emphasising the development of enclosed and more fixed forms of settlement out of a less clearly identifiable Early Bronze Age residency pattern (Brück 2000). However, significant studies of landscapes in alternative contexts are also contributing to debates upon residency patterns, their relationships with agricultural systems, ceremonial monuments and land tenure (Barnatt 2000; Kitchen 2001). Large-scale development in Britain during the 1990s has also provided the opportunity to examine large tracts of landscape through current planning policy. Bronze Age settlement locales have therefore continued to be identified in further locations (McCullagh and Tipping 1998; Garner 2001), whilst more intensive study of settlement sites in southern England has continued (Brossler 2001). Therefore the regional and chronological context of settlement in the Bronze Age is beginning to be more clearly understood. However, significant questions regarding settlement patterns in the period continue to persist.

Themes in Bronze Age settlement studies

The most consistent theme to emerge from the study of Bronze Age settlement is a lack of evidence for Early Bronze Age settlement sites, which contrasts with the evidence for enclosed and nucleated sites in the Middle and Late Bronze Age periods. Structures regarded as domestic in function have, nevertheless, been identified for the Early Bronze Age c. 2500-1500 BC. These are, however, infrequently recorded and largely insubstantial and ephemeral in nature. A significant investment in domestic architecture does not appear to have been made in this period. In the Middle Bronze Age c. 1500-1150 BC settlement forms appear to be more clearly defined in the archaeological record, particularly in the south of England. In the Late Bronze Age c. 1150-750 BC enclosures have been recorded more frequently and consistently across Britain, particularly those on hilltops or in defended positions. However, the nature of occupation within them is by no means clear.

Definitions of 'settlement' in the Oxford English Dictionary (1989) include " the placing of persons or things in a fixed or permanent position" and " the art of settling oneself, or state of being settled, in a fixed place or position, in a permanent abode…". Therefore settlement is defined in terms of permanency and an attachment to a specific place, within a domestic context. A 'settler' is defined as " one who settles in a new country; a colonist." Piggott, for example, described the "eventual colonisation of west Britain after the south-east had been intensively settled…" in an Early Bronze Age context (Piggott 1949, 110). This colonial interpretation implies that settlement is an act culminating in the establishment of a fixed location, to which a group or individual becomes attached or can lay claim to. Recent discussions on the nature of settlement in prehistory have questioned the existence of permanent and definable settlement sites, and have attempted to disassociate the concept of the settlement site with acts of colonial settlement (Carman 1999).

The existence of permanent and fixed settlement sites has been questioned for the Early Bronze Age specifically, where enclosed and definable domestic areas are lacking in the archaeological record. The evidence that has been recorded often suggests transitory, although perhaps recurrent, settlement episodes. A pattern of residential mobility has been suggested as a response to a lack of definable permanently occupied sites (Brück 1999a). The role of funerary and ceremonial monuments within this settlement pattern have been emphasised, and interpreted as influencing patterns of mobility (ibid. 68-69).

Alternative discussions have suggested that funerary monuments were located in close proximity to more permanent settlement and agriculture and served to legitimise land tenure in upland contexts (Barnatt 2000,

83). However, defined tenure over land does not necessarily imply fixed settlement sites occupied on a year-round basis, or preclude the existence of mobile settlement patterns. The mutual benefits of shared rights of access to land or resources and co-operation between groups, has also been emphasised, particularly for zones traditionally regarded as marginal (Young and Simmonds 1999, 205-206).

Where longevity in occupation is suggested, settlement is described as 'sustained' rather than permanent (Barnatt 2000, 3) allowing for its position within a more mobile system. The concept of mobility has permeated the language used in the recent discussion of settlement in prehistory and the Early Bronze Age in particular. Points of occupation are referred to as 'locales' or 'nodes' (Brück 1999a, 67-69; Carman 1999, 23) inferring that they represent transient episodes within a wider network of mobile settlement.

Current interpretations suggest that more permanent and fixed points of residency emerged from mobile patterns in the Middle Bronze Age, c.1500-1150 BC (Brück 2000). It has been argued that structured social interactions in the Early Bronze Age, involving the episodic movement of groups between monuments began to dissolve, and settlement became more fixed as a result (ibid.). There appears to be greater evidence for nucleation and permanency in the mode of residency in the archaeological record for this period when compared with the Early Bronze Age. Groups of structures associated with the residues of domestic consumption and production have been identified within defined and bounded spaces in southern England (Burstow and Holleyman 1957; Drewett 1982; Barrett et al. 1991). Originally regarded as Late or Later Bronze Age, calibrated radiocarbon dates would now place these sites into the Middle Bronze Age.

Discussion of these farmsteads (Burstow and Holleyman 1957, 209) has explored their subsistence economy and the function of individual structures within settlement sites (Drewett 1982). Recent studies have discussed spatial organisation and intra-site mobility (Brück 1999b, 146). The re-building of structures and reorganisation of space has been interpreted in terms of change across generations (ibid. 149-150). Therefore organisation within defined settlement sites was not static and the permanency of their occupation may have been limited. This therefore again implies a degree of mobility in the mid-second millennium BC settlement pattern, but mobility that was restricted to shifts in settlement location, rather than the more frequent and structured mobility that has been envisaged for the Early Bronze Age (Brück 1999a, 68-70).

The most frequent form of settlement enclosure that has been identified outside the south of England appears to have been initiated in the Late Bronze Age. This has been recorded at hillfort sites where phases of enclosure and settlement have been identified in southern, northern and western Britain (Hamilton and Manley 1997; Coombs 1971; Ellis 1993; Musson 1991; Barrett et al. 2000). It has been suggested that the emergence of enclosed and defended sites represented dislocation in existing patterns of settlement. This perceived dislocation was considered a direct consequence of dramatic climatic deterioration and the subsequent pressure on resources, particularly in environmentally marginal locations (Burgess 1985). More recent arguments have emphasised continuity in settlement location, through adaptation to any changing conditions and co-operation between groups (Young and Simmonds 1999; Young 2000).

The nature of domestic settlement within enclosed hilltop sites is not fully understood, since structures have not always been confidently related to dating sequences from circuits of enclosure, and finds are often residual within later contexts. Therefore it is possible that these sites are atypical of a more general settlement pattern, or that their specific function lay beyond the domestic sphere. Therefore the position of these sites within a more widespread pattern of settlement remains ambiguous.

Recent arguments have questioned the assumption that early hill top enclosures in southern England were defensive constructions (Hamilton and Manley 1997, 99). Instead their function has been seen in terms of looking out and surveying surrounding landscapes during intermittent phases of occupation (ibid.101), as opposed to acting as focal points to surrounding groups. However the formal enclosure of a hilltop location would have reinforced and monumentalised its inaccessibility. This suggests that activities within were restricted to specific sections of a community and not accessible to certain outside groups. The technological development of weaponry in the period (e.g. Burgess 1968), together with the development of associated display objects (Burgess et al. 1972, 227), highlights the importance of warfare in the Bronze Age. Therefore it is not unreasonable to assume that defended locations were constructed as a response to conflict and may have become focal points of dispute, particularly if they were centres for the consumption of valuable resources (Osgood 1998, 6). Therefore it could be suggested that such sites were permanently occupied in order to maintain restricted access. To what extent they represent a more widespread settlement pattern is, however, open to question. It is possible that their occupants were at the apex of a hierarchical and competitive society such as that envisaged by Rowlands (1980, 32).

Enclosed and unenclosed sites dating to the Late Bronze Age have also been recorded in alternative riverine and lowland contexts in southern England (Needham and Longley 1980; O'Connell 1986) and there is evidence that certain locations witnessed recurrent and relatively dense occupation (Moore and Jennings 1992, 14; 118).

Therefore alternative locations for settlement to hilltop enclosures existed in the period and some may have played an important role regarding the production and exchange of objects and resources.

It has been argued that the later Bronze Age was a period of "agricultural intensification" in contrast to the earlier Bronze Age, where the archaeological record is dominated by funerary and ceremonial activity (Barrett and Bradley 1980, 9). This theme has been further emphasised, recently, within the context of the Thames Valley (Yates 2001) and a greater intensity of stock management and arable diversification has been suggested for the emergence of enclosed settlements and field systems (ibid. 65-66). Middle and Late Bronze Age settlement sites in Sussex (Drewett 1982) and Oxfordshire (Moore and Jennings 1992; Brossler 2001), for example, have provided evidence of a contiguous association between enclosed and nucleated settlement and cultivation. In the northern English borders a number of unenclosed settlements have been identified in upland contexts in association with field systems and clearance cairns dating to the mid to late second millennium BC (Jobey 1985). Clearly defined boundaries on Salisbury Plain, Wiltshire have also been interpreted as representing agricultural organisation in the late second millennium BC (Bradley et al. 1994, 123).

In Wiltshire it has been suggested that the more formal demarcation and division of land in the later Bronze Age could mirror earlier territories, structured by the location of funerary monuments (ibid. 122). Similarly, it has been suggested that field systems in upland contexts in Derbyshire reflect patterns of landholding established in the Early Bronze Age (Barnatt 2000, 5). Therefore, it is possible that any intensification in agricultural production developed from earlier systems of landholding, and that re-organisation of agricultural practice may have respected established patterns of land tenure. This could suggest a degree of continuity in land use and the adoption of field systems may represent re-organisation rather than dislocation. This, therefore, may also suggest continuity in the location of settlement during the Bronze Age. It is also possible that the formal organisation and division of agricultural landscapes in association with settlement may not be exclusively a Late Bronze Age phenomenon. Pryor for example has argued that the field systems at Fengate were laid out in the early second millennium BC and continued in use throughout the Bronze Age (Pryor 1980, 176; 1992a, 447).

Themes relating to the development of Bronze Age settlement in Britain have emerged from fieldwork and study in regions where field systems or enclosures are readily identifiable, or have been the recipients of a long tradition of archaeological research. It is important to begin to widen the study of settlement to regions which have a relative paucity of settlement evidence, but whose archaeological record contains the widespread products of a populated landscape in the Bronze Age.

The study area

Bronze Age settlement in the Welsh Marches, or borders between England and Wales, reflects the discontinuity in visibility that has been recorded elsewhere in Britain. Settlement sites are rare and reflect the general bias towards the late second millennium BC. Yet the region has significant numbers of monuments and artefacts datable to the Bronze Age.

Current recorded distributions in the Welsh Marches reflect Bronze Age activity in a number of different contrasting upland and lowland environmental contexts. However, the distributions of artefacts and monuments have not been discussed in the region in relation to known settlement locales. It is important therefore to examine these artefact and monument distributions within the context of settlement patterns, in order both to illuminate patterns of residency and to place the distribution of finds and monuments into a wider social and economic context. This is important in order to assess the degree to which existing regional models of development in Bronze Age settlement patterns have a more widespread application.

Settlement foci datable to the Early, Middle and Late Bronze Age are not visible as a clearly defined or closely associated network of sites in this region. Therefore, in order to study their relationship across the period, it is necessary to establish the context of known sites and use this in association with other contemporary activities in the landscape, in order to extrapolate patterns of residency. The defined limits of the study area go beyond the immediate Welsh Marches borders, since widening the area examined allows a greater number of settlement locales to be identified. Therefore the study area has been approached on a scale which incorporates the Welsh counties of Denbighshire, Flintshire, Wrexham, Powys and Monmouthshire and the English counties of Cheshire, Shropshire, Herefordshire and Gloucestershire (Fig. 1).

Prehistoric settlement in the region has been largely identified by the investigation into later more visible monuments. Iron Age hillforts have received continued attention from the mid-twentieth century (e.g. Kenyon 1942; Varley 1948). The Breiddin hillfort, Powys, was one of a number of hillforts in Britain beginning to produce radiocarbon dates belonging to the Late Bronze Age in the 1970s (Musson 1976, 296-298; Savory 1976, 243). Subsequently a number of other hillforts in the region have produced evidence for Late Bronze Age occupation (e.g. Ellis 1993). These sites represent the first form of enclosure during the Bronze Age that could represent

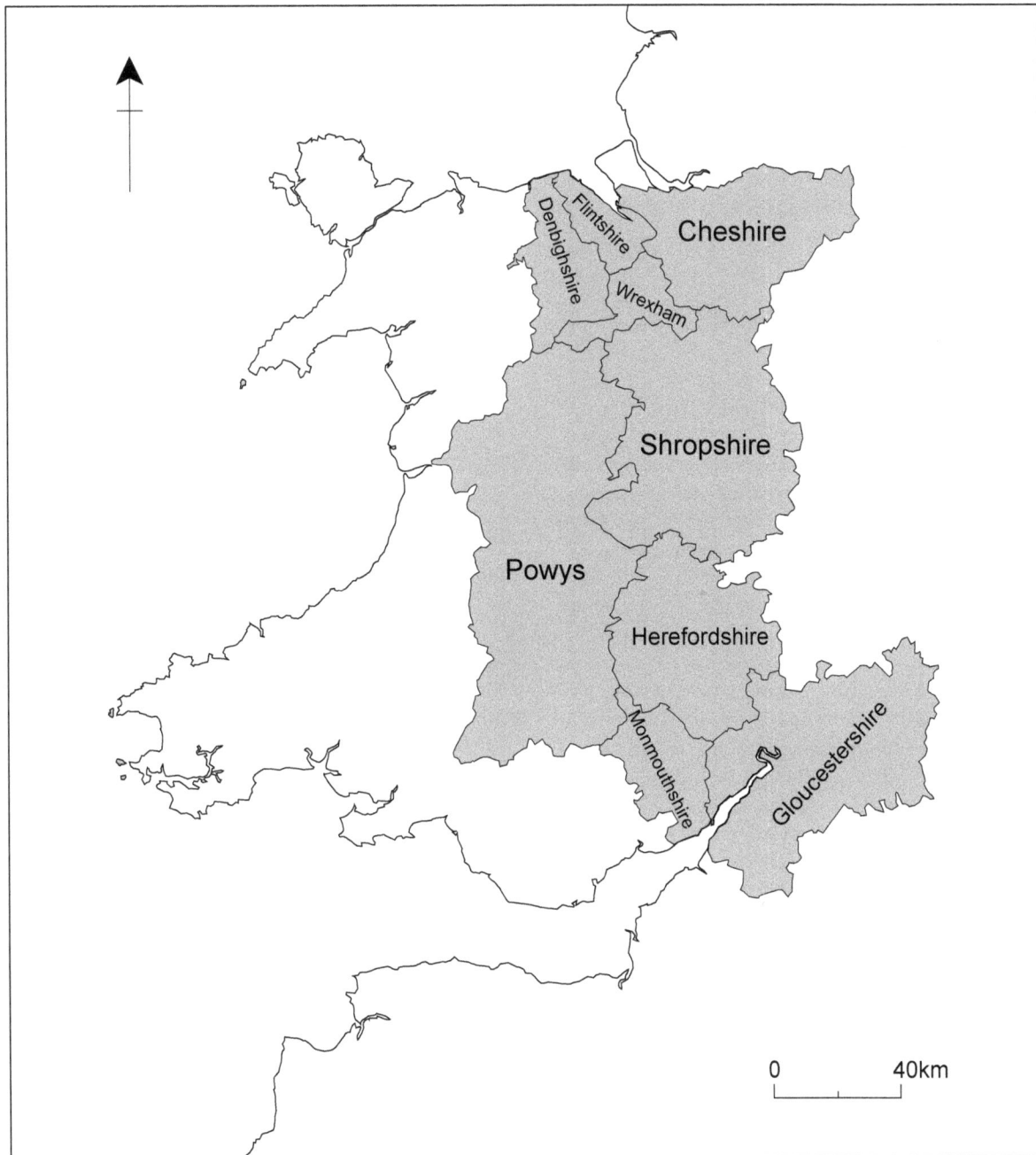

Fig. 1 The extent of the study area

defined areas of settlement in the region. However the nature of their occupancy is ambiguous. Furthermore, the context of enclosed sites upon hilltops, within the development of settlement patterns during the Bronze Age in the Welsh Marches, is poorly understood. It is therefore clearly necessary to establish patterns of settlement that pre-date these enclosures, and also to examine the position which Late Bronze Age defended sites held within wider contemporary patterns of residency.

Few settlement locales dating to the Early Bronze Age have been recorded in the study area, despite a profusion

of Early Bronze Age funerary and ceremonial monuments (3599 round barrows and ring ditches are recorded in the study area). Evidence for settlement dating to the Middle Bronze Age is similarly lacking, and contrasts with the evidence for nucleated settlements recorded in the southern English counties dating from the mid-second millennium BC.

However, recently published excavations (Garner 2001; Higham and Cane 1999; Nevell 1988; Britnell et al. 1997) in Wales and bordering counties have identified a small number of sites which confirm the presence and can begin to illuminate the context of settlement in the study area, from the late third to mid-second millennia BC. There is evidence to suggest that some locations show considerable longevity and continuity in their occupation, raising questions about interpretations that assume settlement patterns and forms necessarily change across established period divisions. These sites have provided an opportunity to begin to examine the context of settlement across the Bronze Age, beyond what have previously been the core regional areas of study in Britain.

Principal themes to be addressed

1. LOCATION OF SITES

The Welsh Marches region has a lack of Early Bronze Age settlement sites which is consistent with the archaeological record in Britain. This lack of settlement evidence also extends into the Middle Bronze Age in the Welsh Marches, which contrasts with the pattern recorded in southern England. It is important therefore to clarify the context of recorded Early and Middle Bronze Age settlement locales, in order that further sites can be identified by excavation in the future.

It is necessary to identify structures associated with the residues of domestic consumption and production which have absolute radiocarbon dates placing them in the Bronze Age. This has been achieved through an examination of recent published excavation reports in local county and national journals or specific excavation monographs. The context of these sites has been illuminated by examining their topographical position in the landscape and their association with drift geology.

In the 1970s it was recognised that hillforts had early phases of enclosure which could be dated to the Late Bronze Age by radiocarbon. A refined chronology for Late Bronze Age and Early Iron Age ceramics (Barrett 1980) contributed to the interpretation of Late Bronze Age occupation on these sites. The fact that a number of hillforts were excavated prior to the identification of Late Bronze Age phases, allows for the possibility that further hillfort sites in the Welsh Marches were occupied in this period. Therefore, early excavation reports from hillforts have been examined closely, in an attempt to identify structural phases or material assemblages which may suggest they were occupied in the Late Bronze Age. The frequent association between Late Bronze Age metalwork finds and hillforts, and the fact that an association with hoards has been recorded in a number of instances (e.g. Savory 1980, 119; Hall and Gingell 1972, 306-308), can also be used to infer the location of further settlement phases at other comparable sites.

The fact that enclosed and unenclosed settlement sites

dating to the Late Bronze Age have been recorded in other landscape contexts in the south of England (e.g. Needham and Longley 1980; O'Connell 1986), requires an examination of the evidence for settlement beyond enclosed hilltop sites in the Welsh Marches. Again, this has been achieved through the examination of recently published excavation reports in journals and monographs for the region.

Once the landscape context of known Early, Middle and Late Bronze Age settlement locales has been clarified, it may be possible to extrapolate settlement patterns by an examination of the distribution of contemporary artefacts and monuments in the study area. The association between known Early Bronze Age settlement nodes and contemporary funerary monuments can be examined in order to assess the degree to which monuments in the landscape can be used to represent the location of domestic residency.

It may also be possible to use the distribution of contemporary metal objects to extrapolate settlement patterns for the Early, Middle and Late Bronze Age. However, despite the fact that metalwork has been recorded at Middle and Late Bronze Age settlements in Britain (e.g. Drewett 1982; O'Connell 1986), a number of factors may have influenced the recorded distribution of these objects in the landscape.

It is important to stress that the distribution of metal objects is not necessarily fully representative of the pattern of metalwork deposition in prehistory. The recovery and recording of artefacts could introduce bias into distribution maps, and these have been regarded as 'maps of recovery', representing the documented archaeological record, rather than a genuine reflection of distribution in prehistory (Needham 1993a, 164). Modern collection biases may have resulted in distributions which are unrepresentative and at least incomplete. Land-use could potentially affect the rate of recovery of artefacts, with land that is actively disturbed perhaps more likely to result in the more frequent discovery of artefacts. The quality of the recording of these artefacts can also affect the detailed examination of their contexts. The masking of certain areas of the landscape by alluvium or colluvium may also affect the rate of recovery of objects and contribute to bias in the perceived distribution of objects.

Processes in prehistory will also have affected the distribution of metalwork. From its point of production an object may have undergone a number of exchanges during its life cycle (ibid. 166). The final deposition of an object therefore represents the culmination of a process of displacement (ibid. 162). Therefore the recorded location of an object may not necessarily equate with contexts in which it once existed (ibid. 165), including nodes of settlement. Therefore areas which show an apparent lack of artefacts do not necessarily represent a lack of activity for the use of these artefacts in prehistory. Such apparent blank areas could represent places from which metal objects were re-distributed (ibid. 164).

The deposition of metal objects, particularly those in wet and non-retrievable contexts, has been interpreted either in terms of votive offerings intended to "placate supernatural powers" (Bradley 1990, 95), or as an act of deliberate consumption designed to enhance prestige (Barrett and Needham 1988, 133). The possibility of intentional deposition could suggest, together with the processes of exchange and displacement in prehistory, that an object's location does not necessarily reflect any utilitarian sphere in which it may have existed during its life cycle. This could suggest that there might be no relationship between the distribution of recorded objects and nodes of domestic activity. Yet even if a mutually exclusive relationship can be shown to exist between the location of known settlement locales and the distribution of metal objects, it may infer areas of contrasting activity in the landscape. All such activity has to be related to a pattern of settlement ultimately.

The association between metalwork distribution and settlement location cannot necessarily be equated directly, yet metalwork distributions may provide an important insight into the relationship between contrasting landscape zones, within the context of settlement patterns.

2. RESIDENTIAL MOBILITY

The degree of residential mobility in the settlement pattern must be assessed, in order to establish whether models for Early Bronze Age southern England (Brück 1999a) can be applied to the Welsh Marches and potentially other regions of Britain. It is also important to assess the validity of the settlement mobility argument as a means of explaining a lack of evidence for permanently occupied sites, since mobility in the settlement pattern does not necessarily preclude the existence of fixed settlement nodes in the landscape.

It is first necessary to examine the degree of longevity evident in Early Bronze Age settlement locales, in order to assess the extent to which they may have been re-occupied, as part of a structured nodal system of mobility. Longevity in the occupation of a settlement locale can be measured by the identification of the reconstruction of buildings, or the accumulation of significant artefact assemblages representing long chronological sequences. Longer-term longevity in the occupation of specific locales can be suggested through sequences of calibrated radiocarbon dates from excavated settlement contexts. Such observations could suggest that mobility was limited, or confined to particular sections of a community. Therefore it is necessary to examine published excavation reports in order to assess the length of occupation of

specific settlement sites.

The frequency of ceremonial activity at monuments has been argued to be an integral part of the pattern of settlement in the Early Bronze Age (Brück 1999a, 68-69). Therefore it is necessary to examine the degree of association between recorded settlement locales and funerary monuments during this period, in order to assess the extent to which events at monuments structured the pattern of settlement. The location of Early Bronze Age monuments and artefact distributions across the study area has, therefore, been examined in relation to the context of recorded nodes of settlement.

The degree to which any mobile settlement patterns dissolved in the Middle Bronze Age to be replaced by more fixed forms of residency, as has been envisaged in southern England (Brück 2000, 285-286), is also significant. Therefore it is also necessary to examine the degree of residential mobility between c. 1500 and 1100 BC.

Burnt mound sites have produced dates which, when calibrated, fall within the mid- late Bronze Age period (e.g. Hannaford 1999, 73; Hodder 1990, 107). They are also regarded as representing temporary, but repeated, episodes of activity (O' Kelly 1954, 137-138). Their function is ambiguous, but nevertheless, they may have played an integral role in the settlement pattern. The context of burnt mounds in relation to that of the few known settlement locales of the Middle Bronze Age has been examined in order to assess the degree of residential mobility that their use may have dictated. In the absence of frequently recorded and clearly defined settlement locales for the Middle Bronze Age in the Welsh Marches, the location of burnt mounds has also been examined within the context of the distribution of metalwork from the period. The context of metalwork depositions in relation to the location of burnt mounds may be able to infer the extent to which activities in the landscape were separated, and the extent to which this reflects mobile patterns of residency.

3. SETTLEMENT AND AGRICULTURE

It is important to assess the extent to which the location and form of residency is dictated by agricultural practice. A mixed agricultural system may involve the use of contrasting environmental zones, with certain areas being more suited to pastoralism and others for cultivation. The movement of livestock could engender forms of mobile settlement and such mobility could also facilitate the reproduction of exchange systems and social relations. Any change in the location of settlement or form of land holding may suggest changing agricultural practice during the Bronze Age and changing social or economic relations.

In order to assess the degree to which agricultural systems

influenced settlement patterns in the Bronze Age, it is necessary to establish the type of agriculture practised at known settlement locales and to assess the degree to which certain landscape zones may have influenced the mode of agriculture. These observations can be used as a means of measuring the extent to which certain landscape zones were occupied in the period.

The position of a settlement locale within the agricultural economy can be most directly evaluated by an examination of specific excavated assemblages from domestic sites. These can include the actual products of cultivation such as charred cereals, or related objects such as quern stones. Pastoralism or animal husbandry may be reflected in bone assemblages from excavated contexts. Such evidence, albeit limited, has therefore been examined in published excavation reports.

In order to assess the type of agricultural practice that may have existed across wider landscape zones it is necessary to evaluate the suitability of specific contexts for cultivation or pasture. The association between recorded settlement locales and the products of agricultural production and consumption can be used as a basis to extrapolate the mode of settlement and agriculture in the Bronze Age across comparable geographical contexts.

Agricultural practice across broad areas of landscape has also been examined through a study of modern land-use and its relationship with drift geology and geographical contexts. It cannot necessarily be assumed that the modern relationship between land-use and geographical context equates with that during the Bronze Age.

However, if nodes of settlement, artefact and monument distributions can be shown to equate with specific geographical contexts, it may support the suggestion that settlement patterns were influenced by agricultural practice. Differences in the distribution of artefacts, settlement sites and monuments across contrasting landscape zones may suggest different modes of settlement or intensities of occupation, reflecting contrasting land-use in the Bronze Age.

4. CONTINUITY AND DISLOCATION IN SETTLEMENT PATTERNS AND FORMS
The degree of continuity in the settlement pattern across the Bronze Age needs to be addressed, in order to illuminate potential social change during the period. The extent of dislocation and discontinuity in patterns of settlement have characterised discussions of, and have contributed to the definition of, the transition between the Early and Middle Bronze Age (Brück 2000) or the earlier and later Bronze Age (Barrett and Bradley 1980; Burgess 1985).

It is important to assess whether settlement nucleation, agricultural intensification or re-organisation identified

in southern English counties, have a more widespread application. Discontinuity manifested in settlement form may reflect changing systems of social or economic interaction (Brück 2000, 290). Therefore, the extent of continuity or discontinuity in the settlement pattern is important as a means of understanding wider changes within Bronze Age society in the region. It is, therefore, also important to establish the chronological horizons at which any dislocation or change in settlement form took place. The distinction between the Early, Middle and Late Bronze Age may be less rigid if patterns of settlement and their influence on social and economic interaction remained the same for much of the period.

Continuity in settlement patterns during the Bronze Age can be assessed by examining the degree of maintenance in the form and location of settlement. Long chronological sequences of absolute dates, or artefact types, at specific sites, can suggest either permanent occupation, or re-occupation as part as an enduring pattern of settlement. A consistent relationship between settlement locales and specific geographical contexts can also be used to suggest continuity in the pattern of residency during the Bronze Age.

Discontinuity in settlement patterns can be most readily envisaged by changes in the form and location of settlement sites. The most recognisable change in settlement form is between unenclosed and enclosed sites. The development of enclosed sites may reflect changing relationships with landholding or social and political relations between groups. The horizon at which changes in settlement form take place can be clarified by calibrating published radiocarbon dates from comparable excavated contexts. Dislocation represented by a change in settlement form can be further emphasised by shifts in the location of settlement locales. More general discontinuity in settlement patterns may be envisaged by the changing context of artefact distributions during the period and changing relationships between settlement and monuments.

Data collection methods

Data used as a basis for this study has been collected from the county Sites and Monuments Records for Cheshire, Shropshire, Herefordshire and Gloucestershire County Councils, Clwyd-Powys Archaeological Trust and Gwent-Glamorgan Archaeological Trust. Further data was obtained from the National Monuments Record, together with published sources. 581 hillforts or possible hillforts, 3599 Bronze Age round barrows, cairns or ring-ditches and 439 Bronze Age metalwork finds, were each given 12 figure co-ordinates and entered into an Access database. Data for a further 430 metal objects in the region was provided by Dr. Peter Northover, Department of Materials, Oxford

University, which was also entered into a database. An attempt to eliminate duplicate data between SMR, NMR and Dr. Peter Northover's sources was made. No data on Bronze Age barrows in Monmouthshire was available from the SMR or published sources. A number of sites and finds lay beyond current unitary authority boundaries, particularly in Denbighshire and Monmouthshire and this relates to changes in county boundaries in 1996. Similarly, finds from Warrington lay beyond the unitary authority boundary of Cheshire, used as the basis for the study area, but have been included in the study as part of the Cheshire SMR database. Each metalwork find has been placed into an Early, Middle or Late Bronze Age context where possible, on the basis of typological affinities. Further subdivision into established chronological metalwork phases has also been made, where descriptions of objects were sufficiently detailed for specific identification. This simply allows artefacts to be examined within a more refined chronological framework.

The data was imported into ESRI ArcView G.I.S. software and plotted graphically against a 1: 625,000 physical map of the study area, digitised using Cartalinx software. This enabled queries to be made of the data, in order to visualise relationships between artefacts, sites and monuments across different periods of the Bronze Age. The use of a large-scale physical map provided a general overview of the data in the region. However, the map's resolution was not fine enough to allow the interpretation of individual and specific geographical contexts, since the accuracy of the physical features decreases when the map is examined at smaller scales. Therefore, in all instances where specific relationships with physical geographical features have been highlighted, contexts were examined through 1:50 000 Ordnance Survey Landranger maps of the region. Nevertheless, the relative association between the location of monuments and artefacts within the ArcView data remains valid, within the limits of the accuracy of specific provenances. British Geological Survey drift geology maps were examined in detail for the areas of Wem, Nantwich, Wrexham and Rhayader, and further 1:50 000 or one-inch to one mile (1: 63 360) drift geology maps were consulted where necessary. The scale of these maps allowed reasonably confident correlations to be made with artefact, sites and monument data. The Ordnance Survey First Land Utilisation Survey of Britain maps produced in the 1930s were also consulted for specific areas.

All radiocarbon dates in the text derived from published sources have been calibrated using Oxcal v. 3.9 software (Bronk Ramsey 2003) unless specifically stated otherwise, in order that consistent comparisons can be made between dates. These calibrations have been included as an appendix. Illustrations have been produced using Adobe Illustrator.

Agenda

This study of Bronze Age settlement is divided into three main chapters which separate the period into Early, Middle and Late phases. Previous discussions on the subject have preferred an earlier or later Bronze Age chronology (Barrett and Bradley 1980, 9). However, the first phases of nucleated settlement sites in southern England appear to emerge between 1500 and 1150 BC (Needham 1996, 133-134). Recent discussion of settlement in the Bronze Age has also emphasised a distinctive Middle Bronze Age phase (Brück 1999b, 145). It has also been argued that the nature of Late Bronze Age settlement differs (ibid. 149), therefore justifying a period distinction at the end of the second millennium BC. Such clear-cut divisions in the settlement pattern have not been discerned outside the southern English counties, but the division of the period into Early, Middle and Late phases is a useful means of measuring change in the study area, against more defined chronological developments recorded elsewhere.

Each chapter of this study addresses the principal themes as outlined above, against a broad British context for modes of residency in each period. Chapter three examines the distribution of round-barrows in relation to the settlement pattern, and discusses the degree of longevity at settlement sites of the Early Bronze Age period. Chapter four discusses the extent to which mobility in the settlement pattern continues and the evidence for the emergence of more nucleated settlement forms which characterise southern English regions in the Middle Bronze Age. Chapter five focuses upon the identification and role of enclosed settlement forms and the extent to which they represent widespread social change in the region in the Late Bronze Age. The distribution of contemporary artefacts, in particular metalwork and its context has been emphasised in each chapter, in an attempt to extrapolate known geographical contexts for settlement and to broaden the context of recorded settlement locales. These discussions are first placed into context by a broad description of the geographical character and contrasting environments that are to be encountered in the study area.

2. The physical environment of the study area; past and present

The physical environment of the study area is dominated by the Welsh upland massif which gives way, via a number of major river valleys, to the lowlands of the English border counties to the east (Fig.2). The Cambrian Mountains in the west of the study area stretch from Denbighshire in the north and through mid- Wales into the old county of Breconshire, reaching heights of over 600m OD. The Berwyn Mountains and Clwydian Range extend these uplands into north-east Wales reaching heights of 800m and 500m OD respectively. Significant outliers of the upland massif extend eastwards into south-west Shropshire forming the Stiperstones, Wenlock Edge and the Clee Hills. In southern Powys the uplands of the Black Mountains and Brecon Beacons dominate the landscape. The Cotswold Hills in Gloucestershire, rising to over 300m OD, form the highest ground in the south-east of the study area, whilst the far north-east incorporates the lower reaches of the Pennines in eastern Cheshire.

The modern upland environments of Wales represent areas that are unsuitable for arable agriculture and are largely given over to rough pasture. In general the higher and more exposed areas equate with the poorest quality agricultural land, based on modern land-use data (Jenckins 1991, 24). It has been emphasised that rainfall increases with altitude and in combination with denser cloud cover and lower temperatures, serves to restrict the growing season for crops and undermines the quality of pasture, by creating podsolized soils (R.C.H.M.W. 1986, 6). High precipitation and poor drainage have also culminated in the formation of widespread peat deposits in both mountain and valley contexts (Davies et al. 1997, 227). The upland environments of Shropshire are similarly characterised by podsolized soils and rough pasture (Rowley 1989, 12-13), although more freely draining soils in the south-west of the county lying between c.245 and 365m OD are regarded as more amenable to cultivation (ibid. 14). The Cotswolds in Gloucestershire also appear to be more receptive to cultivation than the uplands to the west. These hills are formed of an underlying solid geology of Lias clays capped by well-drained oolitic limestones (Firman 1994, 11-12). The impermeable nature of the underlying geology gives rise to numerous naturally occurring springs, providing important water sources (ibid.).

Arable agriculture in the region appears to show a preference for soils covering Limestone geology and pasture for Lias clays in Gloucestershire, when geology is compared with land-use data mapped in the 1930s.

The uplands of the Welsh Marches are drained by a number of broad river valleys which are more suited to settlement and agriculture than the more hostile environments above. Glacial drift deposits laid down in the final Devensian glaciation c. 60,000 – 14, 500 BP (Hebblethwaite 1987, 20) fill these valleys and blanket the lowlands to the east. Alluvial deposits formed during the post-glacial Holocene provide more fertile environments for agriculture and settlement (Herz and Garrison 1998, 22) in the river valleys. Whilst freely draining gravel geology in the lowlands appears to also favour cultivation.

In the north the Denbigh Moors and Clwydian Range are divided by the Vale of Clwyd. Here the uplands are drained via the Clwyd, northwards into the Irish Sea. The valley floor is largely blanketed by glacially deposited boulder clay (Warren et al. 1984, 147) and supports mixed arable and pastoral landscapes in a modern context. To the south the uplands are drained by the River Dee which flows through the Vale of Llangollen, through the lowland Cheshire Plain into the Irish Sea. The alluvial floodplain in the Vale of Llangollen again supports a mixed arable and pastoral economy, based on modern land use, with surrounding uplands having a greater preference for meadow and rough pasture. North and mid-Powys is drained by a network of rivers and streams which flow into the Severn, which flows southwards via the English Border counties into the Bristol Channel. The broad Severn Valley extends into mid-Wales providing more freely draining contexts along its gravel terraces, and more sheltered environments for agriculture, in contrast to the surrounding uplands. The upper Wye Valley and the valley of the River Usk provide relief to the upland environments of the Black Mountains and Brecon Beacons which are largely characterised by steep-sided and restricted valleys which limit land suitable for cultivation (R.C.A.H.M.W. 1986, 3-5).

In the north of the study area the Cheshire Plain is blanketed by glacial boulder clays with sand and gravel deposits being more extensive in the east of the county (Hebblethwaite 1987, 21). Solid outcrops of sandstone punctuate this glacial drift (ibid. 22) notably running in a band of higher ground north-south through the centre of the county. The boulder clays of Cheshire are associated with

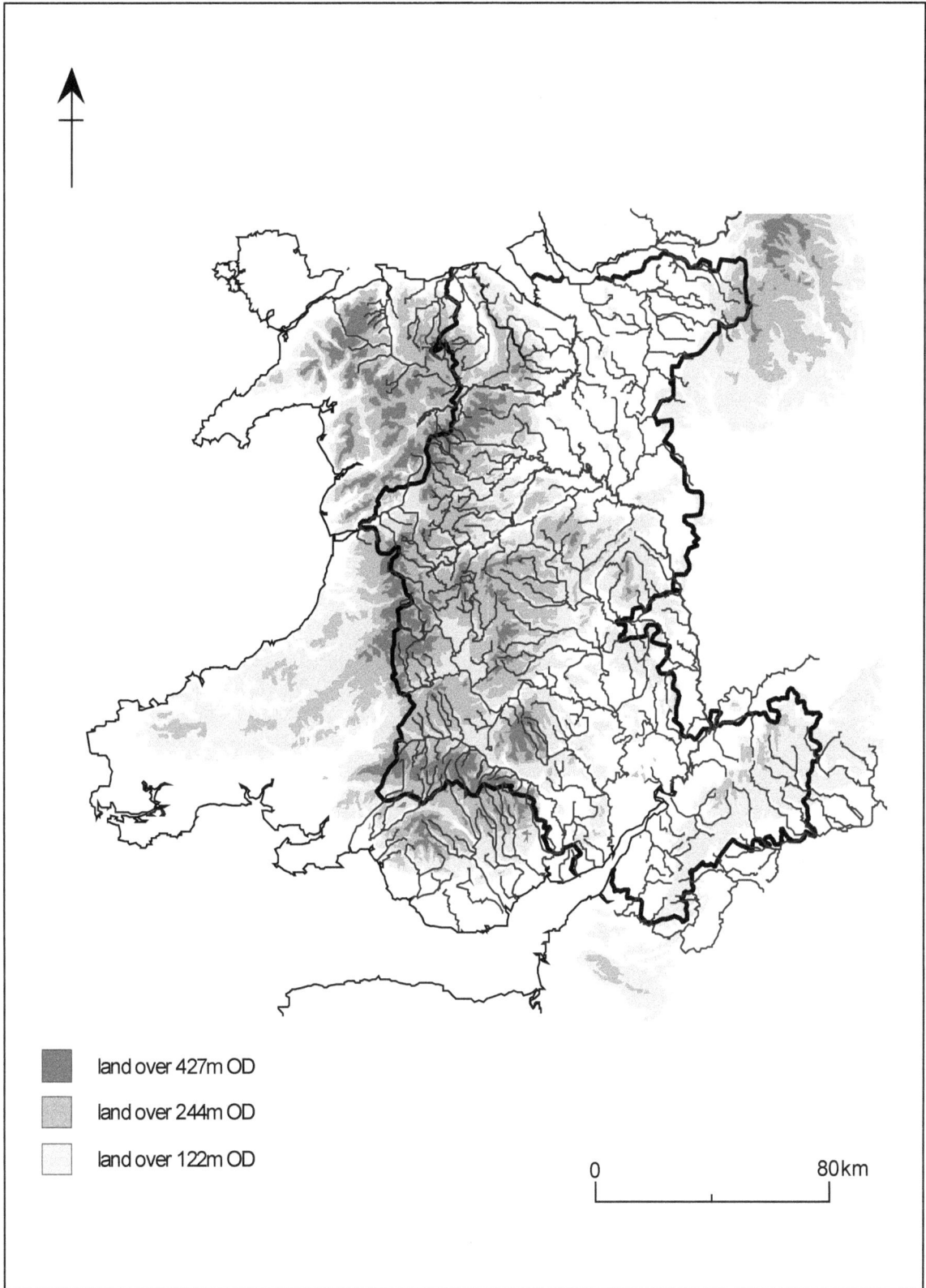

land over 427m OD
land over 244m OD
land over 122m OD

0   80km

Fig.2 General topography of the study area

modern pastoral agriculture and are considered to inhibit cultivation through their tenacious stony components (ibid. 32). It has been noted that the soils overlying the more freely draining sands and gravels are lighter, more freely draining and more amenable to arable cultivation (ibid.). To the south boulder clays again predominate the drift

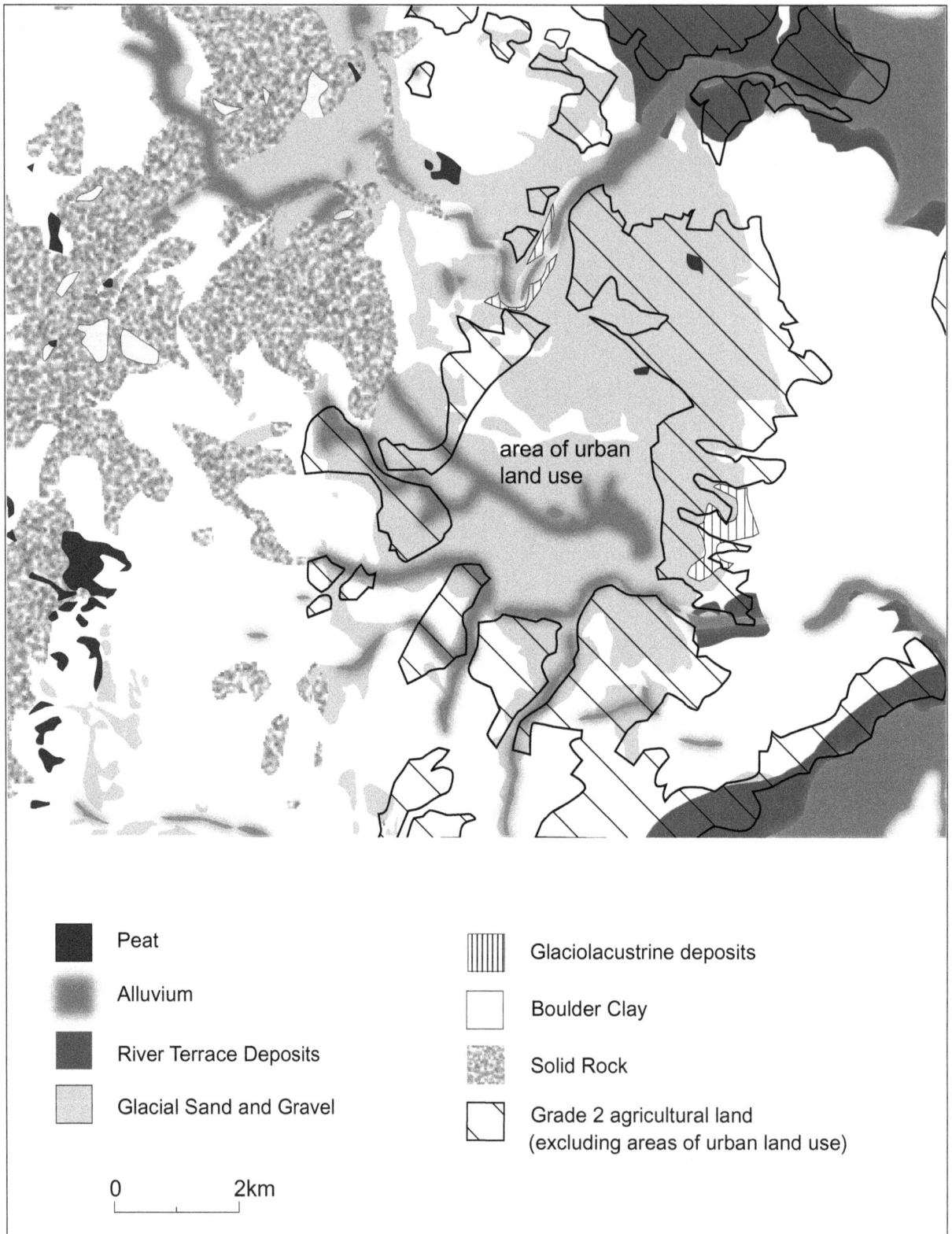

area of urban land use

Peat

Alluvium

River Terrace Deposits

Glacial Sand and Gravel

Glaciolacustrine deposits

Boulder Clay

Solid Rock

Grade 2 agricultural land (excluding areas of urban land use)

0   2km

Fig. 3 Drift geology and best quality agricultural land around Wrexham (after Hains 1991)

deposits, whilst extensive areas of sands and gravels are present around Wrexham (Hains 1991). When equated with modern land-use data (ibid.), sand and gravel deposits and gravel river terraces can be seen to broadly accord with the better quality agricultural land here (Fig. 3). In lowland northern Shropshire the boulder clays are again considered to support poorly drained soils which inhibit effective cultivation and require active drainage to improve their quality (Rowley 1989, 18). Sandier soils overlying sands and gravels are regarded as being more amenable to arable cultivation, however their freely draining properties can also give rise to podsolised soils (ibid.). Indeed it has been noted that soils upon freely draining geology would require careful management and fertilisation to sustain permanent cultivation and offset the effects of leached out nutrients (Hebblethwaite 1987, 32). This could suggest that settlement on such lands in prehistory might have been short-lived or episodic. Alternatively long term occupation of such contexts may be testimony to efficient agricultural practices.

Boulder clays with cobbles and erratic boulders form the undulating landscape of Herefordshire, with sands and gravels more frequent in the north of the county and heterogeneous deposits of gravels, tills and silts characterising areas of the Wye Valley (Brandon 1989, 36-37). The glacial deposits of lowland Gloucestershire include fluvioglacial and river gravels (Green 1992, 157-158) and restricted pockets of boulder clay in the north of the county. The south-east of the study area in Gloucestershire extends into the uppermost reaches of the Thames Valley and its associated gravel terraces.

The physical attributes of the study area also have to be measured against prevailing environmental conditions during the Bronze Age. The Early Bronze Age in Wales is considered to have been characterised by short vigorous summers, allowing occupation of higher altitudes, but followed by long severe winters (Taylor 1980, 123). During the mid-Late Bronze Age a general trend of climatic cooling is considered to have continued and exacerbated, having a more severe effect at higher altitudes, precipitating soil podsolization and restricting growing seasons (ibid. 125).

This trend is perhaps reflected on the Denbigh Moors above 400m OD, where the excavation of a Late Bronze Age enclosure suggests it was preceded by light scrub woodland suitable for rough grazing and subsequently enveloped by acidic soils and Heather moorland (Manley 1990, 524-525). In the uplands of southern Powys at Mynyyd y Drum c. 300m OD, pre-barrow contexts suggest that funerary monuments were constructed in a heath-dominated (Dorling et al. 1990, 244) marginal landscape (ibid. 233), following tree clearance in the Neolithic (ibid. 244). These two examples suggest that changing environmental conditions in upland contexts may not necessarily have followed a uniform sequence.

Two episodes of tree clearance have been recognised in mid-Shropshire, from peat core samples dating to the Late Neolithic/Early Bronze Age and the Middle Bronze Age (Leah et al. 1998, 53). These results have been replicated from peat samples across the north of the county together with evidence for cereal cultivation (ibid. 66-67). This suggests a common sequence of environmental change. The relatively extensive environmental sampling programmes undertaken in the county over a number of decades have enabled the suggestion that Bronze Age clearances and associated human settlement activity were earlier in the south of the county (ibid. 67). Sampling at Lindow Moss in Cheshire supports the evidence for lowland clearances and cultivation in the Early Bronze Age (Leah et al. 1997, 49). However, to what extent these recorded horizons represent widespread colonisation of forested lands in the Early and Middle Bronze Age is open to debate. Comparisons between pollen horizons and associated Early Iron Age radiocarbon dates in peat deposits in the north –west of England, have raised doubts about generalised interpretations of climatically affected environmental change (ibid. 61). Therefore sequences of change recorded in pollen records dated to the Bronze Age cannot necessarily be applied to any more than a local context. Furthermore the degree and rate at which climatic change, particularly the onset of adverse conditions, affected the location of settlement in the Bronze Age has recently been questioned (Young 2000, 73).

The identification of settlement sites in the following study refers to the influence of specific environments in their siting. The distribution of contemporary artefacts and monuments is also examined in relation to the location of settlement and used to illuminate its wider social context.

3. Settlement in the Early Bronze Age

Background: Early Bronze Age settlement in Britain

Settlement sites of the Early Bronze Age in Britain are an elusive feature of the archaeological record. Apparently meagre evidence for domestic activity has therefore been interpreted as representing a transient pattern of residence. In the early twentieth century Childe emphasised a temporary settlement pattern, where movement in a semi-nomadic system was explained in terms of repeated soil exhaustion (Childe 1930. 159-160). Attempts to identify settlement evidence through the recognition of domestic structures have met with limited success. Nine excavated examples from Britain and Ireland were identified by Simpson (1971, 132-135). The paucity of settlement sites dating to the period is underlined by a more recent summary of the evidence from Ireland, which has recorded only eight house structures dating to the Early Bronze Age (Doody 2000, 143). Artefact concentrations in association with hearths have been recorded in low-lying contexts in the south-east of England, but associated structures appear to be ephemeral (Bamford 1982, 8-20). Deposits and structures sealed beneath stratigraphically later monuments such as round barrows have been interpreted as settlement episodes which have been favourably preserved (Gibson 1982, 36-37). It is debatable, however, to what extent pre-barrow features represent activity that is unrelated to the construction of the barrow or use of the site for ceremonial activity. Furthermore, it has been argued that a lack of evidence for Early Bronze Age settlement sites is not necessarily due to masking by post depositional processes, such as the development of colluvium or alluvium (Brück 1999a, 54).

It has been suggested that later patterns of enclosed and nucleated settlement may have influenced our expectations for the Early Bronze Age (Gibson 1992, 41). The historical use of the terms 'settlement' and 'site' have also been examined and have been used to question our interpretation of settlement in prehistory (Carman 1999). It has been argued that our notion of settlement has been influenced by Early Modern concepts of the act of settlement in foreign lands, where sites were intentionally and clearly bounded (ibid. 21). Instead, settlement sites are seen as " nodes of more concentrated activity within a larger area." (ibid. 23).

Fleming built upon Childe's theory of temporary settlement by suggesting that populations moved in a systematic seasonal cycle which incorporated the use of funerary monuments (Fleming 1971). Barrow distributions in Dorset and Wiltshire were examined and patterns in the spacing of barrow groups across the landscape were identified and interpreted as territorial markers (ibid. 155). Fleming did not consider that barrows were necessarily contiguous with permanent settlement sites. Instead, a seasonal pattern of transhumance was envisaged whereby populations converged upon monuments situated in grazing areas during the summer months (ibid. 159). The fact that barrows were often situated near to water sources was a factor to support this theory, and it was also suggested that linear barrow cemeteries could be aligned upon droveways (ibid. 162-163). However, this regularity of movement, is perhaps belied by a fact highlighted by Barrett, that death is haphazard and irregular, unless it is a deliberate act (Barrett et al. 1991, 138). This would not allow for a settlement pattern where funerary monuments were only visited seasonally, since deaths could occur at any time. Fleming argued that cremation burial could fit into this system (Fleming 1971, 160), as cremated bone is portable. However, whilst funerary monuments could witness the interment of the dead or the enactment of a ceremony during the seasonal occupation of associated lands, it is equally possible that they were used on a year-round basis.

Recent arguments have emphasised the relationship between the settlement pattern and monuments (Brück 1999a, 63). Episodic domestic activity has been interpreted as centring upon monuments (ibid.), in a mobile pattern that was less regular than the seasonal one envisaged by Fleming. It has also been argued that investment in arable agriculture did not necessarily require an associated settlement site for the duration of the season (ibid.67) allowing for a more mobile pattern of settlement (ibid.). Barnatt has suggested that barrows occupy locations with contrasting land-use patterns and settlement contexts in the Peak District (2000, 83).

Considerable investment can be seen to have been made in monument construction during the Early Bronze Age.

16

The fact that burials within ring ditches begin in the mid to Late Neolithic (Warrilow et al. 1986, 64) and continue to attract secondary cremations into the Middle Bronze Age (ibid. 85) shows continuity in at least the focus of funerary practices (Fig. 4). Continuity in the location of funerary practices suggests continuity in the settlement pattern also, although it does not necessarily suggest that this settlement pattern included permanently occupied settlement sites.

However, there is a suggestion from sites in Britain that longevity was a feature of settlement locales in the Early Bronze Age. This suggests that mobility in the settlement pattern was either restricted, or structured in a way that made repeated reference to specific places. At Lairg in north-eastern Scotland two round-house structures were identified as succeeding each other, separated by a cultivation horizon (McCullagh and Tipping 1998, 38). A radiocarbon date (Gu-3308) obtained from House 1 calibrates to between 1780 and 1510 BC at 95.4% confidence. The replacement of structural timbers (ibid.) suggests the structure was the focus of prolonged occupation. The succeeding structure has a series of later radiocarbon dates between 1600 and 1400 cal BC (McCullagh and Tipping 1998, 47) suggesting a later, but broadly concurrent, phase of occupation.

The fact that the structures were rebuilt in the same location suggests that settlement continued to focus upon an established locale. It is possible that any period of abandonment between phases of round-house construction could have witnessed occupation elsewhere on the same site, since other structures of a comparable date have been recorded here (McCullagh and Tipping 1998, 42-44). The reorganisation of space within later enclosed settlement sites of the Middle Bronze Age in southern England has been emphasised and has been shown to include the rebuilding of structures elsewhere on the same site (Brück 1999b, 146). Therefore the possibility of longevity in the occupation of settlement locales from the Early to Middle Bronze Age and the potential reorganisation of settlement space, can be suggested here in a highland zone context.

An Early Bronze Age domestic site in a contrasting lowland coastal context has been recorded at Stackpole Warren in Dyfed (Benson et al. 1990). Evidence for up to three Early Bronze Age round-houses was excavated here. Broad continuity in settlement between the Early and Middle Bronze Age is represented by radiocarbon dates (ibid. 187; 239) which calibrate to between 2060 and 1730 (CAR –475) BC and 1780 and 1490 BC (CAR –100) at 95.4% confidence. The fact that the stratigraphic interpretation of structure 146 suggests two phases (ibid. 189) separated by an episode of burning and destruction, is comparable to the relationship between the two phases of round-house construction highlighted from Lairg. This activity suggests continuity, but again allows for a period of dislocation. To what extent this dislocation is representative of a wider settlement shift or merely the abandonment of an individual

structure, is again uncertain.

At Stackpole Warren Collared Urn sherds and flint were found in association with charred cereal grains of barley (ibid. 187). Lairg House 1 was associated with a saddle quern and carbonised naked barley seeds (McCullagh and Tipping 1998, 38). It can be argued therefore that both sites had a relationship with arable agriculture and were occupied at least seasonally. It is possible therefore that both upland and lowland settlement locales in the Early Bronze Age are broadly comparable. These sites suggest that sustained or at least recurrent settlement episodes may have taken place in dramatically contrasting geographical regions. This supports recent discussions which have questioned the notion of environmentally and economically marginal locations as having inhibited settlement (Young and Simmonds 1999).

A permanent attachment to a particular settlement locale is more readily envisaged when landscapes are formally divided for agricultural purposes. This represents significant investment in a particular place. It has been argued that field systems in Britain could belong in the Early Bronze Age. However the dating of such field systems to the Early Bronze Age is inadequate and cannot be used to infer the presence of permanently settled fixed agriculture elsewhere.

In the lowlands of East Anglia field systems have been recorded in association with more marginal fenlands considered to have been used for common grazing on a seasonal basis (Pryor 1999, 93-94). The complex system of ditched enclosures at Fengate, has evidence to suggest origins in the Early Bronze Age, and continuous usage into the Late Bronze Age (Pryor 1992b, 519).

Collared Urn sherds have been excavated from ditch fills (Pryor 1980, 92) and radiocarbon dates give weight to the suggestion of an Early Bronze Age phase (ibid. 177-178). These dates however are weighted earlier than the currency of Collared Urns, and are more likely to be contemporary with Beaker pottery in the early Phase 1 and 2 periods of the Early Bronze Age (Needham 1996). This could therefore suggest that the material sampled for dating is residual from earlier activity. It is equally possible that the Collared Urn sherds found in boundary ditches at the site are also residual. Therefore the dating evidence from Fengate is ambiguous. The fact that other Early Bronze Age settlement evidence in East Anglia suggests intermittent occupation (Bamford 1982, 19-20) also undermines the interpretation that organised field systems and significant investment in particular locales are contemporary. This would, however, depend on the extent to which systems of fixed agricultural organisation were incorporated into wider mobile patterns of residency.

Attempts have been made to correlate field systems with

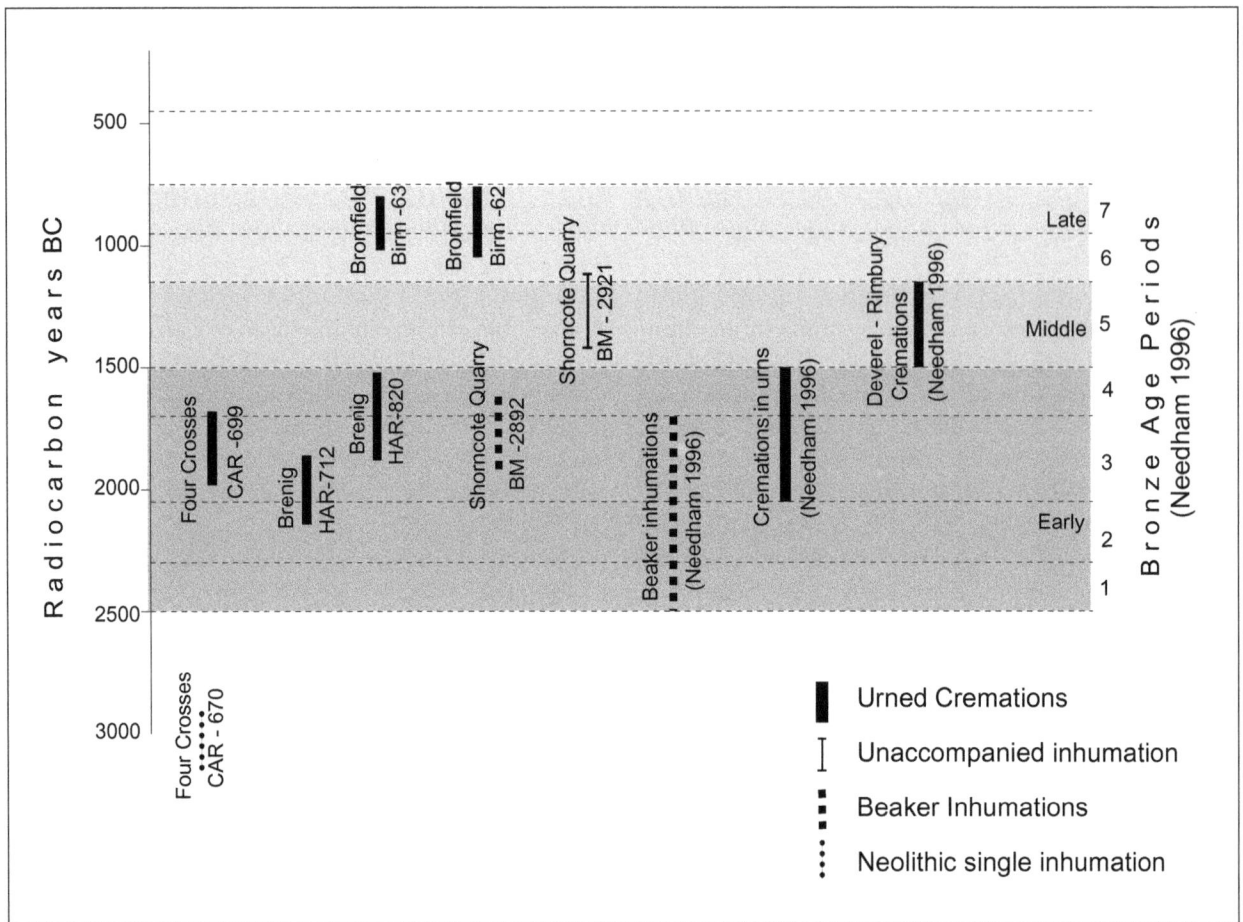

Fig. 4 Calibrated radiocarbon dates from burials at ring-ditches and round barrows in the study area

evidence for Early Bronze Age settlement in upland contexts also, yet the dating evidence is again inconclusive. At Houseledge-Black Law in Northumbria round-house structures have been identified in an upland context at 300m OD and appear on spatial grounds to be associated with field systems (Burgess 1995). However, Early Bronze Age pottery on the site cannot be seen to be securely associated with stone round-houses and their field systems, which may post-date any Early Bronze Age activity.

Nevertheless, the excavation of monuments frequently produces evidence which suggests a relationship with settlement activity in the Early Bronze Age either earlier, contemporary with, or later than the monument. At Newgrange in Ireland Beaker domestic activity has been recorded post-dating the use of the main passage grave and a partial stone circle (O'Kelly et al. 1983). However, the fact that this activity was contemporary with a concentric arc of pits c.80m in diameter (ibid.18), suggests that the occupation was contemporary with associated ritual activity. At Cranborne Chase a group of ten pits were found to pre-date a pond barrow at the site of Firtree Field (Barrett et al. 1991, 118). An assemblage of flintwork including utilised flakes, scrapers and knives together with

animal bone, beaker and food vessel pottery are considered in terms of domestic activity (ibid.). However, the presence of such activity may equally be seen as a prelude to later funerary and ceremonial events, and may not simply be the chance survival of unrelated domestic occupation, and this could apply to all such instances. The presence of quern stones and animals in a burial context at Cranborne Chase (Barrett et al. 1991, 132-134) suggests that deposits referring to the domestic sphere were intentionally placed in a non-domestic context. It was suggested that stake circles beneath round barrows represented preserved domestic structures (Gibson 1982, 36). However, in the light of further excavations, these features can be seen as part of an ordered construction of these monuments (Warrilow et al. 1986, 55). Therefore it appears questionable that material recorded beneath monuments represents domestic activity that has been favourably preserved.

The most common relationship recorded between areas of potential settlement activity and funerary monuments is that between flint scatters and round barrows or ring-ditches. At Biddenham, situated on a gravel terrace near the River Great Ouse in Bedfordshire a number of ring-ditches have been recorded (Woodward 1978; Malim 2000, 80).

Systematic field walking recovered a flint assemblage which included an Early Bronze Age component (Woodward 1978, 44). The distribution of tools, and specifically scrapers was interpreted as representing habitation foci nearer the river than the ring ditches (ibid.). The fact that the monuments themselves appear to lie no further than 0.5km from the river reinforces their potential relationship with the settlement activity. Therefore phases of settlement in proximity to monuments can be suggested, but to what extent they represent sustained or more episodic events is uncertain.

Brück has suggested that the ceremonial and domestic spheres cannot be separated (Brück 1999a, 62). Within a system of residential mobility groups would congregate periodically for specific events at monuments and associated domestic activity has been interpreted as being representative of the settlement pattern in southern England (ibid. 68-69). But to what extent other areas of the landscape were occupied, for how long and at what distance removed from monuments is again uncertain.

In order to examine settlement patterns during the Early Bronze Age in the study area it is first necessary to identify nodes of domestic settlement. The sequence of dating from individual excavated sites can be used to indicate the extent of longevity in their occupation and therefore the question of residential mobility. The examination of the distribution of contemporary artefacts located in non-funerary contexts can be used to infer a wider settlement pattern, and its relationship with ceremonial events or agricultural cycles. An examination of the relationship between settlement and funerary monuments can also be used to explore the centrality of ceremonial events to the settlement pattern.

Settlement sites in the study area: location and longevity

There is a general lack of Early Bronze Age settlement sites recorded in the study area, which is consistent with the archaeological record for the rest of Britain. All recorded contemporary metalwork finds and barrows in the Welsh Marches have been plotted against a topographical background for this study (Fig. 5). This distribution highlights the widespread activity in the study area during the Early Bronze Age in both upland and lowland zones and demonstrates the fact that the evidence for Early Bronze Age domestic structures is severely limited.

The greatest evidence for structural remains dating to the Early Bronze Age comes from the north of the study area in Cheshire, with more ephemeral evidence having been recorded in Shropshire and Powys. The siting of Early Bronze Age settlements can be seen to have been influenced by rivers, streams or other water sources in all cases where evidence for domestic structures can be

demonstrated. There is also some evidence to suggest that nodes of settlement in the Early Bronze Age witnessed longevity in their occupation and sustained settlement phases.

At Rock Green, Ludlow, Shropshire, ephemeral evidence for settlement activity has been recorded (Carver and Humler 1991). A hearth in association with Beaker pottery was recorded in the vicinity of a flint scatter including waste flakes and a scraper (ibid. 87). A barbed and tanged arrowhead recorded twenty metres away (ibid. 93) could suggest hunting in the vicinity. The position of the site lies around 1.5 km from the River Corve and 1km away from two tributaries, suggesting only a loose relationship with water sources and perhaps a transient settlement episode.

Similar ephemeral evidence for Early Bronze Age activity has been recorded on a number of hilltop sites in the study area that were subsequently to become hillforts.

However, the fact that archaeological features have been truncated by later activity on these sites leaves the nature of Early Bronze Age occupation ambiguous. At the Breiddin hillfort, Powys a radiocarbon date (HAR −470) associated with intercutting bowl hearths (Musson 1991, 22) calibrates to between 1950 and 1680 BC at 68.2% confidence, which would place activity within Period 3 of the Bronze Age (Needham 1996, 130-132). Food Vessel, Beaker and possible Beaker domestic sherds (Lynch and Gibson 1991, 116-118) found from residual contexts on the Breiddin would also be contemporary with Period 3 (Needham 1996, 130-131) as would the jet and amber beads found on the site (Musson 1991, 19). It is possible therefore that the hilltop witnessed settlement activity in the Early Bronze Age. The presence of jet, faience and amber beads (ibid.) could, however, suggest that the focus of activity was funerary or ceremonial rather than domestic, since these finds are often associated with inhumations and cremations of the period (e.g. Lynch 1991, 163-164).

Possible Beaker pottery has also been recorded in secondary contexts at Llwyn Bryn-dinas hillfort in Powys (Musson et al. 1992, 270) and at the Wrekin in Shropshire (Stanford 1984, 73). At Beeston Castle, Cheshire, Early Bronze Age sherds of Beaker, Urn, Food Vessel and Accessory Cups in secondary contexts have been interpreted as representing the presence of barrows upon the crag (Ellis 1993, 20). This is not necessarily incompatible with a settlement phase, since a comparable assemblage of material has been recorded at Oversley Farm, Cheshire, in a settlement context (Garner 2001). At Sharpstones Hill, Shropshire, Beaker sherds were considered to be residual from earlier settlement phases (Barker et al. 1991, 21). However, the excavation of two ring-ditches with cremations in a Collared Urn and an Enlarged Food Vessel, again suggests that the focus of the site in the Early Bronze Age was funerary and ceremonial rather than domestic.

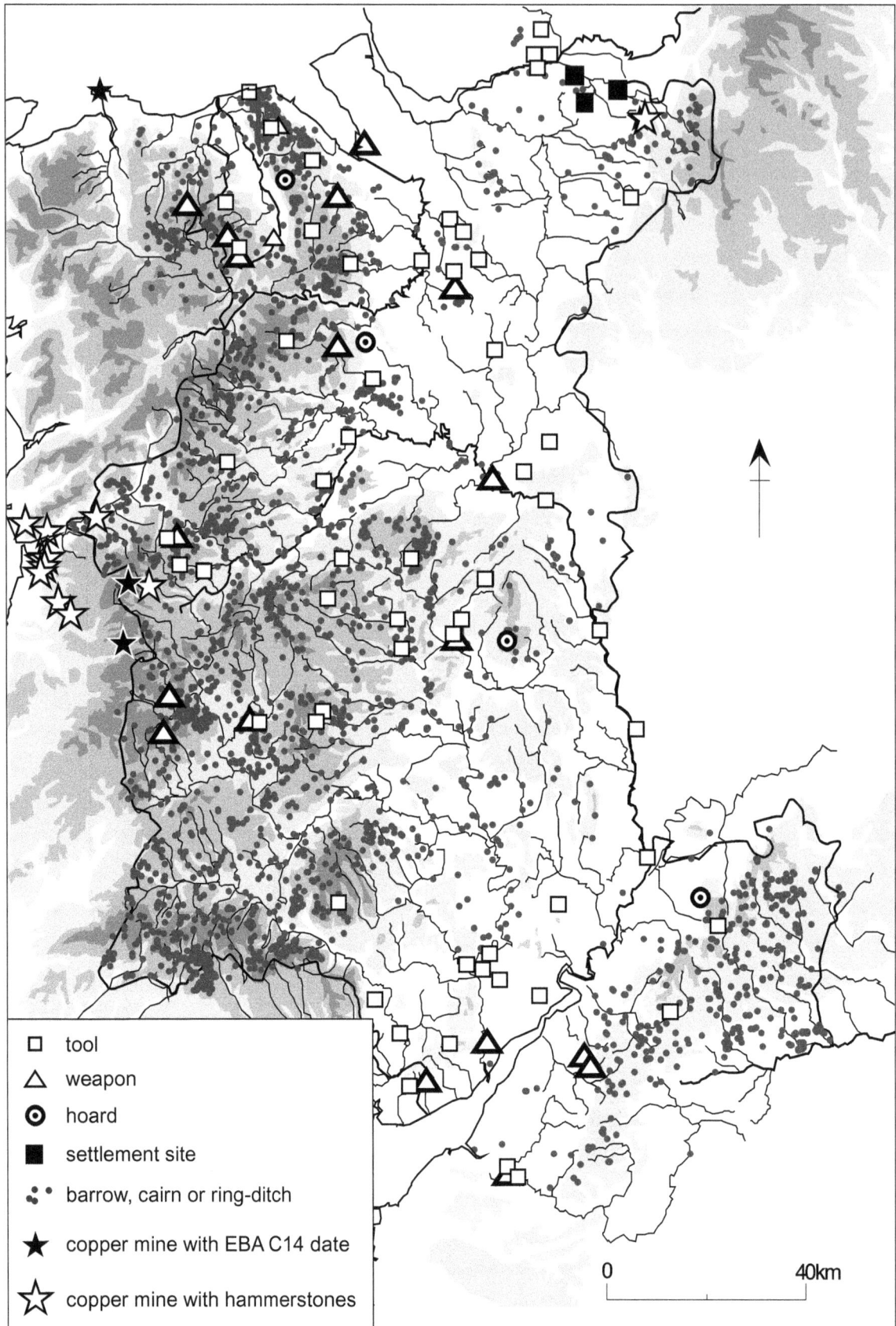

Fig.5 Early Bronze metalwork, settlement sites, funerary monuments and mines in the study area

Legend:
- □ tool
- △ weapon
- ◉ hoard
- ■ settlement site
- ∴ barrow, cairn or ring-ditch
- ★ copper mine with EBA C14 date
- ☆ copper mine with hammerstones

0   40km

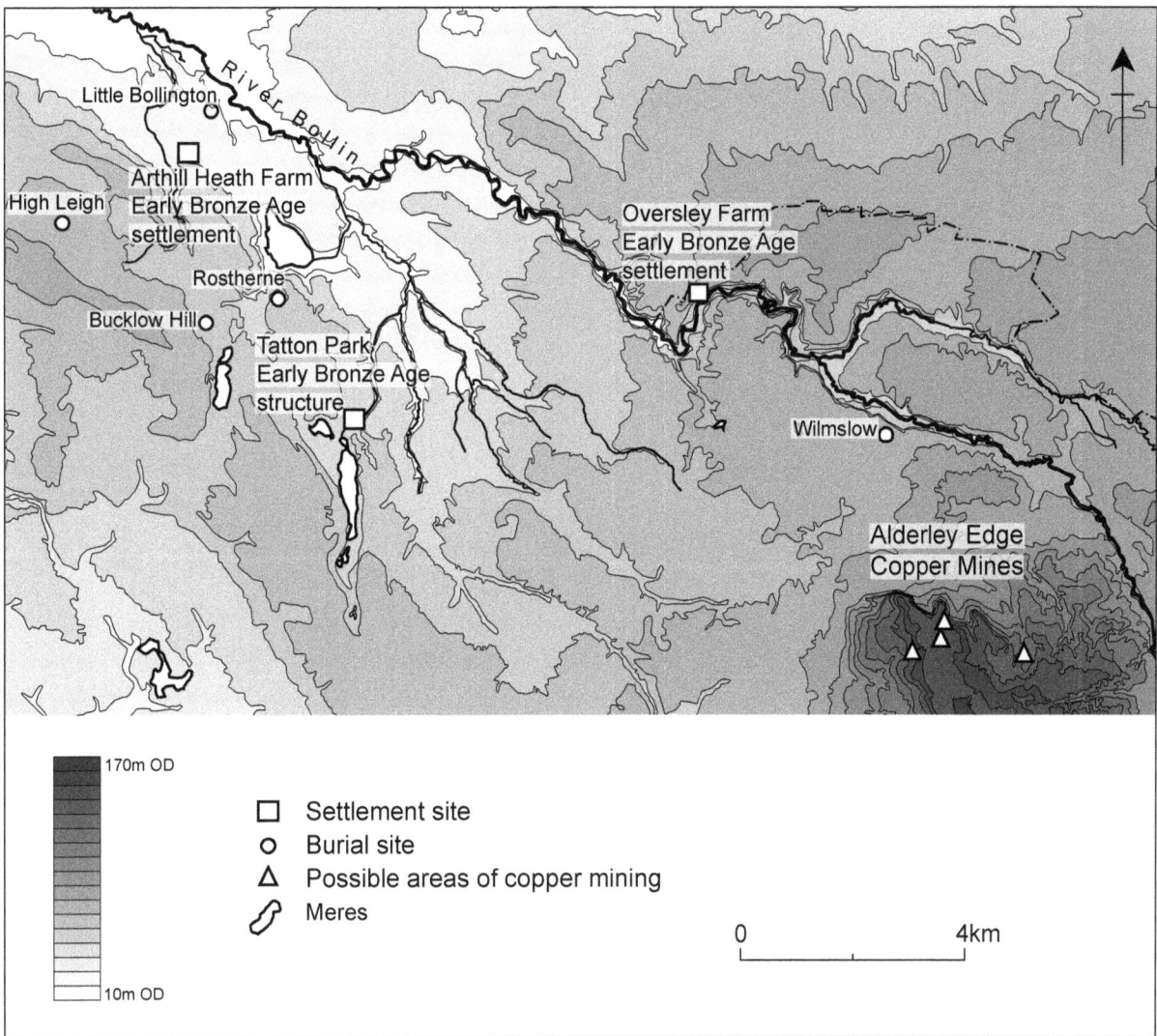

Fig. 6 Early Bronze Age settlement sites and Bronze Age copper mines in Cheshire

It is possible therefore that the Early Bronze Age phases at hillfort sites do not represent sustained domestic occupation, but rather activity associated with episodic ritual events. It is possible that these locations were considered distinctive natural features of the landscape (cf. Bradley 2000) which may therefore have served as a focus for ceremonial events in the Early Bronze Age.

A site in Cheshire which shows slight evidence for Early Bronze Age settlement structures, has been recorded near the mere at Tatton Park (Fig. 6), lying at around 50m OD (Higham and Cane 1999) and situated on free draining sands and gravels (ibid. 1). The site was located through excavation which had been designed to investigate later Medieval occupation of Tatton village (Ibid. 4). Here an ambiguous but possibly sub-rectangular arrangement of postholes has produced a radiocarbon date (HAR-5716), which calibrates to between 2200 and 1600 BC at 95.4% confidence, or 2030-1740 at 68.2%

confidence. This is considerably later than radiocarbon dates from Neolithic pits and postholes on the site (ibid. 32), and would place the structure in Period 3 of the Bronze Age (Fig. 7), contemporary with late Beakers, Collared and Cordoned Urns and Food Vessels (Needham 1996, 130-132). It has been suggested that this 'late' date could be due to contamination of the sample by root activity (Higham and Cane1999, 32). However it can be shown that other domestic sites in comparable contexts along the River Bollin in Cheshire, at Arthill Heath Farm and Oversley Farm, date to the Early Bronze Age (Fig. 7), and therefore activity at Tatton could be contemporary.

More substantial evidence for settlement is represented by four circular structures at Arthill Heath Farm, Cheshire, which lies at 30m OD on a plateau 1 km from the River Bollin (Fig. 6), on well drained glacial sands and adjacent to a spring line (Nevell 1988, 5). The site at Arthill Heath Farm was preserved by clay surface deposits relating

21

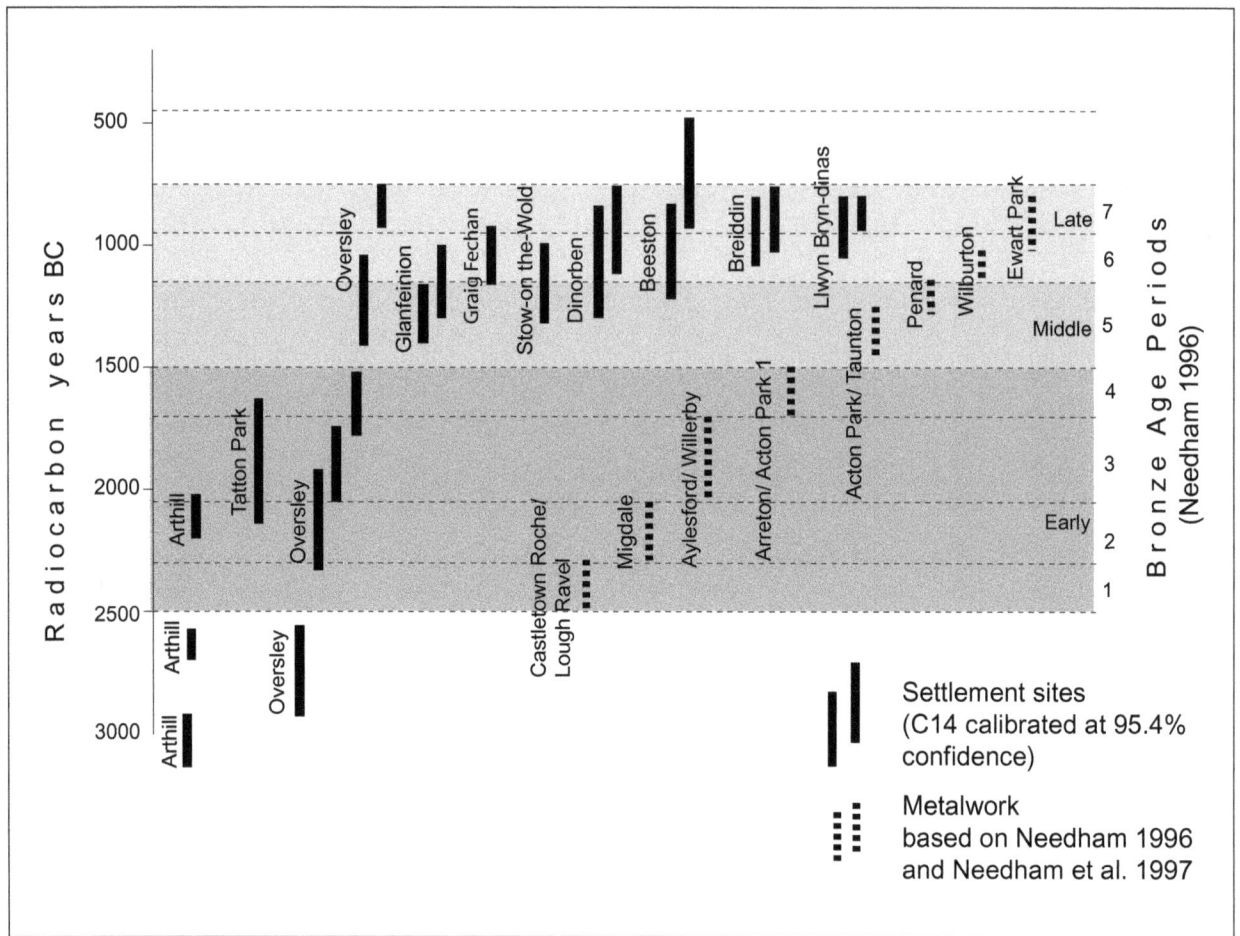

Fig.7 Radiocarbon dates from Bronze Age settlement sites in the study area and metalwork chronology

to a later Romano-British settlement on the same spot (Nevell 1988, 10). The identification of the site through the excavation of later more visible settlement traces can be compared with the site at Tatton Park.

All structures have a ring of post or stakeholes within construction trenches. Structures 1 and 4 are c.8m in diameter (ibid. 7), Structure 2, c.6m and Structure 3, c.5m. All features are recorded as having been filled with large quantities of charcoal or black organic material. The presence of carbonised seed, waste flint flakes and 'button' scrapers (ibid. 8-10) suggests food processing and a domestic function for the site. The black material could also be interpreted as the remains of cooking, comparable with midden deposits recorded elsewhere on Bronze Age sites

A sustained period of occupation is suggested by more than one phase, with circular structures 3 and 4 appearing to intercut (ibid. 8), although the relationship is unclear. There appears to have been a paucity of pottery from the organic contexts on the site, and that recorded appears to

have been too small and friable for identification (ibid. 11). This could suggest that the site was not occupied for a long period. Alternatively a sustained period of occupation could have destroyed and abraded sherds present on the site, particularly if the midden deposits were not removed from the immediate settlement area.

The 'button' scrapers from the site, although not illustrated, could be comparable to the 'thumbnail' scrapers associated with Early Bronze Age stuctures elsewhere (Benson et al. 1990, 224-225). The radiocarbon dates from the site are earlier than the date from the Tatton Park structure (Fig. 7). A date from Structure 3 (Grn-15906) calibrates to between 2210 and 2020 BC at 95.4% confidence. This would place the structure within Needham's Peiod 2 of the Early Bronze Age, contemporary with Beaker burials and narrow butted Migdale flat bronze axes (Needham 1996, 128-30). The date from Structure 4 (Grn-15905) appears to be considerably earlier, calibrating within a number of date ranges centring on the early to mid-third millennium BC (Fig. 7; Appendix). It is likely that this site therefore belongs to the Late Neolithic and Early Bronze Age, and

22

that more than one phase of activity is represented at a settlement locale which either remained occupied, or was episodically re-occupied over a long period.

Another Early Bronze Age site in Cheshire also lies at around 70m OD, 150m from the River Bollin (Fig. 6), on comparable glacial sands and gravels to Arthill and Tatton. The site at Oversley Farm was discovered during the course of random trial trenching during the construction of the Manchester Airport Runway 2 in 1997-8, and its location was not predicted by non-intrusive evaluations of the site (Garner 2001). This compares with the discovery of Early Bronze Age settlement at Tatton Park and Arthill Heath Farm that had not been predicted in advance.

Longevity in the use of the site, however, can be seen not from the structures but from an extensive midden deposit which overlay a metalled trackway. Several hundred sherds of Early Bronze Age pottery were found within a black deposit rich in charcoal and containing significant quantities of burnt stone (ibid.). The pottery mainly comprised collared urns representing over 100 vessels, together with Food Vessel, Cordoned Urns and Pygmy Cups (Garner forthcoming.). The lithic assemblage included flint tools and debitage, and a number of perforated stones (ibid.). This midden deposit was stratified and a number of Beaker and Beaker domestic ware sherds were found towards the lower horizons (Garner 2001, 47 and forthcoming).

The quantity of pottery in the midden deposit suggests that this site was occupied over some considerable time when compared with the material assemblages from Tatton and Arthill Heath Farm, although factors of preservation could have affected the degree of survival of deposits at these two sites. The range of Early Bronze Age pottery suggests that the midden at Oversley Farm accumulated during Needham's Period 3 (2050-1700 cal. BC) which witnessed the contemporary use of Late Beakers, Collared Urns, Cordoned Urns and Food Vessels (Needham 1996, 130-131). Radiocarbon dates from features on the site (Garner 2001, 55) suggest that it had witnessed occupation from the Neolithic in the early to mid-fourth millennium BC (Appendix). Dates of 3050-2450 BC (Beta –127174) and 2350 – 1920 BC (Beta 133370) calibrated at 95.4 % confidence, allow for the possibility of continuity in the settlement of the site between the Late Neolithic and Early Bronze Age. The Bronze Age dates from the site suggest that it was occupied in the earliest phases of the period contemporary with both Arthill Heath Farm and Tatton Park and that this occupation continued into at least the Middle Bronze Age (Fig. 7) if not the Late Bronze Age (ibid. 53-54).

The radiocarbon dates show a broad longevity in the occupation of the site at Oversley Farm. They do not however reveal the extent to which settlement on the site was punctuated by any settlement shifts. If occupation here was part of a mobile system then the position of the site must have remained as a fixed feature in the landscape, which was returned to repeatedly within any patterns of movement.

The presence of charred cereals on the site and a saddle quern (Garner 2001, 47-48), represents grain processing and arable agriculture, and could suggest that the site was settled permanently. Although it has been suggested that arable agriculture did not necessarily require an attendant permanent settlement (Brück 1999a, 67), the evidence from Oversley Farm does suggest that settlement was at least sustained. Lipid samples from pottery on the site suggest the presence of pig and sheep/goat (Garner forthcoming). The latter could suggest that pastoral agriculture was practised by the site's occupants alongside cereal cultivation. The presence of pigs may also suggest a permanently occupied locale, since these animals are unlikely to be suited to controlled movements through the landscape. This may have required the seasonal movement of stock into areas of pasture, and could allow for a degree of mobility in the settlement pattern. However, the evidence for the sustained accumulation of burnt stone, charcoal and pottery in a midden on the site, together with the radiocarbon dates, suggests that Oversley Farm remained a focal point for settlement activity, and that any mobility in the settlement pattern did not lead to wholesale abandonment of the site. The rate at which such a midden deposit may have accumulated is open to question, but the quantity and range of ceramics could suggest it represents a significant length of time.

A number of factors can result in the formation of midden deposits and these have been recently discussed with regard to Late Bronze Age sites in southern England (Needham and Spence 1997). The creation of a midden involves the deliberate and cumulative disposal of waste over time. Such a site may not have been specifically selected as a midden but "could have progressively emerged as a midden both physically and conceptually" (ibid. 80-81). Therefore this also suggests longevity in the occupation of an associated settlement. The accumulation of material in a certain location could be dependant upon the type of fuel used or mode of cooking on a site with stones used as pot boilers for example (ibid. 82). A significant quantity of burnt stone from the midden deposit at Oversley perhaps reflects intensive or repeated cooking activity of this kind. Other factors could include a greater frequency and quantity of imported goods, centralised storage of foodstuffs, or the location of exchange centres attracting people, artefacts and livestock (ibid.).

The presence of a trackway at the Oversley Farm site may favour the latter interpretation, if this served to facilitate exchange with other groups, particularly in conjunction with the nearby River Bollin. The quantity of pottery in the midden could represent symbolic deposition through

Fig. 8 Location of detailed drift geology study

feasting (Needham and Spence 1997, 85), or perhaps a slower cumulative deposition through less intensive events.

The degree of longevity in settlement at Oversley Farm could be influenced by its position in relation to Early Bronze Age copper mines at Alderley Edge to the east (Fig. 6). Together with characteristic hammer stones found during nineteenth century ore extraction and the identification of contemporary mine shafts, a wooden shovel discovered in the early twentieth century has been dated to the Early Bonze Age (Lewis 1998, 54-55). This date (OXA-4050) calibrates to between 1890 and 1680 BC

at 68.2% confidence. This would place activity at the site within Period 3 (2050-1700 cal BC) of the Early Bronze Age (Needham 1996, 130-132). This date is comparable with the material assemblage and radiocarbon dates from the midden deposit at Oversley Farm (Garner 2001, 51 and forthcoming.). The relationship of Alderley Edge (as with other Early Bronze Age mines in Britain), with the location of the production of bronze objects does not appear to be well understood. It is, however, possible that settlement sites such as Oversley Farm, c. 7 km away, were involved in the exchange and redistribution of material produced here, facilitated by a river system which links the uplands of the Pennines with the Mersey Estuary and the Irish Sea (Fig. 5).

It is evident that Early Bronze Age settlement locales in the study area have parallels with settlement recorded elsewhere in Britain. Transitory settlement episodes can be suggested from the more ephemeral signs of occupation. Such activity may, however, have taken place away from more permanently settled and fixed locales. There is evidence to suggest sustained domestic activity in lowland river valley contexts, which may be associated with locations expedient for agriculture or exchange. This reflects evidence from elsewhere in Britain that Early Bronze Age settlement locales show evidence for longevity in their occupation.

The distribution of artefacts in the study area and their relationship with settlement locales

It may be possible to extrapolate the settlement pattern and place it into a wider context by examining the distribution of contemporary artefacts in the landscape (Fig. 5). It has been noted in the Cotswolds that flint assemblages with an Early Bronze Age component show a preference for areas with a good water supply (Marshall 1985, 47). In Cheshire it has been suggested that the distribution of perforated stone implements datable to the Early Bronze Age show a preference for the well-drained sands and gravels in the county and may represent areas of settlement (Cowell 2000, 121). The presence of perforated stone implements at Oversley Farm (Garner forthcoming) and Tatton Park (Higham and Cane 1999, 38), both on sands and gravels, may support this suggestion.

Flint assemblages with an Early Bronze Age component have been recorded in association with rivers. At Saintbridge in Gloucestershire for example a flint assemblage was recorded in a lowland context around 30m OD on a sand and gravel terrace 150m from the River Twyver (Darvill and Timby, 1986). This location is again comparable to settlement evidence elsewhere in the study area. The presence of contemporary flintwork upon the recorded settlement sites in the north of the study area could suggest that flint scatters represent nodes of settlement in the landscape. However to what extent they reflect nodes of sustained, rather than episodic activity, is difficult to address without the identification of associated features through excavation. An assemblage of flint containing an Early Bronze Age component was recorded in a residual context at Barnsley Park, Gloucestershire (Webster 1981). The assemblage was interpreted as representing episodes of re-occupation, in that flint debitage was re-used (Barfield 1981, 44). To what extent the re-use of flintwork represents the re-occupation of a settlement locale, inferring residential mobility, is open to debate.

It has been shown that the recorded settlement sites in Cheshire at Oversley Farm, Arthill Heath Farm and Tatton Park all lie upon sand and gravel geology apparently in preference to boulder clay deposits. Modern day agricultural land-use in Cheshire favours boulder clay till for pasture (Hebblethwaite 1987, 32), whilst lighter sandy soils on glacial sands and gravels, sandstones and river terraces are considered to be more favourable for arable cultivation (ibid.). The majority of Early Bronze Age metal finds in the county have been recorded in locations that would place them on boulder clay rather than sand and gravel deposits. This suggests that they could represent areas of contrasting land use than the recorded location of known settlement sites.

The best quality agricultural land around Wrexham to the south also favours sands and gravels and river terrace deposits (Fig. 3). If an area of drift geology is examined covering north-east Wales, north-west Shropshire and southern Cheshire (Fig. 8) it can, again, be seen that Early Bronze Age metal finds around Wrexham and north-west Shropshire, do not necessarily show a preference for these areas (Fig. 9). Therefore the locations chosen for the deposition of metal objects, or the areas in which these objects were lost in the Early Bronze Age, may reflect activities at locations which were less suitable for arable cultivation and which contrast with the context of known settlement locales recorded in Cheshire. It is possible therefore that metal objects were deposited in areas more suited to pastoralism. If these areas did not witness the more sustained forms of settlement reflected at Oversley Farm, then it could be suggested that they represent areas of seasonal land use within systems of transhumance.

In Denbighshire and Flintshire there appear to be a greater number of metal objects recorded on the limestone, sandstone, mudstone and shale solid geology of the higher ground at altitudes ranging between 280 and 400m. The land utilisation survey of 1932-5 (Sheet 42) in Denbighshire suggests that the higher ground around the Vale of Clwyd, characterised by mudstones and sandstones, has a greater proportion of land given over to meadow. The highest areas on the Denbigh Moors and Clwydian Range in Flintshire are also characterised by heath moorland, commons and rough pasture. It would appear therefore that as with finds from the lower land in counties to the east, recorded Early Bronze Age metalwork lies upon lands which in a modern context are more suited to grazing than arable agriculture.

In Gloucestershire the distribution of Early Bronze Age metal objects also show a preference for the solid limestone and sandstone geology of the higher ground in the Cotswolds between 150 and 250m OD. However, unlike the areas examined in north Wales, the Land Utilisation Surveys of 1931-4 (Sheets 92 and 103) suggest that the land upon higher ground is more suited to cultivation. A clear distinction can be seen between the oolitic limestones

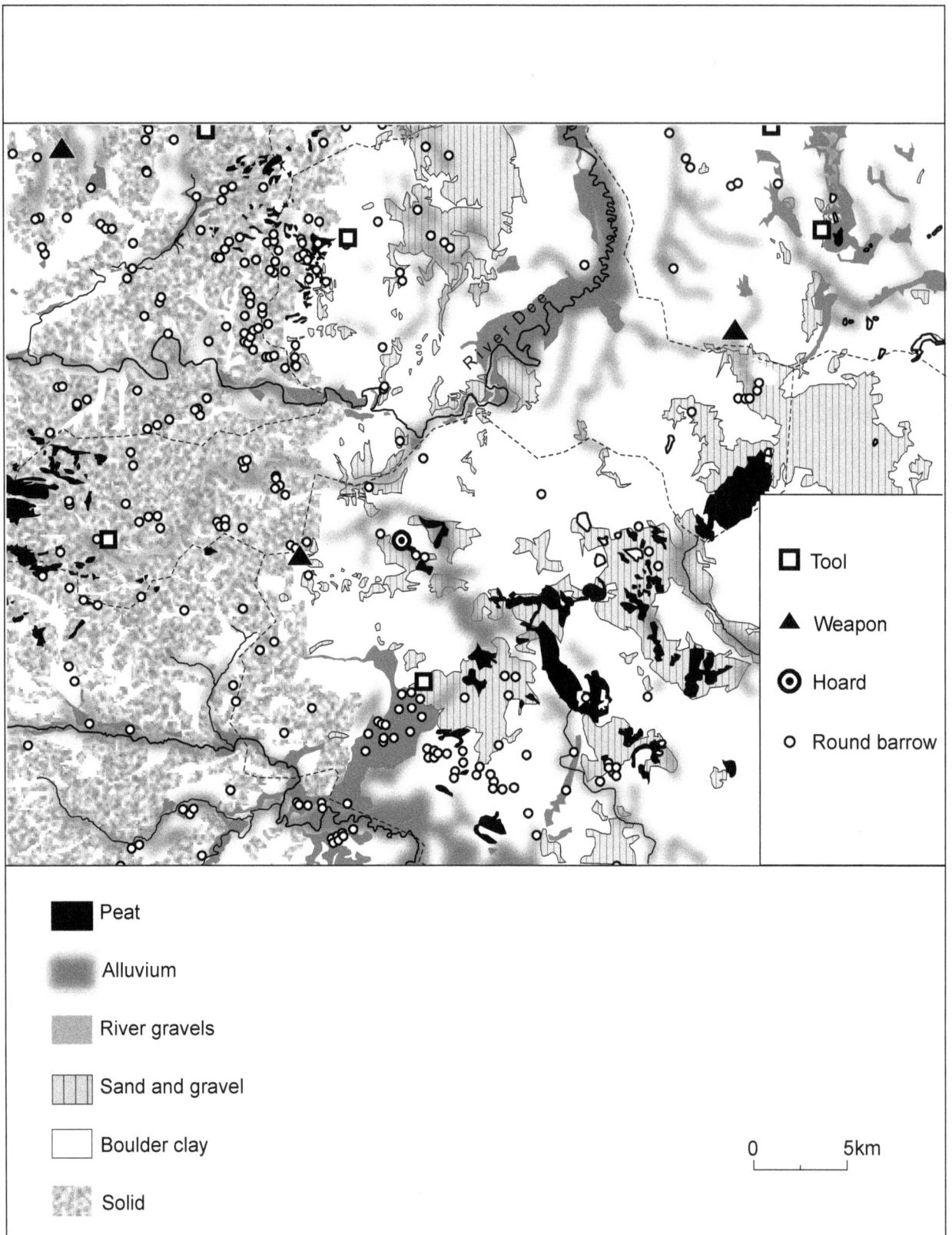

Fig. 9 Round barrows, Early Bronze Age metalwork and drift geology in north-west Shropshire, south-west Cheshire and north-east Wales (see Fig.8)

Legend:
- □ Tool
- ▲ Weapon
- ◉ Hoard
- ○ Round barrow

- Peat
- Alluvium
- River gravels
- Sand and gravel
- Boulder clay
- Solid

0   5km

of the Cotswolds, with significant areas of arable land and the lias clays to the west characterised by meadowland. The meadowland can be seen to predominate up to around 130m OD, with a greater amount of arable land between 130 and 270m OD. Sandstone geology to the west, however, appears to show a greater correlation with meadowland, suggesting that the metalwork recorded here was deposited in areas more suited to pastoralism.

Therefore the distribution of metalwork in Gloucestershire is ambiguous in terms of any geological preference, with metalwork having been recorded in locations suitable for both arable and pastoral agriculture. It is possible that this reflects a relationship between contrasting landscape zones in the region, settled as part of mixed agricultural systems during the Early Bronze Age.

It has been highlighted that the majority of Bronze Age metalwork from non-funerary contexts in Lancashire and Cheshire is located within 5km of a major river or the coast (Davey 1976, 6). However a closer association with rivers can be witnessed for a number of finds, which may reflect areas of settlement comparable to the location of domestic structures recorded in northern Cheshire. A haft-flanged axe of Needham's Bronze Age Period 4 has been recorded at Grappenhall, Warrington, Cheshire. The axe is recorded in a position c. 0.5km from the Mersey at c. 20m OD. This is comparable to the position of the sites to the south-east in Cheshire on the River Bollin, itself a tributary of the Mersey. It is possible therefore that the deposition of the axe reflects areas of further settlement along this river system.

However, the fact that this axe is deposited on boulder clay geology, contrasts with the siting of known settlement sites along the Bollin and may suggest that the axe was not deposited in a settlement context. The location of the axe on geology which could be argued to be more suitable for pastoral rather than arable agriculture, based on modern land-use surveys, is consistent with the recorded distribution of metal finds in Cheshire, north Wales and northern Shropshire. This could suggest alternative modes of agriculture and settlement along river systems in the region. However, the fact that no metalwork has been recorded on known settlement sites is further evidence to suggest that the deposition of objects was removed from locations of sustained residency. Metal objects recorded in association with rivers and less well-drained land may reflect alternative activity in the landscape. Their relationship with settlement locales could, nevertheless, reflect seasonal, episodic or contemporary activity, in association with nodes of settlement sited in specifically well-drained locations nearby.

A number of other metal finds in the study area appear to reflect the association with rivers recorded for settlement sites in northern Cheshire. For example a broad–butted

early flat axe has been recorded in a valley context below 50m OD, adjacent to the River Severn near Ironbridge, Shropshire. At Trederwen, Llandrinio, Powys, a bronze flat axe has also been recorded at 1km from the Severn at 60m OD. There are further examples which appear to show a preference for valley contexts where surrounding ground rises to higher altitudes. In Monmouthshire a flat axe has been recorded at Monmouth Secondary School within 150m of the Wye and 300m of the Monnow at 30m OD, below surrounding higher ground which rises up to 250m OD (Fig. 10). Similarly at Clunbury, Shropshire a flat axe has been recorded at 200m from the River Clun at 150m OD in a valley context below hills which rise to over 300m OD (Fig. 10). A flat axe at Gwernafon Farm, Trefeglws, Powys has also been recorded 200m from the River Trannon within a valley context surrounded by mountains rising up to 400m (Fig. 10).

The location of these finds at lower altitudes reflects the apparent preference of the majority of early Bronze Age metalwork finds in the study area to be found below 122m OD (Fig. 11). To what extent this reflects a fieldwork bias is open to debate, since Early Bronze Age artefacts in Denbighshire and Flintshire, for example, appear to show a preference for higher ground, rather than the Vale of Clwyd (Fig. 5), which has been favoured for cultivation in modern times and may be expected to have produced more finds.

The majority of Early Bronze Age metalwork from the study area has been recorded in locations which are characterised by small streams and tributaries. An association between small streams and metal finds can be shown both in lowland and upland contexts. It has been shown that possible Early Bronze Age settlement at Tatton Park, Cheshire, is in close proximity to a mere and streams and further hints at settlement activity have been recorded at the Sugar Brook, south of the River Bollin (Garner 2001, 45). An Early Bronze Age flat axe has also been recorded c. 0.75km from Deer Park Mere at Bickley, Chester, Cheshire. Therefore it is possible that nodes of settlement elsewhere in the study area focussed upon similar water sources, and that the recorded distribution of metalwork reflects this.

The possibility that Early Bronze Age metal objects were deposited in locations that were intentionally removed from the domestic, and possibly the agricultural sphere must also be explored. This is particularly relevant since no metalwork has been associated with the limited number of settlement locales that have been recorded in the study area.

It has been argued above that recorded Early Bronze Age material from hillfort sites could represent funerary and ceremonial activity rather than settlement. A number of Early Bronze Age finds can be seen to be associated with hillfort sites in the study area, some of which can be seen

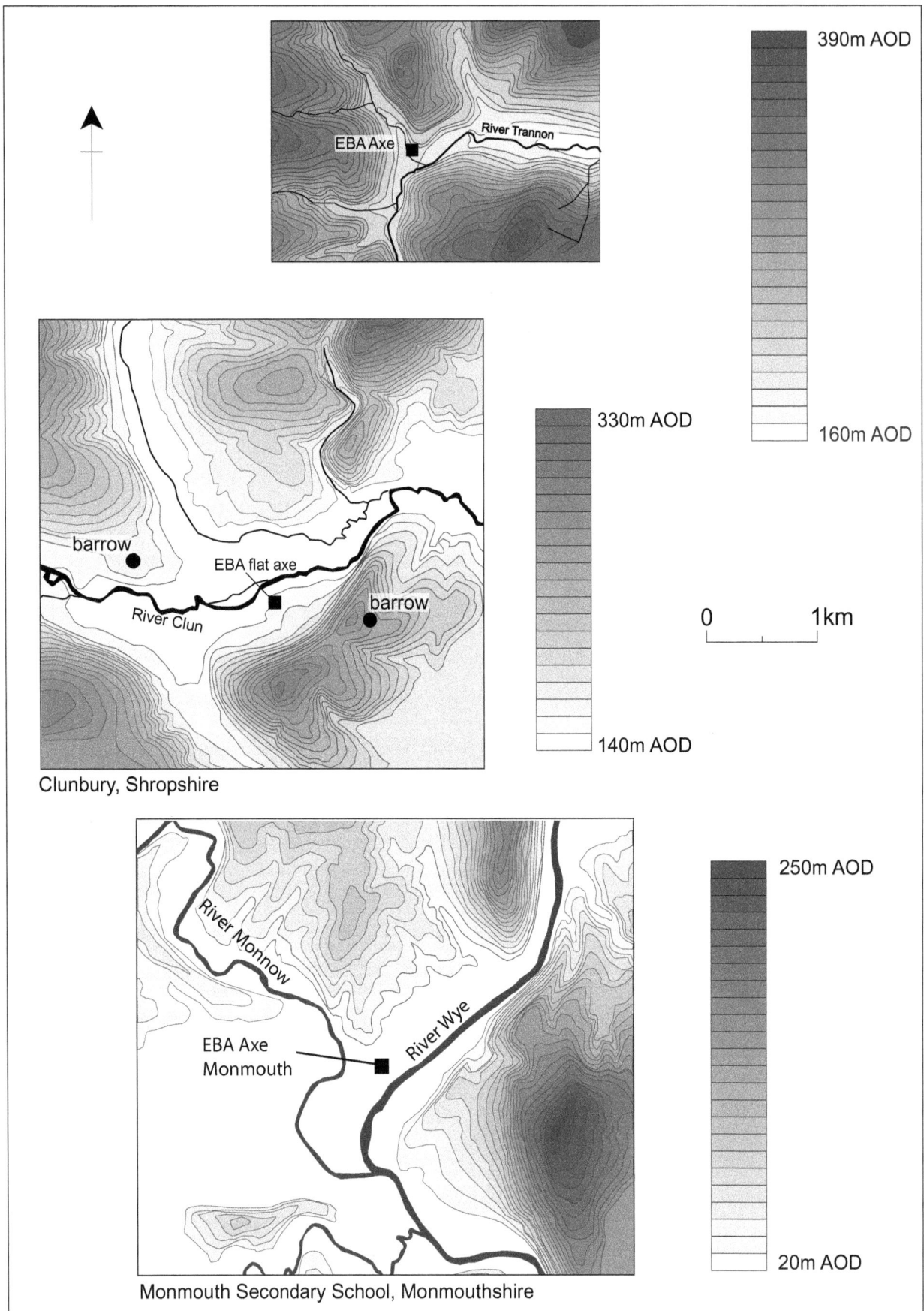

Labels within the figure:
- River Trannon
- EBA Axe
- 390m AOD
- 160m AOD
- 330m AOD
- 140m AOD
- barrow
- EBA flat axe
- River Clun
- barrow
- 0   1km
- Clunbury, Shropshire
- River Monnow
- River Wye
- EBA Axe Monmouth
- 250m AOD
- 20m AOD
- Monmouth Secondary School, Monmouthshire

Fig. 10 Examples of Early Bronze Age metalwork in river valley contexts

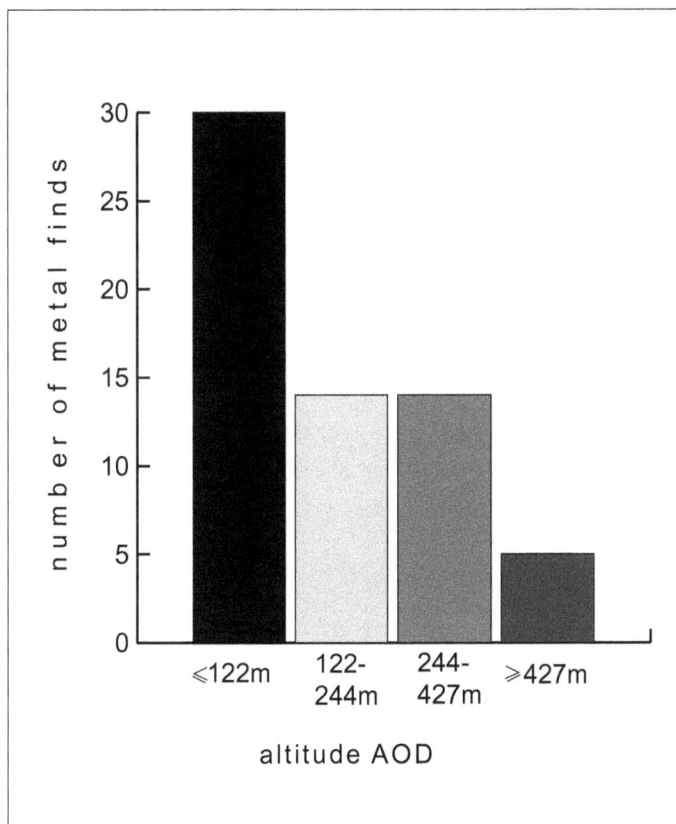

Fig.11 Numbers of Early Bronze Age metalwork finds
in relation to increasing altitudes above OD

associated with burials. Nevertheless, the deposition of metal axes both in hoards and singly at these sites could represent intentional deposits, associated with places perceived as special and associated with funerary rites or other ritual events. It has been argued that natural features in the landscape may themselves have been imbued with a special significance in prehistory (Bradley 2000). Pre-Christian societies in northern Europe have been shown to have undertaken acts of propitiation at significant points in the landscape, including mountains, water and caves (ibid. 11-13). It has been argued that these natural features may have attracted later monuments to them (ibid. 35). Therefore the location of Early Bronze Age metalwork at hillfort sites may reflect specific events intentionally removed from sites of settlement.

A number of notable depositions appear to have been made on mountain tops at higher altitudes in the study area (Fig. 5). In Powys an ogival dagger has been recorded at Llanwrthwl at 500m OD, and a halberd at Glannau Wood, Rhayader at 470m OD. It could be suggested that these weapons or display objects, were votive depositions in locations that were not easily accessible from nodes of settlement at lower altitudes. Such acts may have been confined to groups engaged in activity away from areas of more permanent domestic settlement.

Similarly, daggers and a halberd have also been recorded from wet peat bog contexts at Derwen, Denbighshire and Bwlch y Ddaufaen, Powys (R.W.B., 1885, 156). The halberd found in the Dee Estuary, Flintshire can also be seen to come from a marsh location. Again these objects may have been deposited as votive offerings in locations removed from settlement locales.

The axe recorded around 300m from a brook at Weaveram Cum Milton, Vale Royal, Cheshire is described as "miniature" (SMR, 2378) and may also represent the votive deposition of a symbolic object. The location of this find can be seen to be generally representative of Early Bronze Age metal artefact distribution in the study area. Therefore, this raises the question of the extent to which metalwork finds in the landscape represent votive depositions, and the extent to which these depositions are separated from settlement locales, or incorporated within settlement patterns.

In order to broaden the context of metalwork deposition in the Early Bronze Age landscape it is also necessary to

to represent rare associations in hoards, and also rare and potentially significant objects.

At Moel Arthur, Flintshire a hoard of three flat axes was discovered within the hillfort (Forde-Johnson 1964) at 450m OD. A possible hoard comprising a flanged axe (Burgess and Cowen 1972, 179) and a decorated flat axe were also found on Titerstone Clee, Shropshire (Chitty 1926, 235-236) at c.450m OD. A flat axe has also been recorded at Little Wenlock, below the Wrekin in Shropshire.

A dagger in Denbighshire is recorded as having been found at or near Adwy Wynt hillfort (SMR, 100925). A hoard comprising a miniature tanged dagger and plough share (SMR 5446) possibly belonging to the Early Bronze Age have been recorded in Tewkesbury, Gloucestershire. The provenance of the find is not specific, but their recorded location places them at around 200m OD on Cleeve Hill, which rises up to 300m OD and has a number of later defended enclosures upon it. Another tanged dagger was found on Brackenbury Camp, Gloucestershire (see SMR; SAM 34).

It is possible that weapon finds from these sites represent disturbed grave goods, as with Beaker pottery, faience, amber and jet beads found at the Breiddin (Musson 1991, 19). However, metal axes of the period are not generally

examine further nodes of activity represented by funerary monuments. It is only through an examination of the landscape context of all recorded activity in the period that we can attempt to understand settlement in the Early Bronze Age.

The relationship between monuments, artefact distributions and settlement

It is important to establish the relationship between known settlement locales and funerary monuments in the study area in order to understand the extent to which ceremonial activities influenced the location and pattern of settlement in the period. The relationship between the two could contribute to understanding the degree of mobility in the settlement pattern in the Early Bronze Age, and the extent to which the location of barrows reflects settlement nodes in the landscape. The degree of association of metal finds in the landscape with funerary monuments may also illuminate the extent to which they were deposited within areas characterised by ceremonial activity and the extent to which they represent areas of settlement.

It has been suggested that the location of Early Bronze Age barrows in Cheshire shows a correlation with the agriculturally favourable sands and gravels at the expense of heavier boulder clays (Longley 1987, 61) in the same way as the recorded settlement sites. However, settlement sites in the north of Cheshire appear to have a relationship with barrows that suggests settlement and burial could have been related, but that they were not necessarily contiguous (Fig. 6). The nearest barrow to Arthill Heath Farm lies c.800m to the north at Little Bollington, and another lies c. 2.5km to the south-west at High Leigh. Two further barrows lie c.3km to the south-east of Arthill at Rotherene and Bucklow Hill. These barrows also lie at c.2.4km and 2.7km respectively from the settlement evidence at Tatton Park. Therefore it is possible to suggest that funerary monuments were located in situations that were distanced, but did not require wholesale movement from, settlement sites in the vicinity. The nearest recorded barrow to Oversley Farm, is that at Wilmslow c.4 km away. However, it is also possible that monuments have been recorded outside the study area to the north in Greater Manchester, or have been destroyed by the previous development of Manchester Airport. Indeed the data only represents a recorded proportion of the sites of settlement, burial or ceremony that could have existed in prehistory.

Similarly, fieldwork in the vicinity of funerary and ceremonial monuments in the Walton Basin, Powys (Gibson 1999), has identified a number of flint scatters with Early Bronze Age components (Bradley 1999, 53-66) which may reflect settlement activity. The majority of the recorded flint scatters lie between 250m and 750m of recorded barrows, which may again suggest a degree of separation between the use of monuments and activities associated with domestic production and consumption. The duration of activity represented by flint scatters in the vicinity of monuments is, however, unknown and cannot be fully resolved without an attempt to identify associated structures through excavation.

The relationship between settlement locales and funerary monuments may be reflected in the recorded distributions of metal tools in the study area. The majority of single finds appear to have been recorded between c.0.5 and 2km from monuments (Fig. 12). This could suggest that these objects were deposited in locations that were relatively close to funerary monuments, but not directly adjacent to them. This suggests that funerary monuments did not form a specific focus for the deposition of these objects, and that the location of metal tools represent activity in alternative contexts.

Elsewhere in the study area round-barrows and ring-ditches show similarities with the location of settlement recorded in Cheshire, though without further recorded settlement locales any relationship with domestic activity remains vague. If an area of drift geology is examined to the east of the uplands of Powys and Denbighshire, barrows appear to show a preference for glacial sands and gravels and gravel river terraces in lowland contexts. Fifty one barrows lie on gravel, while 36 lie on boulder clay (Fig. 9). This could suggest that the position of barrows is related to better quality arable land and therefore that they may have an association with settlement sites. It has also been suggested that in Shropshire the location of ring-ditches may have a genuine correlation with the sand and gravel terraces of the Severn (Watson 1991, 12). However, the division between monuments on boulder clay and those on gravel is not distinctive enough to suggest an exclusive relationship with a specific landscape context. Furthermore, the majority of barrows have been recorded on the higher ground in the study area (Fig. 5). This may suggest a relationship with upland settlement locales that have not been recorded. Barrows may be situated in areas characterised by either temporary or seasonal land-use together with more sustained residency at sites in valley or lowland contexts.

Interpreting the archaeological record: the context of Early Bronze Age settlement in the region

It can be seen that there is evidence of sustained settlement activity in Cheshire in locations favourable to arable cultivation and areas potentially expedient for exchange transactions and communications between groups. The identification of all instances of Early Bronze Age

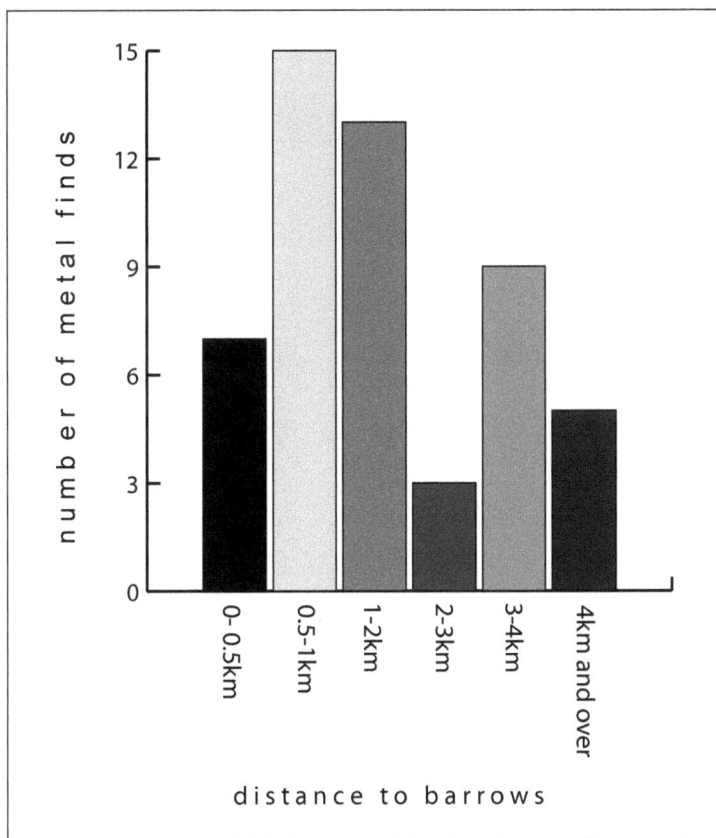

Fig.12 The distance between Early Bronze Age tools and barrows, cairns and ring- ditches in the study area

settlement activity show that they were the result of excavations upon later more identifiable archaeological features or that they were not predicted in advance. This suggests therefore that other comparable sites existed elsewhere in the study area.

The few recorded settlement locales appear to be located in river valleys. Metalwork has been recorded in comparable river valley contexts elsewhere in the study area, suggesting that this pattern of settlement can be extrapolated. It is not possible, however, to equate directly the location of a recorded metal object with the location of a settlement site, since no direct correlation between metal objects and domestic structures has yet been made in the Welsh Marches. These artefacts could nevertheless represent activities related to associated settlement nodes, as part of agricultural cycles or ceremonial events subtly removed from the domestic sphere. They may therefore provide an indication of settled areas in the lowland zone.

The location of metal objects in upland contexts, away from river valleys, may suggest alternative settlement foci. It has been demonstrated elsewhere in Britain that sustained or at least recurrent settlement activity can take place in upland contexts (McCullagh and Tipping 1998). Furthermore, the

concept of ecological or economic marginality may have been less apparent or influential in prehistory (Young and Simmonds 1999). However, the location of artefacts in upland contexts may equally reflect settlement mobility in the Welsh Marches and represent the deposition of objects at specific places removed from more permanently settled locations in valley contexts.

Such mobility may also have existed in the lowland zone. Ceremonial activity may have engendered a degree of mobility in the settlement pattern. Objects can be shown to have been placed into irretrievable wet contexts or at significant natural features in the landscape such as conspicuous hilltops. Such locations may have been distanced from sites of more sustained settlement activity. The degree of distance between such locations and specific settlement locales is unknown, although the deposition of objects into streams or rivers may reflect the presence of domestic sites nearby. The relationship between recorded settlement locales, flint concentrations, metalwork and funerary monuments, suggests that domestic activity may have taken place in relative proximity, but nevertheless maintaining a degree of separation. This would suggest, in a lowland context at least, that ceremonies at monuments could have been enacted within a system where permanent settlement locales remained occupied.

The presence of metal objects and barrows upon geology which appears to contrast with that favoured for recorded settlement locales, could reflect a degree of mobility in the pattern of settlement. Lands less suitable for fixed nodes of residency may have been occupied on a seasonal basis within a system of transhumance. Within the cyclical occupation of these lands, metal objects may have been deposited. Ceremonies at barrows may have been designed to reiterate or establish claims to the access of seasonally occupied lands, whose tenure may have been more fluid, beyond more permanently settled locales.

It is possible to suggest that permanent settlement locales existed during the Early Bronze Age in the study area, but that settlement at these sites may have been punctuated by seasonal movement of a proportion of their occupants. These movements may have incorporated the use of funerary monuments and witnessed the votive or conspicuous deposition of metalwork, but these practices were not necessarily divorced from the more sustained settlement locales that existed elsewhere. A comparable pattern of settlement can be argued to have persisted into the later second millennium BC in the study area.

4. Settlement in the Middle Bronze Age

Background: Middle Bronze Age settlement in Britain

Settlement in the Middle Bronze Age from 1500-1150 BC (Needham 1996, 133) appears to have witnessed a shift towards nucleated settlement forms in southern England. At Itford Hill (Burstow and Holleyman, 1957) and Black Patch (Drewett 1982), Sussex, for example, settlements are suggested to have enclosed nuclear or extended family groups engaged in a mixed arable and pastoral economy. It has been suggested from the evidence in the sequence of structures on settlement sites in the south of England that many have a single phase of occupancy only (Brück 1999b, 147). The re-building of structures within these settlements (ibid.146) has been associated with a re-ordering of space across a generation (ibid.150), but longer sequences of occupation have been argued against (ibid.149).

Enclosed sites could reflect acts of settlement within newly colonised lands (Carman 1999, 21). If such enclosures represent newly established settlement locales then this suggests dislocation with earlier patterns of settlement. Recent arguments have emphasised fragmentation in the Early to Middle Bronze Age transition (Brück 2000). It has been argued that this fragmentation restricted mobility envisaged in the Early Bronze Age, and that a greater emphasis was consequently placed upon the extended family group, rather than wider kinship or exchange networks (ibid. 285-286). However, the exact mechanism for this fragmentation is not postulated (ibid. 295).

Alternatively, there is evidence to suggest continuity rather than dislocation in the settlement pattern between the Early and Middle Bronze Age. At Down Farm, Dorset, a phase of round-houses has been shown to pre-date a palisaded enclosure (Barrett et al. 1991, 186) and at South Lodge Camp, Dorset, field lynchets have also been shown to pre-date the enclosed phase of settlement (ibid.149-151). Whether this represents the transition between the Early and Middle Bronze Age is less clear. Nevertheless, these sites appear to represent the transition between unenclosed and enclosed settlement at the same location in the landscape, suggesting continuity in the settlement pattern.

Continuity between the Early and Middle Bronze Age in the burial record has been emphasised and could also be used to suggest continuity in the pattern of settlement. The continuing practice of placing cremations at existing barrow sites is well attested (Ellison 1980a, 119), as is continuity in the mode of burial in newly constructed barrows (ibid. 115-116). Middle Bronze Age Burials within barrows and ring-ditches have been shown to be contemporary with nearby settlement sites at Itford Hill, Sussex (Ellison 1972, 110) and Down Farm, Dorset (Barrett et al. 1991, 211). It has been suggested that burials and settlements were constructed with specific spatial reference to one another and that settlement and burial sites were closely associated in the Middle Bronze Age (Bradley 1981, 100).

Therefore, it is necessary to establish the location of Middle Bronze Age settlement locales in the Welsh Marches study area, in order to assess the degree of continuity or discontinuity in their siting with earlier patterns of residency. It is also necessary to address the degree of residential mobility in the settlement pattern, if the southern English model of a shift towards more fixed and nucleated sites can be applied to the study area. This can be achieved by examining the context of contemporary artefacts, sites and monuments in the region and comparing them with earlier distribution patterns. These distributions can be examined in terms of the agricultural economy and also with regard to ceremonial events or social interactions in the landscape which may have influenced the degree of mobility in the pattern of settlement.

The evidence for the location, form and date of settlement locales in the study area will be examined, followed by an examination of the context and role of burnt mound sites and their relationship with settlement locales. The distribution of contemporary metalwork will again be examined in an attempt to extrapolate the known settlement pattern and to examine activity in contrasting landscape contexts.

Settlement evidence from the study area

The evidence for enclosed settlement sites dating to the Middle Bronze Age, as recorded in southern England, is not mirrored in the Welsh Marches study area. The evidence for settlement locales instead appears to mirror earlier patterns of residency, although the number of recorded sites is again limited in comparison with the recorded distribution of artefacts (Fig. 13).

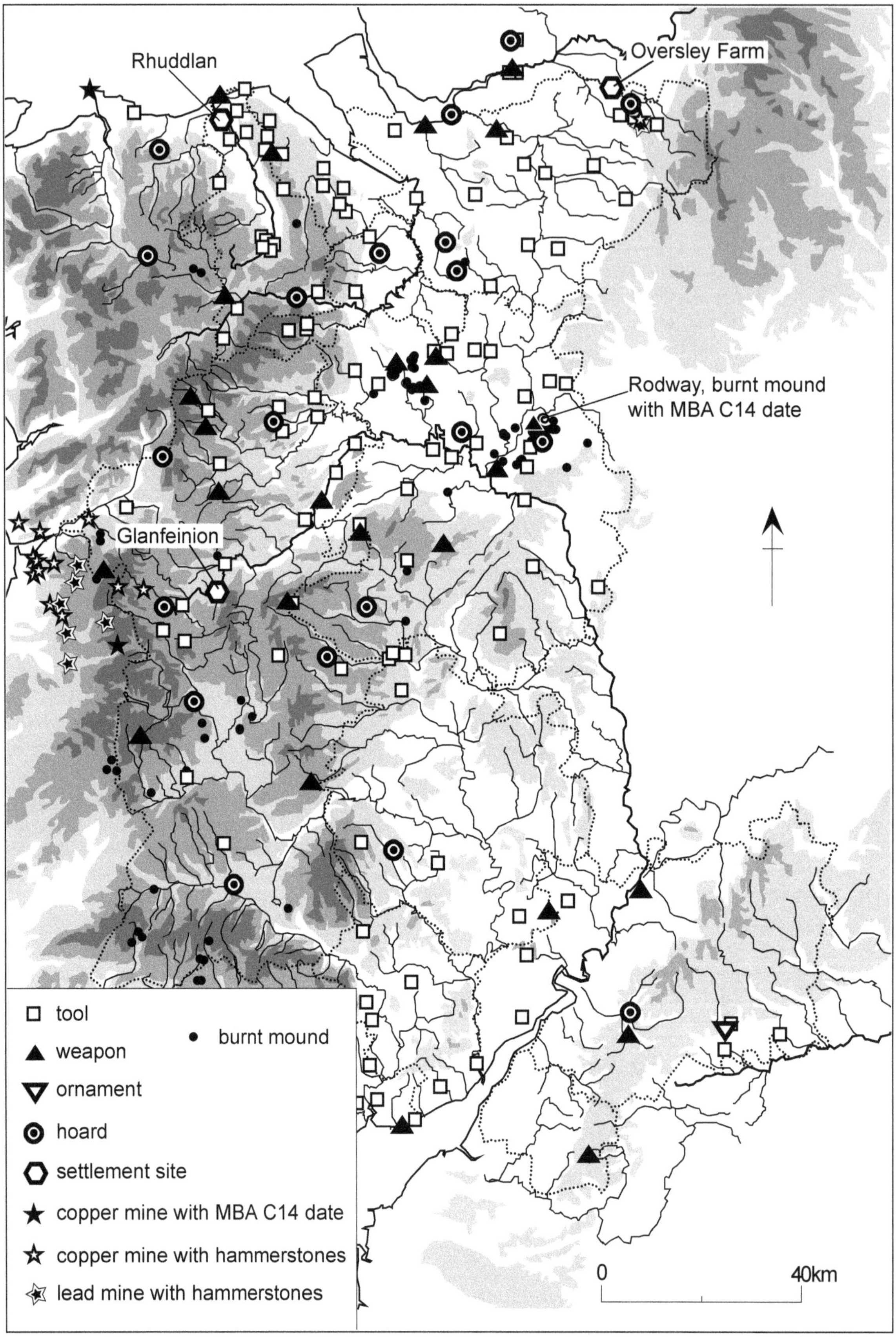
Rhuddlan
Oversley Farm
Rodway, burnt mound with MBA C14 date
Glanfeinion
tool
weapon
ornament
hoard
settlement site
copper mine with MBA C14 date
copper mine with hammerstones
lead mine with hammerstones
burnt mound
0
40km

Fig.13 Middle Bronze Age metalwork, settlement sites, burnt mounds and mines in the study area

Radiocarbon dates allow for the possibility that defended sites were emerging in the period, although many recorded enclosures in the region remain unexcavated. Radiocarbon dates from pre-hillfort enclosures could allow for a late Middle Bronze Age origin (Fig. 7). A date (V -123) from Dinorben, Denbighshire (Savory 1976, 245-6) from a pre- rampart phase, calibrates to between 1400-800 BC at 95.4% confidence. A date from Beeston Castle, Cheshire (HAR –4405) could also allow a late Middle Bronze Age origin, calibrating to between 1270 and 830 BC at 95.4% confidence. However, narrower date ranges from these sites calibrated at 68.2% confidence can be placed more firmly into the Late Bronze Age, at 1220-970 BC and 1130-910 BC respectively. The artefactual assemblage at Beeston also supports occupation in the Late rather than Middle Bronze Age (Needham 1993b; Royle and Woodward 1993). Similarly the Parc-y-meirch hoard from Dinorben represents activity in the Late Bronze Age (Savory 1980, 59-60), although does not preclude earlier occupation.

Radiocarbon dates from Camp Gardens, Stow on the Wold, Gloucestershire, suggest a possible enclosure in the late Middle Bronze Age. A date from a ditch context (OxA -3801) calibrates to between 1390 and 970 BC at 95.4% confidence and 1270-1040 at 68.2% confidence (Parry 1999, 82). Ceramics from the site have, however, been compared with post Deverel-Rimbury forms from Late Bronze Age settlements elsewhere in Gloucestershire (Woodward 1999, 83). Limited excavations at Stow-on-the-Wold leave the nature of the occupation unresolved, although the dimensions of the excavated ditch have been compared to those at Rams Hill, Berkshire (Parry 1999, 81). Here a univallate enclosure has produced a radiocarbon date from a ditch terminal (BM-2790) which calibrates to between 1320 and 910 cal BC at 95.4% confidence (Needham and Ambers 1994, 234).

Therefore the dating evidence from enclosed hilltop sites is ambiguous. Radiocarbon dates allow for the possibility of enclosure in the Middle Bronze Age, but only at the earlier extremities of the calibrated date ranges. Furthermore, the artefactual assemblages from the sites confirm a later date for activity. It could also be argued that the size of these enclosures would be larger, if they mirror later circuits of enclosure, than the nucleated settlement forms recorded in southern England in the Middle Bronze Age. This could be further evidence to suggest they are not contemporary.

A large number of univallate enclosures have been recognised by aerial photography in the Welsh Marches. Within an area of 50 by 60 km in eastern Clwyd and Powys, Shropshire and the northern extremities of Hereford and Worcester (Whimster 1989, 4), 335 examples have been recorded (ibid. 35.). This sample includes later datable forms including Roman camps (20) and Medieval moats (1), and it is considered likely that the majority belong in the Iron Age or Romano-British periods (ibid. 35). However,

few have been excavated (ibid.), and it is therefore possible that examples of enclosed Middle Bronze Age settlements akin to those in southern England do exist, though on present evidence it is not possible to demonstrate this.

It is equally possible that enclosed Middle Bronze Age sites are not substantial enough to be visible from aerial photography and that they cannot be predicted easily by the current archaeological methodology of desktop and field survey. It has been highlighted that the enclosed settlement at Down Farm, Dorset, was only discovered during pipeline excavations, and was not visible from the air (Barrett et al. 1991, 183). The only visible archaeological evidence on the ground was a "poorly defined flint scatter" (ibid.). The only apparent evidence for a clearly defined Middle Bronze Age domestic structure in the Welsh Marches study area was similarly discovered by chance during pipeline construction in the upper Severn Valley in Powys (Britnell et al. 1997, 179). Therefore it appears likely that any such settlement evidence in the Welsh Marches could suffer from a lack of visibility, alongside a lack of fieldwork upon known enclosure sites.

No enclosure was recorded in association with the single round-house excavated at Glanfeinion, Powys (ibid. 194-195). Areas around the structure do not appear to have been excavated, and the possibility of at least a timber palisade, if not a ditched enclosure remains open (ibid.). This is perhaps supported by the fact that the round-house shares a number of features with excavated structures at enclosed Middle Bronze Age sites in the south of England. The building is orientated south-south-east for example, comparable with the majority of Middle Bronze Age round houses in southern England which face south-east (Brück 1999b, 155). In terms of date the site would appear to be broadly contemporary with phases of settlement recorded on enclosed sites (Fig. 7). One date (BM-2972) of 1270-1110 BC (at 68.2% confidence) accords well with a date (GrU-6167) of 1220-1110 BC (also at 68.2% confidence) from Itford Hill, Sussex (Holden 1972, 88). A date from Black Patch, Sussex of 1320-1040 BC (HAR-3735) at 68.2% confidence is also broadly comparable (Drewett 1982, 391).

Another date (BM-2971) from Glanfeinion also calibrated at the same 68.2% confidence level could suggest slightly earlier phase of occupation at the site ranging between 1320-1250 BC. This may suggest a degree of longevity in settlement here, but the evidence for the replacement of the entrance posts is the only physical indication of continued occupation (Britnell et al. 1997, 180).

The partial rather than wholesale rebuilding of structures on Middle Bronze Age settlements in the south of England has been noted (Brück 1999b, 146). However, a re-ordering of space within enclosed settlements has been argued to have been a common feature, with structures often being

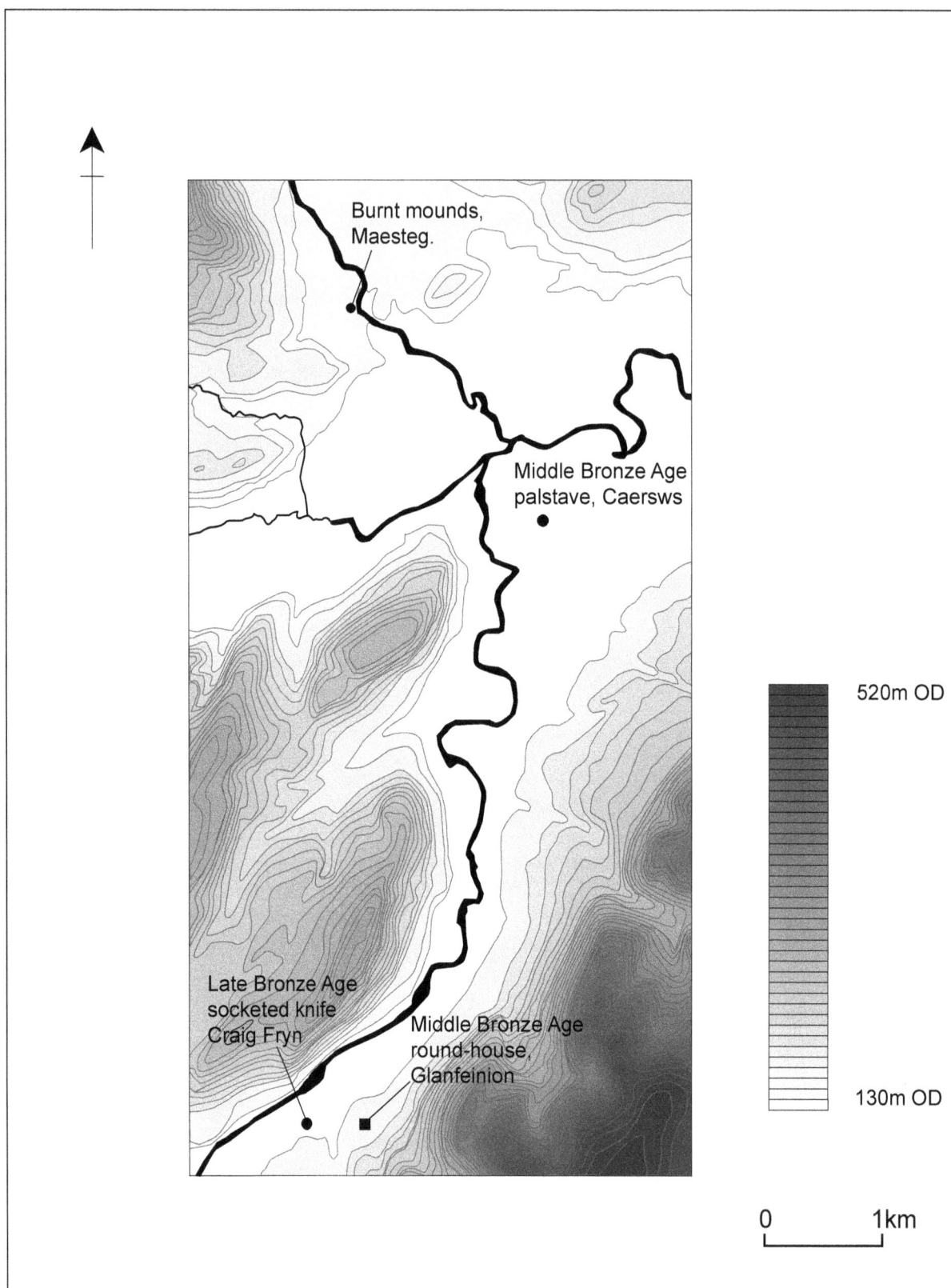

Fig. 14 Middle Bronze Age round-house, burnt mound and artefacts in the Upper Severn Valley, Powys

rebuilt completely, elsewhere on the same site (ibid.). This could suggest that other structures existed at Glanfeinion as part of a larger settlement, and that this settlement was occupied beyond the use of a single structure.

The fact that no hearth was recorded within the post-ring of the Powys structure (Britnell et al. 1997, 187) could suggest that it was not a domestic residence, and that it might originally have been associated with other buildings. A number of features of the structure suggest it could have had specific functions during its life. A pit with evidence of burning and charred cereal grains has been interpreted as a drying oven for example (ibid. 186), and the evidence for crop processing is represented by the presence of wheat chaff (ibid.186) and a saddle quern (ibid. 193). The possibility of the presence of loom weights could also suggest that the building was used for textile production. At Black Patch Hut Platform 1, Drewett argued that contemporary buildings could have had specific functions involving food preparation, craft production and storage (Drewett 1982, 340). This could again suggest that other structures existed at Glanfeinion as part of a larger nucleated settlement. However, this cannot be demonstrated without further excavation.

Although the date and form of the Glanfeinion structure is comparable with Middle Bronze Age nucleated sites in southern England, there is no firm evidence to suggest that it represents a departure from earlier settlement patterns in the study area. The structure is located on a well-drained gravel terrace c. 150m from the floodplain of the River Severn (Fig. 14). This location can be seen to be directly comparable with the Early Bronze Age settlement locales at Arthill Heath Farm and Oversley Farm on the River Bollin in Cheshire. The fact that the site at Glanfeinion shows evidence for arable agriculture involving the cultivation of barley and wheat supports the suggestion of a permanently settled location, in that the investment of time and labour in cultivation was mirrored in an attendant settlement. The evidence for the consumption of cattle and sheep/goat in the form of calcined animal bone (Britnell et al. 1997, 188) also suggests that a mixed agrarian and pastoral economy was in place. The cultivation of cereals coupled with the suggestion of animal husbandry is again comparable to the agricultural system that appears to have been employed at Oversley Farm, Cheshire (Garner 2001, 51-52).

The site at Rhuddlan, Denbighshire, is also in a comparable position to Glanfeinion and Ovesley Farm, in that it is situated upon fluvio-glacial gravels and is above the floodplain of a major river in the region, the Clwyd (Fig. 15; Quinell and Blockley. 1994, 1- 4). Postholes on the site have been considered to represent structures (ibid.), but unlike Glanfeinion no structure plan was discernible. No evidence for an enclosure was recorded, though it is important to note that the Bronze Age phase of the site was heavily truncated by later activity.

The fact that a pit was recorded here containing charred wheat (ibid. 163) and Middle Bronze Age pottery (ibid. 138) is comparable to the evidence from Glanfeinion. Therefore it appears likely that the location of the site was chosen for its suitability for arable agriculture and that this was practised in close proximity to the settlement. Its location next to a major river, flowing into the Irish Sea to the north (Fig. 15) could also suggest that the site was situated in a location expedient for exchange. A similar interpretation has been suggested for Oversley Farm in the Early Bronze Age, and could equally be applicable to Glanfeinion on the River Severn.

Further excavation in Rhuddlan at Gwindy Street, has recorded a pit containing twenty-four sherds of Bronze Age pottery together with some possible postholes (Rogers, 1995, 45). Subsequent analysis has compared the assemblage with the Middle Bronze Age assemblage from Glanfeinion (Gibson 1997, 190). Therefore the activity at Gwindy Street may represent more extensive settlement in the Middle Bronze Age at Rhuddlan, or the possibility of settlement shifts across generations as envisaged by Brück (1999b, 149).

Nevertheless, a degree of uniformity in the location of settlement sites can be seen in the study area, which suggests continuity rather than dislocation in the settlement pattern between the Early and Middle Bronze Age. Furthermore, at Oversley Farm, Cheshire, continuity between Early and Middle Bronze Age settlement can be demonstrated in the same location.

A number of radiocarbon dates have placed Oversley Farm into the early second millennium BC (Garner 2001, 55). However, a date of 1740-1380 BC at 95.4% confidence or 1620-1430 BC at 68.2% confidence (Beta-127173), suggests continuity at the settlement during the mid-second millennium BC. A further date of 1430-1040 cal BC at 95.4% confidence or 1390-1190 at 68.2% confidence (Beta-127177), also suggests that settlement activity continued on the same site into the Middle Bronze Age (Fig. 7).

The evidence from Oversley Farm therefore suggests that settlement sites in the study area were settled for much longer than the one or two generations postulated by Brück for southern English sites (1999b, 150). It is possible that a broad longevity of settlement at any one particular place was punctuated by settlement shifts or even abandonment. However, it could be argued that the re-occupation of a site suggests that it was current in the memory of those who returned to it and therefore that any abandonment was short-lived. This allows for the possibility that the settlement sites at Rhuddlan and Glanfeinion echo the location of earlier occupation. The fact that these two sites also lie upon glacial sands and gravels, in close proximity to a major river, is further evidence to support the suggestion

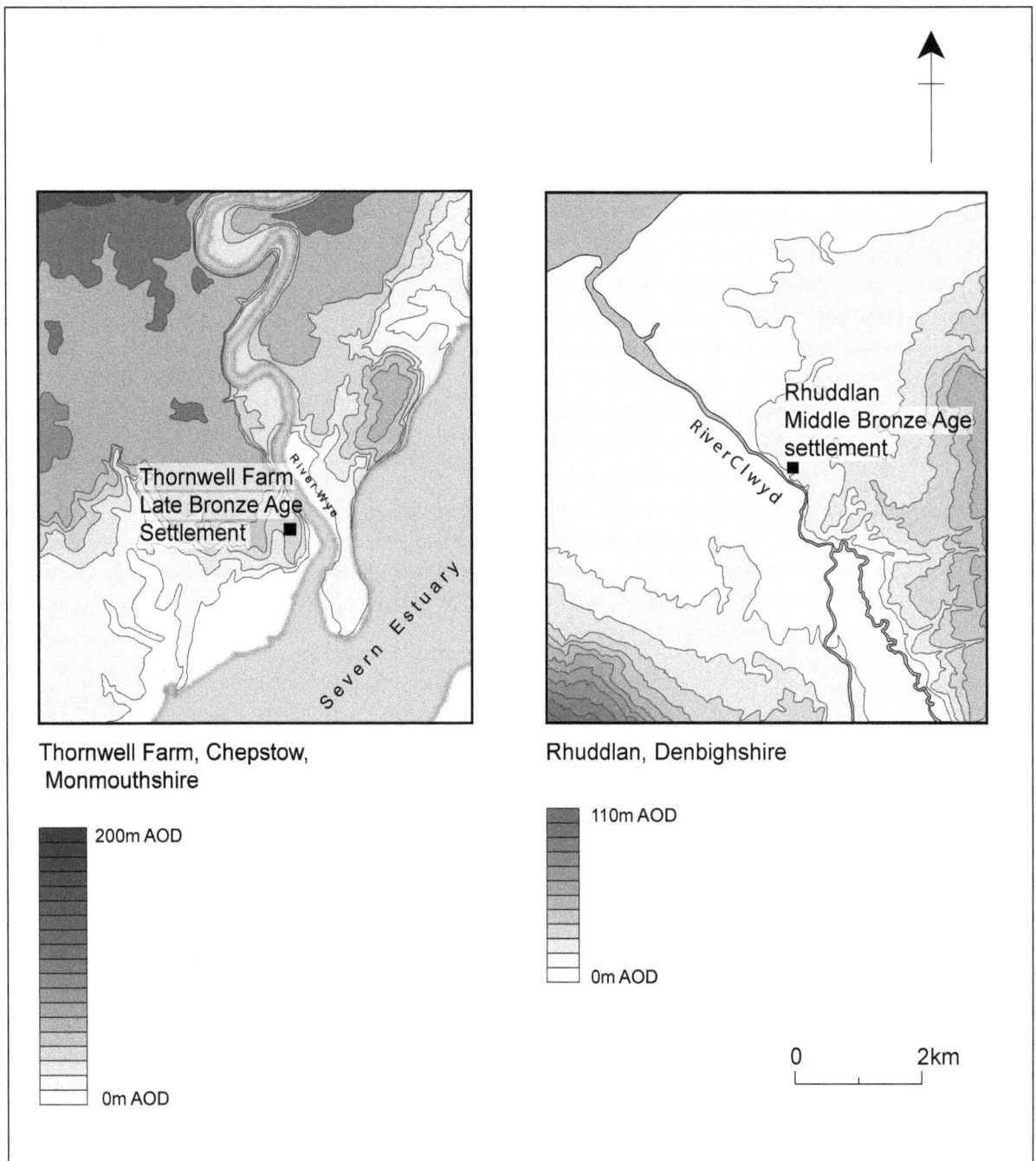

Fig. 15 Midle and Late Bronze Age settlement sites in Monmouthshire and Denbighshire

that they may represent a continuity of occupation with a pattern of settlement established in the Early Bronze Age.

There is also a suggestion that Middle Bronze Age settlement locales may have been sited in reference to earlier barrow cemeteries, perhaps emphasising a link with earlier patterns of land holding. At Rhuddlan, Denbighshire, the presence of an Early Bronze Age cremation in a Collared Urn (Quinell and Blockley 1994, 139) c. 20m from the Middle Bronze Age postholes suggests a potential relationship between an existing funerary monument and

subsequent activity. A pit with charred grain and Middle Bronze Age pottery also lies c.200m from the cremation.

Bradley (1981, 100) has highlighted that settlements most frequently lie between 50 and 300m of contemporary cemeteries in southern England. However, there is nothing to suggest that any funerary activity was contemporary with a Middle Bronze Age settlement phase at Rhuddlan. This is consistent with a general lack of evidence for Middle Bronze Age burial in the study area, with the only notable burial activity dated to the period having been recorded

38

at Shorncote Quarry, Gloucestershire (Barclay and Glass 1995, 31-37), with residual Middle Bronze Age sherds having been recorded at Four Crosses, Powys (Warrilow et al. 1986, 85). At Glanfeinion, Powys, the nearest barrows have been recorded on higher ground between 1.5 and 2km from the settlement site. This perhaps reflects the distance apparent between Early Bronze Age settlement sites recorded in the study area and contemporary barrows. This distance would also be maintained at Oversley Farm, Cheshire, during a Middle Bronze Age settlement phase. These sites therefore suggest that a relationship with contemporary burial activity was not necessarily close in the Middle Bronze Age.

Furthermore, where Middle Bronze Age burial has been recorded, evidence for settlement is lacking. The mid-Late Bronze Age cremation cemeteries at Bromfield, Shropshire are situated on a freely draining gravel terrace at 90m OD above the River Onny (Stanford 1982, 279). Such a location is geologically suitable for arable agriculture, and the location at the confluence of three rivers (ibid.) is also suitable for the watering of animals. However, no Middle Bronze Age settlement was recorded during excavations, despite a wide area having been topsoil stripped (ibid. 281).

Similarly the barrow cemetery of Four Crosses, Powys (Warrilow et al. 1986), is situated in a comparable location with Early and Middle Bronze Age settlement sites recorded in the study area, lying at 65m OD on a gravel terrace above the River Vyrnwy, and its suitability for agriculture has been noted (ibid. 53). Pit alignments have been recorded on this gravel terrace, which show regular spacing and have been suggested to represent a field system (ibid. 55). Barrows lie within these land parcels, but no physical relationship can be demonstrated, and the alignments are undated, despite sample excavations (Owen and Britnell 1989). Where pit alignments have been recorded elsewhere in Britain their association with Bronze Age monuments is equally ambiguous (e.g. Malim 2000, 80). Iron Age ceramics and radiocarbon dates from pit alignments recorded in Staffordshire (Coates 2002, 13-15) may suggest that they are not contemporary with the use of Bronze Age funerary monuments.

Therefore a relationship between Middle Bronze Age settlement locales in the study area and contemporary burial monuments has not been demonstrated, although the close relationship between the site at Rhuddlan and earlier funerary activity allows for the possibility that barrows influenced the siting of settlement in the period. To what extent this allows parallels with Middle Bronze Age settlements in the south of England, is open to debate. This is further undermined by the fact that there is at present no evidence to demonstrate that settlement sites of the Middle Bronze Age in the Welsh Marches were enclosed or nucleated.

There remains the possibility that defended hilltop enclosures may have emerged in this period, though such sites are more likely to belong to the beginning of the Late Bronze Age. Therefore the evidence for settlement sites in the study area shows greater evidence for continuity with Early Bronze Age settlement patterns rather than dislocation or re-organisation. A degree of residential mobility has been suggested for Early Bronze Age settlement in the region. However, unlike Brück's (1999a) interpretation of the residency pattern, it has been suggested that the occupancy of permanently settled locales was maintained within this pattern. If the Middle Bronze Age is to be seen in terms of the emergence of more fixed settlement locales (Brück 2000, 285-286), then it is necessary to assess the potential for residential mobility in this period also. This can be achieved by comparing the context of other contemporary sites and artefacts in the landscape with those of known settlement locales.

Burnt Mounds and Middle Bronze Age Settlement

Radiocarbon dates from burnt mounds suggest they were in use throughout the Bronze Age and reinforce the continuity represented by the evidence from settlement sites and the location of burials. A number of these sites have been recorded in the Welsh Marches (Fig. 13). The earliest dates from outside the study area suggest that they were in use as early as Periods 1 and 2 of the Bronze Age, contemporary with the earliest Beaker inhumations beneath round barrows (Needham 1996, 124-130). A date (CAR-469) from Felin Fulbrook, Dyfed (Williams et al. 1987, 231) calibrates to between 2500 and 2130 BC at 95.4% confidence. Dates from Graeanog, Gwynedd suggest that the site was in use during the Early Bronze Age and saw a second phase of activity in the late second and early first millennium BC (Kelly 1992). Other dates from south-west Wales confirm use during the Middle Bronze Age, such as the date (calibrated at 95.4% confidence) of 1690-1310 BC (CAR-498) from Carne, Fishguard, Pembrokeshire (James 1986, 256). Burnt Mounds in the West Midlands to the east of the study area have also provided dates in the Middle Bronze Age (Hodder 1990, 106-107). A radiocarbon date from the site at Cob Lane has provided a date within the Middle Bronze Age which calibrates to between 1520-1310 BC at 68.2% confidence (Birm-1087). The date from Sandwell (Birm-1268) ranges between the mid-Late Bronze Age calibrating to 1400-990 BC at 68.2% confidence, although the error margin at +/-160 is large for this sample). An excavated burnt mound from the study area in Shropshire has produced a Middle Bronze Age calibrated radiocarbon date of 1312-1168 BC (Hannaford 1999, 73). The West Midlands and Shropshire dates therefore fall largely within Period 5 of the Bronze Age, contemporary with Deverel-Rimbury ceramics (Needham 1996, 133)

Burnt stone accumulations appear to have been recorded on a number of settlement sites in the Bronze Age. Burnt stone and charcoal has been recorded in an Early Bronze Age midden deposit at Oversley Farm, Cheshire (Garner 2001, 51), and a large quantity of burnt stones was also recorded in association with Middle Bronze Age postholes at Rhuddlan, Denbighshire (Quinell and Blockley 1994, 57). Outside the study area an association between burnt stones and domestic structures has been recorded at the Midddle Bronze Age settlements at Black Patch, Sussex (Drewett 1980, 385) and South Lodge, Dorset (Barrett et al. 1991, 161). The presence of burnt stone in quantities upon Early and Middle Bronze Age settlement sites could therefore suggest that burnt mounds represent further comparable settlement elsewhere.

However, the association of burnt stone with domestic settlement appears to differ in form from that recorded at burnt mounds. The repeated association of a water trough with mounds of burnt stone is not a feature represented on settlement sites (Barfield 1991, 61). Burnt mounds also regularly have a 'horseshoe' accumulation of burnt stone around these water troughs (O'Kelly 1954, 127) which is not a feature of burnt stone accumulations in association with domestic structures. Their position within peat bogs (ibid. 106) and contiguous with streams also suggests that they are at some remove from areas of more permanent settlement (Barfield 1991, 60). The fact that settlement sites recorded in the study area lie upon freely draining sand and gravel geology, above the floodplain of associated rivers, also argues against burnt mounds representing permanent nodes of settlement. Therefore it can be argued that the location and morphology of burnt mounds represents a different function to that resulting in the accumulation of burnt stone at recorded settlement sites.

The association of burnt stones, water troughs and hearths has been considered to represent the location of cooking activities. Experiments have suggested that a single burnt mound would have been the product of a number of cooking episodes (O'Kelly 1954, 121-123). These episodes were interpreted as representing seasonal hunting forays (ibid. 138). Hunting and cooking meat at burnt mounds suggests a degree of autonomy from those settled at more permanently occupied nodes in the landscape. However, the regular hunting and cooking of meat away from settlement sites, which have evidence of arable agriculture and animal husbandry, appears to be unnecessary unless undertaken in contexts some distance away. Therefore, if burnt mounds are to be interpreted as cooking sites, they must be seen in a context whereby distance from permanent settlement sites was deemed necessary. The use of burnt mounds may have performed a specific social role that was intentionally removed from the domestic sphere in order to restrict access. Alternatively burnt mounds may have been used alongside other episodic or seasonal activities in the landscape which necessitated movement away from

settlement locales.

It could be suggested that burnt mounds represent short-lived or seasonal episodes relating to the movement of livestock within a system of transhumance. This would accord with their location in more marginal contexts, arguably less suitable for cultivation. These locations may have only been suitable for occupation in summer months. The regularity and frequency inferred for the use of burnt mounds could also suggest that they were used seasonally over long periods.

The repeated use of burnt mound sites suggests the repeated occupation of a particular place. The fact that groups of mounds can be found located together (O'Kelly 1954, 127-128) also suggests the re-use of a specific location. The long radiocarbon date range from specific sites (e.g. Kelly 1992, 85-86) can be used to suggest the repeated use of a specific place potentially over the whole second millennium BC. This may reflect long-standing access to lands which may have been held in common between groups for seasonal activities, in areas set apart from more sustained and perhaps defined settlement locales and territories elsewhere. Therefore it may be possible to envisage the occupation of specific areas, seasonally and during livestock movements, repeatedly from one generation to the next.

The actual activities undertaken by people at burnt mounds may not necessarily relate to cooking, although this does not preclude their use during seasonal movements of people and animals. The function of burnt mounds required a constant supply of water, greater than that available at settlement sites, since they are regularly recorded physically adjacent to streams or waterlogged locations such as peat bogs. The cooking of meat does not require this constant supply of water. It has been suggested that burnt mounds were not used for cooking on the basis that the sites show no evidence in the form of associated artefacts or animal bone, even where conditions would allow preservation (Barfield and Hodder 1987, 371). An alternative interpretation of the sites as sweat houses/saunas has instead been given (ibid.). These could have been used for stimulation associated with medicinal or ritual activities (ibid. 373-374). The latter could suggest a social function (ibid.) which perhaps necessitated their removal from areas of settlement elsewhere in the landscape. Other explanations for the use of burnt mounds have include their use in dyeing and fulling textiles (Jeffrey 1991), but to what extent such processes would be removed from domestic sites, which themselves have evidence for the use of hot stone technology and textile production, is open to debate.

Therefore the activity at burnt mounds can perhaps be seen as being related to short- lived but repeated episodes of activity at a distance from more permanently settled locations. The function of burnt mounds suggests their use in a specialised activity or role that was not undertaken on settlement sites elsewhere. This activity was repeated over significant time periods and it could be suggested that it was influenced by mobility related to the subsistence economy. The burnt mounds themselves may have performed a social role restricted to limited numbers of individuals, during the seasonal occupation of lands beyond the limits of more permanently occupied locales.

The lack of evidence for settlement sites in the study area means that the relationship between recorded burnt mounds and settlement is difficult to demonstrate specifically. The structure at Glanfeinion, Powys, lies c.8 km from the nearest burnt mound (Fig. 14). If this is a genuine reflection of the association between areas of domestic settlement and burnt mound sites then this could confirm that burnt mounds were intentionally situated away from more permanently settled positions. However not only is there a lack of evidence for Middle Bronze Age structures in the landscape, but the distribution of burnt mounds does not necessarily mirror that in prehistory.

The distribution of burnt mounds in the archaeological record is potentially biased, and is considered to reflect areas of archaeological fieldwork (Ehrenberg 1991, 43). The work of O.T. Jones and T.C. Cantrill in south-west Wales has been shown to have produced a disproportionate number of burnt mounds within the areas surveyed (Jones 1986, 263). The work of Cantrill for the Geological Survey in Shropshire is also likely to be responsible for the relatively large numbers of burnt mounds recorded here (Leah et al. 1998, 70). The fact that only one burnt mound appears to have been recorded in Cheshire (Leah et al. 1997, 141) could represent this fieldwork bias. The density in the recorded distributions of burnt mounds does not necessarily reflect densities of their original distribution therefore and distinctive clusters of burnt mounds may reflect fieldwork bias in the study area (Fig. 13). However, both Cheshire and Shropshire have been the subject of systematic fieldwork by the North West Wetlands Survey (Leah et al. 1997; 1998) and this could suggest that the distribution is genuine.

The burnt mound at Maesteg north of the structure at Glanfeinion, Powys, appears to be an outlier of the main distributions of these sites to the south in the former counties of Radnorshire and Breconshire (Fig. 13). Again it is possible that this distribution of burnt mounds in Powys could be the product of fieldwork bias. This could suggest that a closer relationship between Glanfeinion and burnt mounds may have existed. The presence of the burnt mound in the valley of the River Carno, near the confluence with the Severn in Powys, is comparable to the location of the site at Glanfeinion (Fig. 14). However, the settlement site is situated on freely draining gravels, whereas the burnt mound appears to be closer to the Severn, in a presumably permanently waterlogged situation. Therefore it is possible that settlement and burnt mounds could have existed in closer proximity, but exploited contrasting areas of the landscape.

It has been shown that sites that have been recorded in the study area are situated on well-drained glacial sands and gravels and that these areas can be equated with the better quality agricultural land. If a concentration of burnt mounds is examined in north-west Shropshire (Fig. 16), it can be seen that the majority lie upon either peat or boulder clay, reflecting their preference for impermeable locations, which has also been highlighted for burnt mounds to the east of the county (Ehrenberg 1991, 49). Those that do not lie in such positions are nevertheless likely to be located next to water sources. The nature of the geology in north-west Shropshire is such that these areas of waterlogged ground are surrounded by large expanses of sand and gravel, suitable for arable agriculture and settlement. The majority of burnt mounds (ten examples) actually lie within 500m of areas of sand and gravel, with a further four lying upon sand and gravel, next to water sources. Six others lie within a kilometre of sand and gravel, with only one within the large peat expanse at Hordley, lying over one kilometre away. Therefore it is possible to suggest that burnt mounds were located specifically at water away from settlement sites which may have existed upon more freely draining land nearby. This could be further evidence to support that burnt mounds are situated within areas used for the seasonal grazing of livestock, that a component of a settlement site moved alongside and engaged in specific activities away from more permanently settled locations.

The distribution of Middle Bronze Age metalwork in the study area

Middle Bronze Age settlements in the south of England have been shown to have an association with metal objects, which have been recorded within round-house structures. These appear to be either personal ornaments, such as bronze finger rings or small tools such as awls (Drewett 1982, 333). It has been suggested that both ornaments and weapons have a closer association with enclosed settlement sites in the south of England than tools, and that these sites engaged in the exchange and distribution of these more specialised metal objects (Ellison 1980b, 134-135). It is possible therefore that the distribution of metalwork might reflect further settlement in the Welsh Marches (Fig. 13), or show an association with settlement locales.

No metal objects have been recorded on the excavated Middle Bronze Age settlement sites in the study area. Tools appear to show a closer relationship than weapons, though this is likely to reflect their dominance in the metalwork assemblage of the period for this region . Two Acton

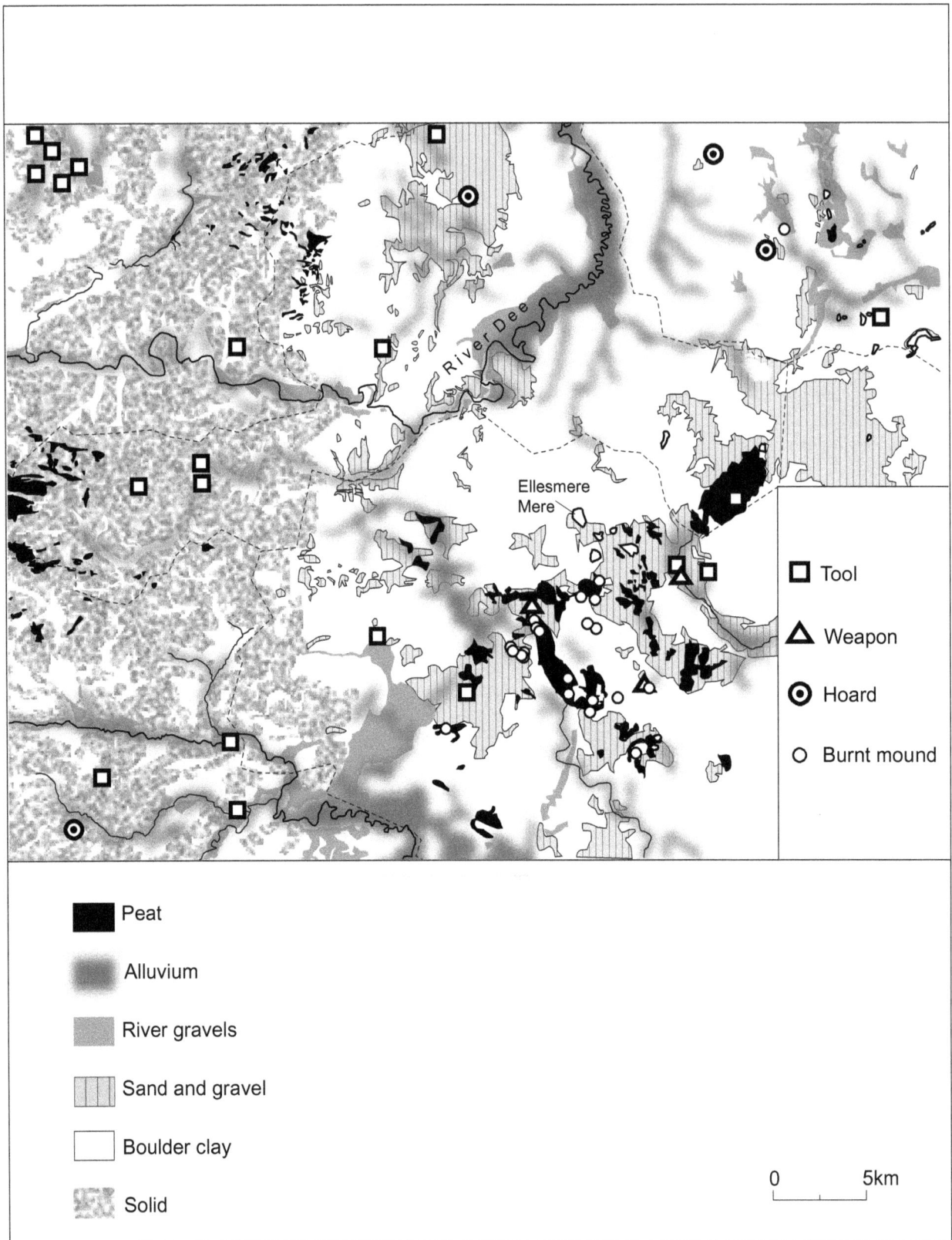

Fig.16 Burnt mounds, Middle Bronze Age metalwork and drift geology in north-west Shropshire, south-west Cheshire and north-east Wales (see Fig. 8)

Park palstaves lay between c. 3.5 and 4 Km from the Middle Bronze Age settlement activity recorded at Rhuddlan.

The closest recorded deposition of metalwork to Oversley Farm, Cheshire is a hoard of palstaves from Wilmslow c.4.5 km away. At Glanfeinion, Powys, the nearest recorded metal object is an Acton Park palstave at Caersws, c.5 km distance from the recorded round-house (Fig. 14). Therefore contemporary metal objects can be seen to have been deposited in the environs of Middle Bronze Age settlement locales, but as with recorded Early Bronze Age depositions, the location of metal objects cannot be shown to equate directly with specific points of domestic residency (Fig. 13).

Therefore, the recorded distribution of metal objects can only be used at best to infer general areas of domestic and associated agricultural activity. The specific context of individual finds has to be examined further in order to understand more fully the nature of depositions in the period, and how these may have related to settlement patterns

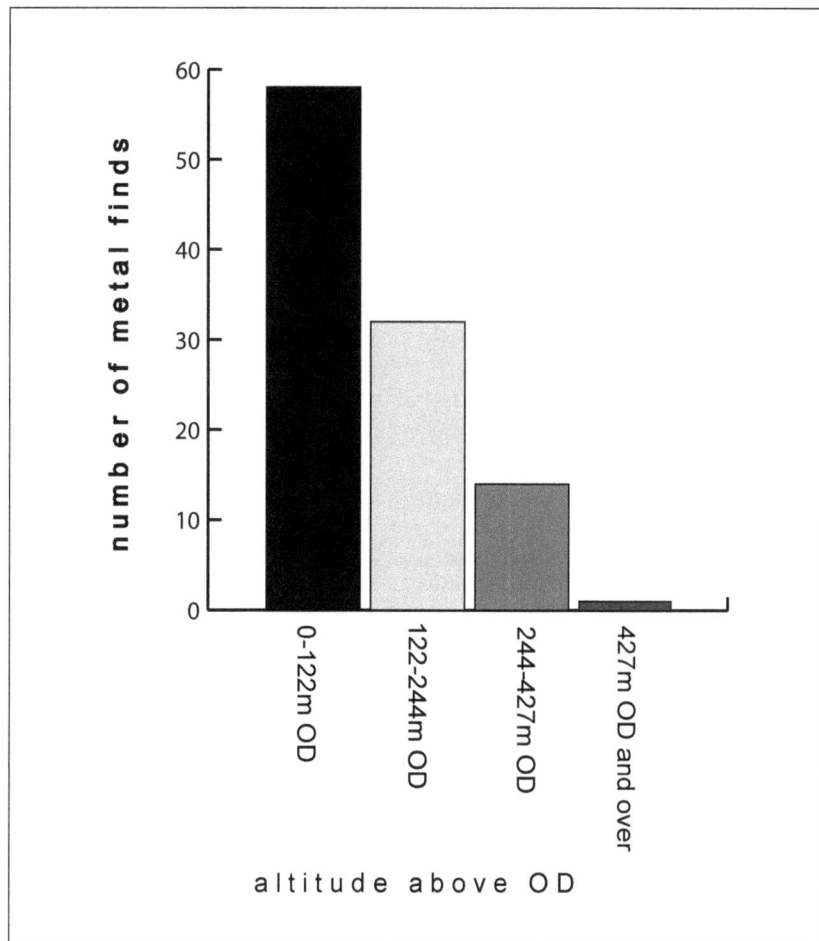

Fig.17 The altitude of Middle Bronze Age tools in the study area

It has been shown that Middle Bronze Age settlement sites recorded in the study area appear to lie upon glacial sand and gravel geology, that these have evidence for arable agriculture and can equate with what is considered to be better quality arable land. In a lowland context in Wrexham, north-west Shropshire and south-west Cheshire there appears to be a preference in the distribution of metal tools with sand and gravel geology (Fig. 16). It is possible therefore that these depositions represent areas of settlement in locations suitable for arable agriculture, akin to the settlement sites excavated in lowland contexts in the study area.

In Cheshire metal objects have also been recorded in association with the major rivers of the county, within a distance comparable to the location of Middle and Early Bronze Age settlement sites in the study area. Three single palstaves have been found within 250m of the River Dee at Huntington, the River Bollin at Prestbury and the River Weaver at Henhull. In Powys a palstave at Caersws has been recorded in the Severn Valley in a situation comparable to the site at Glanfeinion (Fig. 14).

A number of recorded Middle Bronze Age hoards also lie in contexts close to, but above, river valleys and can be compared with the location of recorded settlement. A hoard of transitional palstaves lies at 70m OD at c.500m from the River Bollin and is comparable to the location of Oversley Farm, which lies c.4.25 Km to the north-west. Another hoard in a comparable lowland context is hoard of palstaves from Vowchurch, Herefordshire, at c.120m OD, some 600m from the River Dore. A hoard of two looped spearheads at Rodborough lies at c.120m OD, 650m from the River Frome in Gloucestershire also. Therefore it can be argued that metalwork could be deposited in similar contexts to the known location of settlement sites and that this may reflect further sites of settlement in the study area. The finds, however, may not equate directly with the location of settlement. structures.

The majority of metalwork finds from the study area are from the lower altitudes below 122mm OD, with the number of tool finds (representing the bulk of the assemblage)

decreasing with altitude (Fig. 17). This may support the evidence for the location of recorded settlement sites in the study area, which appear to favour lowland valley contexts. Activity at higher altitudes may have been less frequent and less sustained. Equally these distributions may reflect fieldwork bias and a decrease in the number of recorded finds at higher more marginal contexts in modern times.

However, there are examples of finds from higher altitudes which appear to contrast with the location of recorded settlement sites in relative proximity. For example, at the head of the Clwyd valley in Denbighshire six palstaves have been recorded. Three of these at Pwll Callod, Eyarth and Coed Marchen, have been recorded at 300m, 350m and 500m from the Clwyd respectively, between 150 and 190m OD. These finds contrast with the location of the Rhuddlan settlement at c.20m OD to the north (Fig. 13). There are also a higher number of Middle Bronze Age tools recorded to the east of Rhuddlan on the higher ground of the Clwydian Range (Fig. 13). This demonstrates the use and potential settlement within contrasting landscapes to those in which settlement locales have been recorded.

The location of a number of metal finds also suggests that they may have a relationship with rivers, despite being deposited at significantly higher altitudes. A hoard of two palstaves from Coed y Llan, Llanfylin has been recorded at 250m OD, c.2 km from the River Cain, Denbighshire. The co-ordinates of this find are less specific, although Coed y Llan itself lies above the river valley. In Powys a palstave has been recorded 400m from the River Dulas at 230m OD at Upper Glandulas. The Cemmaes hoard of palstaves has also been recorded at c.280m OD around 250m from the Rivers Dugoed and Clwedog in Powys.

The fact that a number of artefacts have been recorded near streams may reflect activity close to water sources at higher altitudes. It is possible therefore that these items were deposited during movement of people from lower ground, perhaps seasonally as part of the agricultural cycle and a system of transhumance.

It is also possible that objects were deposited intentionally away from more permanently settled locations, as votive offerings. Indeed it is possible that metal objects were deposited intentionally as a means of ensuring the reproduction of a subsistence economy (e.g. Brück 1999b, 154). Such interpretations are applicable to both upland and lowland contexts.

However, metal objects found at the highest altitudes in the study area (Fig. 13) may have been deposited in locations that witnessed only transient and seasonal settlement episodes. Therefore the deposition of weapons and ornaments in such contexts may be significant in their distance from more sustained nodes of residency at lower altitudes. For example a hoard of two side-looped

spearheads was found at Waun Goch, Trefyglws, Powys, at 400m OD near a stream, 2.5 km south of the River Severn. Similarly, a hoard of bar-twisted torcs at Cwm Jenkin, Beguildy, Powys, has been recorded at 350m OD in an upland context near a stream. It is possible that remote and inaccessible locations provided a context where events, restricted perhaps to selected individuals, could take place. A hoard of twisted gold bar torcs from Llanwrthwl, Powys, has been recorded at 360m OD, where the land slopes steeply down to the river valley of the Wye on all sides of the mountain. It has been highlighted that specific natural places may have held symbolic significance (Bradley 2000, 11-13). It is possible therefore that hoards of significant objects were placed at specific and distinctive locations away from areas of settlement.

The deposition of metalwork in these upland and potentially more marginal locations may have taken place during seasonal activities away from lowland settlements. However, their altitude may also suggest alternative settlement locales, that were unrelated to domestic activity in river valleys, or required more permanent occupancy. It is not possible, however, on the evidence of metal finds alone to suggest the frequency of activity at specific locales and whether this necessitated the construction of dwellings that may have been regularly or permanently occupied.

A number of metal objects appear to have been deposited in locations away from river valleys and in closer association with smaller streams at lower altitudes. These locations do not reflect the known location of Middle Bronze Age settlement sites in the study area and instead reflect activity at other locations in the landscape.

In Cheshire for example a number of finds have been recorded at a greater distance from major rivers than recorded settlement evidence from the study area. There appears to be a greater association between the deposition of Middle Bronze Age tools and the location of smaller streams. The majority of finds have specific provenances and appear to be located either adjacent to, or within 250m of stream channels in the county. It is possible therefore that the deposition of these objects represents activity away from the more sustained settlement locales in river valleys. It is possible that this activity was associated with settlement close to stream channels, or more transient activity.

The deposition of metalwork in these contexts may be able to be illuminated further in areas where burnt mounds have been recorded. It has been suggested that the location of burnt mounds may reflect regular activity at locations set away from more permanent settlement sites, and that they may have been located in more marginal areas where animals were taken to graze seasonally. There is a general relationship between the recorded distribution of metalwork and burnt mounds in Shropshire (Ehrenburg

1991, 48-53) and there are recorded instances of metal objects having been found in burnt mounds (Cherry 1990, 50-53). However, the location of metal tools and burnt mounds in Shropshire does not appear to correlate closely. The only metal tools to be found within a kilometre of a burnt mound in the county appear to be those deposited as part of the Preston Hoard from Eyton-upon-the-Weald Moors, which appears to be c. 750m from the nearest burnt mounds. Similarly in Powys there appears to be no association within a kilometre of a recorded burnt mound. The closest example appears to be a Palstave at Llanafanfechan, Treflys, around 1 km from a possible burnt mound. The Palstave recorded from the upper Severn Valley at Caersws is in a broadly comparable location to the burnt mounds at Maesteg to the north, but is c.2.5km away (Fig. 14).

There are examples of a closer association between weapons and burnt mounds (Fig. 13). A spearhead recorded at Petton, Shropshire is c.285m from the nearest recorded burnt mound. A rapier at Church Stretton is c.550m from a burnt mound situated on higher ground. However, other examples appear to be at a further distance from recorded burnt mounds. A spearhead from Cherrington at 1km from a burnt mound and a side-looped spearhead from Wroxeter at 1.2km from the nearest burnt mound. Therefore there is insufficient evidence to suggest that weapons and burnt mounds show a close relationship.

It would appear therefore that burnt mounds did not provide a specific focus for the deposition of metal objects in the Middle Bronze Age. It is possible that the activities at burnt mounds were separated from locations where metalwork was deposited. This separation could reflect specific contexts in which metalwork was being intentionally deposited, away from activities at burnt mounds. However, metalwork deposition may have taken place during the use of burnt mound sites, in similar landscape contexts, if not specifically adjacent to them.

A number of metal finds from the study area appear to have been deposited in wet locations. This supports the suggestion that metalwork could have been deposited away from areas of sustained occupation, although may have taken place within the context of more transient activities at burnt mounds. The deposition of weapons and ornaments into water could signify the deliberate deposition of significant objects into non-retrievable contexts (Bradley 1990, 106-107).

In Cheshire examples of Middle Bronze Age weapons deposited in wet places include a side-looped spearhead from Ince Marshes and a hoard of looped socketed spearheads from Frodsham Marsh. A side-looped spearhead from Twemlow, Congleton, is recorded as coming from an alluvium context, which may reflect a waterlogged situation in prehistory. The hoard of palstaves from Preston upon the Weald moors, Shropshire, may also have been deposited in a wet context. In Shropshire a rapier with a broken tip is recorded as having been found close to a stream (Leah et al.1998, 26). A possibly broken palstave "fragment" is also recorded on the SMR (70302) as having been found at Lake Vyrnwy, Powys, "below the water-level".

Ornaments can also be seen to have been deposited in potentially wet contexts. The SMR (1780) records a hoard of gold twisted coil torcs from Egerton Hall, Cheshire. This is an area of extensive alluvium and meres (Leah et al. 1997, 135-141), although the actual provenance of the nineteenth century find does not record a wet context (Eogan 1967, 143). The flange-twisted torcs from Tan y Llywyn, Llantysilio, Denbighshire, have been recorded in the valley of the River Dee upon the alluvial floodplain, which also suggests deposition in a wet context. Therefore it appears that prestigious personal objects of metal were also deposited in non-retrievable contexts in the late Middle Bronze Age.

The fact that one of the torcs at Hampton, Cheshire has a terminal missing (ibid.) may also suggest that it was deliberately broken. The potential deliberate breakage of metal objects has been recorded elsewhere, at Flag Fen for example (Pryor 1992a, 448), where metalwork began to be deposited in the Penard period of the Late Middle Bronze Age (Coombs 1992, 504-506).

It is possible that the deposition of intentionally broken weapons and tools, and groups of objects within hoards in wet places, represents the intentional consumption of metal objects (Bradley 1990, 39). Placing valuable objects into wet contexts has been seen in terms of enhancing prestige (ibid.) both in terms of the act of display (ibid.) and the removal of objects from circulation and from rivals (ibid. 138). The evidence from Flag Fen suggests that the deposition of metalwork (Pryor 1992a, 448) may be associated with areas of settlement and agriculture (Pryor 1992b, 518-520).

The extent to which such activity took place in proximity to settlement locales in the study area is open to debate. Metalwork distributions in the Welsh Marches appear to suggest that whilst metalwork has been recorded in comparable contexts to known settlement, its deposition may have taken place in locations intentionally removed from these sites.

Continuity during the mid-second millennium BC

Between c. 1500 and 1100 BC it is possible to see continuity in the pattern of settlement in the Welsh Marches. The location of settlement can be seen to be comparable with the Early Bronze Age and there is evidence that some sites may have witnessed occupation throughout the second millennium BC.

The presence of an Early Bronze Age cremation in close proximity to Middle Bronze Age settlement evidence at Rhuddlan, Denbighshire, may reflect a desire to make a conscious reference to established monuments. Such a relationship may be comparable with Middle Bronze Age settlement sites in southern England (Bradley 1981, 100). It may also suggest that a shift in the location of settlement locales which were moving towards a closer relationship with earlier monuments. This contrasts with the location of known Early Bronze Age settlement sites, which appear to be situated at a distance from barrows great enough to emphasise a physical separation. However, there is no evidence to suggest that settlement was located in close proximity to contemporary burial sites in the Middle Bronze Age in the study area, and not all recorded settlement locales show a close relationship with earlier monuments. The number of settlement sites recorded for the Middle Bronze Age in the study area is also too few to allow general trends to be interpreted with certainty.

Continuity in the location of burial, in the few instances where it has been recorded, suggests that an association with long-standing traditions remained important. However, the lack of Middle Bronze Age burials recorded in the study area may equally reflect dislocation in funerary rites, which is not paralleled in the limited settlement record.

Absolute dates from burnt mounds suggest that they were in use throughout the Early and Middle Bronze Age, further reinforcing the suggestion of continuity in the settlement pattern. The location of burnt mounds suggests mobility in the settlement pattern reflecting repeated activity away from contexts where settlement sites have been recorded. It is possible that their locations represent areas of the landscape utilised during the movement of stock on a regular seasonal basis. Activities at burnt mounds may not equate with nodes of settlement specifically and it could be suggested that they performed a social role, associated with seasonal episodes of occupation.

Similarly the deposition of metal objects can be shown to have taken place at points in the landscape at a distance from recorded settlement sites. As with burnt mounds, it is possible that metalwork was deposited at points in the landscape that were regularly used during the movement of livestock by a component of more permanent settlement sites elsewhere. The association between burnt mounds and metal objects is not consistent enough to suggest a specific relationship, though the two may be related within episodes of transient settlement activity away from more permanently occupied locations. The deposition of metal objects may have taken place at specific and possibly isolated places, but nevertheless may reflect general settlement activity within certain landscape zones.

Continuity in the settlement pattern across the Early and Middle Bronze Age may reflect stability in the economies of production and exchange. The deposition of artefacts into wet contexts may also reflect continuity in ritual practice during the Middle Bronze Age. The deposition of potentially valuable hoards of gold ornaments into bogs or alluvial floodplains has been recorded in two instances, reflecting the deposition of a number of individual axes into similar contexts during the Early Bronze Age. The deposition of gold hoards on mountain-tops also reflects the deposition of rare axe hoards in similar contexts in the Early Bronze Age. However, the fact that prestigious objects were no longer deposited with burials has been suggested to represent a degree of change in the location of expressions of prestige in the Middle Bronze Age (Barrett and Needham 1988, 130-133). Evidence for structured mobility in the landscape through the use of burnt mounds and the deposition of metalwork, reflects a landscape divided conceptually in the Middle Bronze Age. This does not necessarily, however, imply a dislocation in the mode of settlement between the Early and Middle Bronze Age in this region.

Despite the apparent continuity between the Early and Middle Bronze Age in the study area a period of instability may have been developing from a previously more stable social and economic system, encouraging the construction of defended hilltop sites in the Late Bronze Age. The following chapter examines the construction of defensive sites in the Welsh Marches and their context within a society where conflict and ostentatious display appear to be more readily identifiable. However, a degree of continuity in the location of unenclosed sites with earlier periods can also be seen, suggesting that dislocation in the settlement pattern may not have been universal.

5. Settlement in the Late Bronze Age

Background: the emergence of defended enclosures

In the Late Bronze Age c.1150-750BC new forms of settlement emerged in a settlement pattern which may have remained relatively unchanged since at least the late third millennium BC. Evidence from hilltops in the Welsh Marches in this period show the first clear indications of enclosure. The fact that these enclosures pre-date the locations of Iron Age hillforts, suggest that they were also designed with defence in mind in naturally suitable locations. The deposition of increased numbers of hoards in the Late Bronze Age (Fig. 18; Fig.19) may reflect increased conflict and insecurity. The deposition of hoards of weapons near enclosed sites and in contexts which rendered them irretrievable may also reflect a desire for conspicuous consumption and display. There is also evidence to suggest that agricultural land was being formally enclosed and divided, a process which has not been demonstrated for earlier periods in the study area. Therefore it can be suggested that the Late Bronze Age witnessed the first major dislocation in the pattern of Bronze Age settlement in the Welsh Marches.

It has been argued that this dislocation was precipitated by climatic deterioration which resulted in a reduction of available resources and a significant population downturn (Burgess 1985). It has also been suggested that there was a disruption in the supplies of copper ores in the Late Bronze Age and that the primary sources in this period lay in central Europe (Northover 1982). Radiocarbon dates from British Bronze Age copper mines would appear to support the suggestion that the majority may have gone out of use by this period (Ambers 1990).

Therefore a restricted supply of resources in the Late Bronze Age may have been more closely controlled, and consequently the focus of dispute. It has been emphasised that an accumulation of wealth at sedentary settlements "could have been a source of antagonism and conflict amongst groups" (Osgood 1998, 6). It is possible that settlement sites in the Welsh Marches were designed to protect resources and that they were therefore enclosed and constructed in defensible positions.

It can also be argued, however, that there was some continuity with the previous pattern of settlement. Recent arguments have rejected the concept of dislocation in the settlement pattern in the Late Bronze Age (Young 2000). Instead an attachment to specific settlement locales and a

sense of place has been emphasised (ibid. 75). The ability of groups to counter changing environmental conditions through adaptation has been stressed. Increased economic co-operation, changing methods of production and expedient engagement in exchange, have been suggested as means of addressing adverse economic circumstances (ibid. 73).

It has been argued that continuity can be seen in the pattern of settlement in the Early and Middle Bronze Age in the study area, and that longevity can be seen in the occupation of certain locales. There is evidence to suggest that the settlement pattern established in the Early Bronze Age continued into the early first millennium BC, at least in the types of location that were chosen for occupation and cultivation.

Evidence for upland agriculture in the Late Bronze Age may also allow a degree of continuity in the settlement pattern to be recognised, counter to claims that marginal locations were abandoned in the period. The presence of unenclosed settlement sites in the study area and the wider system of agricultural organisation beyond defended hilltops, may be able to address the extent to which any dislocation in the Late Bronze Age permeated a wider settlement pattern.

In order to illuminate the nature of any dislocation in the Late Bronze Age it is first necessary to examine the frequency of enclosed sites within the study area, their date and their function. This can be achieved through an examination of excavated sites together with the distribution of artefacts, which may shed light on the role of enclosures and their position within a wider social context. The dominance of enclosed hilltops in the archaeological record can be balanced by an examination of the evidence for settlement locales in other contexts.

The identification of Late Bronze Age enclosures in the Welsh Marches

The Welsh Marches is an area of Britain which has a high density of hillforts. These stretch from the promontary fort of Sudbrook Camp on the River Severn in Monmouthshire, through a line along the border between England and Wales

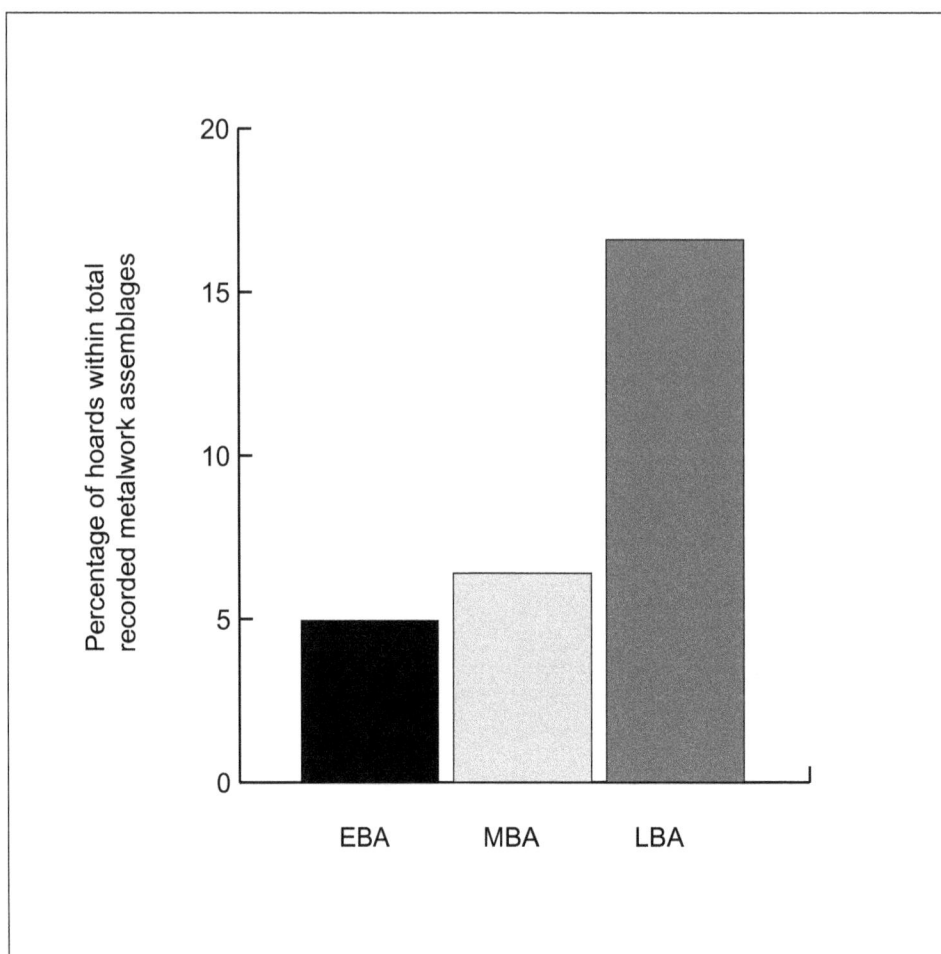

Fig.18 Percentages of recorded hoards within Early, Middle and Late Bronze
Age metalwork assemblages in the study area

to Moel Hirraddug on the north Wales coast in Flintshire and north-east towards Beeston Castle in Cheshire. Between these northern and southern points are a range of multivallate, bivallate and univallate enclosures forming defensive positions upon the hilltops of the counties of Denbighshire, Flintshire, Wrexham, Cheshire, Shropshire, Powys, Herefordshire and Gloucestershire.

The realisation that these hillforts had phases of enclosure and settlement which pre-dated their Iron Age earthworks began to emerge in the early 1970s. Radiocarbon Dates from Mam Tor, Derbyshire, suggested that round-houses lay within a defensive circuit during the Late Bronze Age (Coombs 1971, 101-102). The re-excavation of earlier cuttings through the ramparts at Dinorben, Denbighshire, provided Late Bronze Age radiocarbon dates which appear to have been associated with the first phase of rampart construction and a possible pre-rampart palisade (Savory 1971, 251-254). A Late Bronze Age interpretation was brought into doubt when subsequent radiocarbon dates from the site were published (Guilbert 1980). However, a number of excavated hillfort sites in the Welsh Marches

now have both radiocarbon and artefactual evidence which supports the suggestion that hilltops were occupied and enclosed during the Late Bronze Age (Fig. 20).

Evidence from elsewhere in Britain confirms that this phenomenon was not restricted to the Welsh Marches. In the south of England for example, Harrow Hill and the Caburn in Sussex have timber palisade enclosures associated with early first millennium bc pottery (Hamilton and Manley 1997, 95-97; Drewett and Hamilton 1999, 19-20). South Cadbury hillfort in Somerset also has evidence for mid-Late Bronze Age activity on the hilltop (Barrett et al. 2000, 88) and at the foot of the monument (Tabor 1999; Coles et al. 1999).

This can be used to suggest that the enclosure of hilltops in this period was widespread, but it cannot be suggested that all Iron Age hillforts and enclosed hilltops necessarily equate with Late Bronze Age settlement. Phases of Late Bronze Age activity have not been recorded at Maiden Castle, Dorset (Sharples 1991, 57) for example, or Danebury, Hampshire (Cunliffe 1995, 19), despite

48

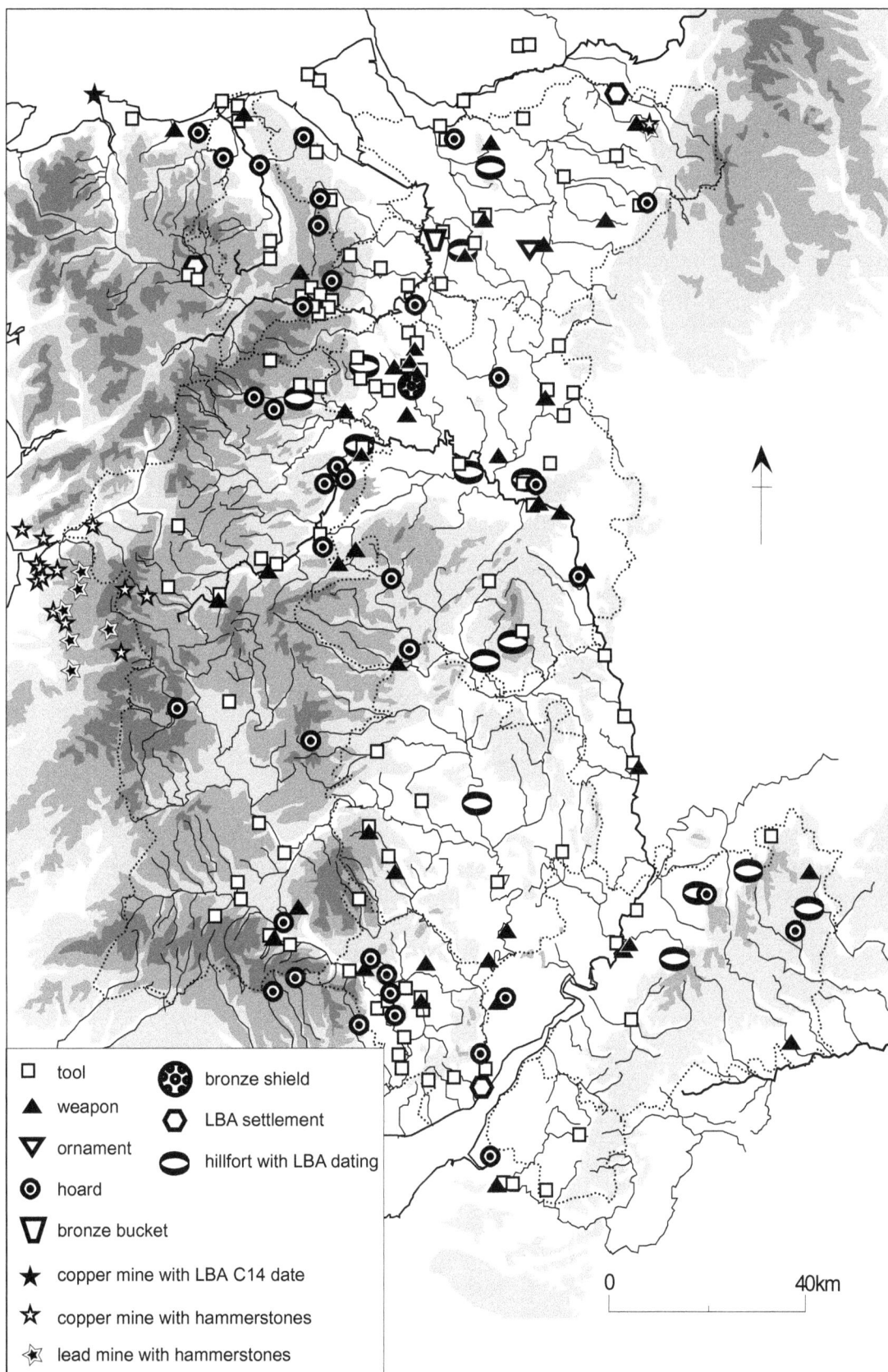

Legend:

□ tool

▲ weapon

▽ ornament

◉ hoard

⬯ bronze bucket

★ copper mine with LBA C14 date

☆ copper mine with hammerstones

✦ lead mine with hammerstones

◉ bronze shield

⬡ LBA settlement

⬭ hillfort with LBA dating

0   40km

Fig.19 Late Bronze Age metalwork, hilltop enclosures, settlement sites and mines in the study area

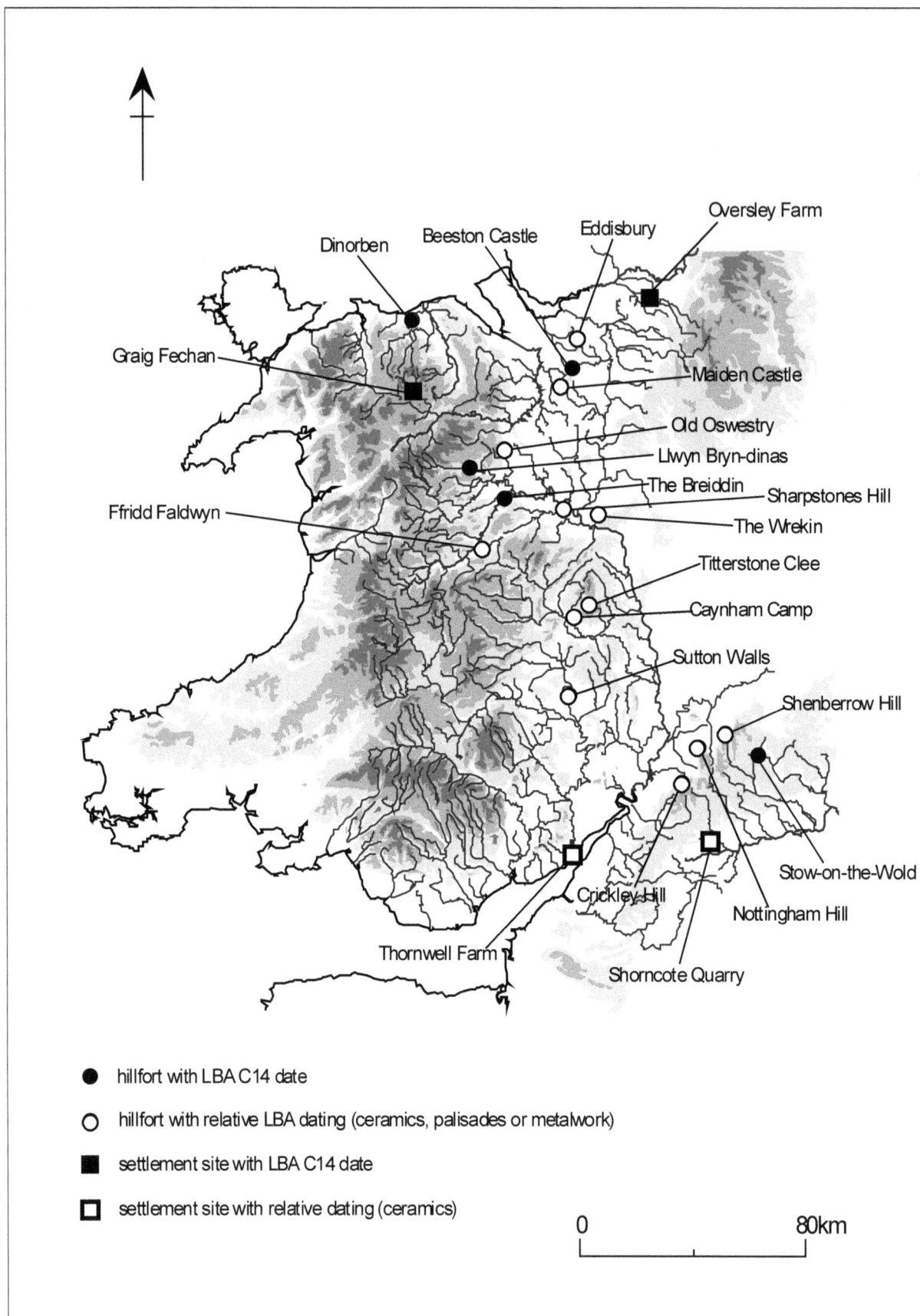

Fig.20 Late Bronze Age settlement sites and enclosures in the study area

extensive excavations. Excavations within the Welsh Marches study area at Llanymynech Hill, Powys, also have not produced evidence for Late Bronze Age activity (Musson and Northover 1989) and excavations at Moel Hiraddug, Flintshire, also appear to have revealed features that date to the Iron Age only (Brassil et al. 1982, 82). Therefore the extent and density of hilltop enclosures in the Late Bronze Age can only be addressed by further fieldwork, and all such sites cannot be assumed to have been occupied in the period.

Four hillfort sites in the Welsh Marches have provided radiocarbon dates from early rampart phases which fall within the Late Bronze Age (Fig. 7). A date (V-122) from Dinorben (Savory 1971, 254) calibrates to between 1300 and 810 BC at the 95.4% confidence level. A comparable date (HAR-4405) from a rampart context at Beeston Castle, Cheshire (Ellis 1993, 85), calibrates to between 1270 and 830 BC at 95.4% confidence. These dates suggest that the construction of ramparts at Dinorben and Beeston may have begun as early as the late Middle Bronze Age. However when calibrated at the 68.2% confidence level the dates from Dinorben and Beeston fall into a tighter band between 1130-890 BC and 1130-910 BC respectively. This places the construction of the ramparts firmly in the Late Bronze Age and Needham's Period 6, contemporary with post Deverel-Rimbury ceramics and Wilburton Metalwork (Needham 1996, 134-135).

Radiocarbon dates from rampart contexts at Llywyn Bryn-dinas (Musson et al. 1992) and the Breiddin (Musson 1991) support a later position within Needham's Period 7 of the Bronze Age, contemporary with Ewart Park metalwork and plain post-Deverel Rimbury pottery (Needham 1996, 136). When calibrated at the 68.2% confidence level dates from Llywyn Bryn-dinas (CAR-802) and the Breiddin (BM-878) calibrate to between 905-805 BC and 920-830 BC respectively.

It could be suggested therefore that rampart construction at Dinorben, Denbighshire, and Beeston Castle, Cheshire, was earlier than the sites at the Breiddin and Llywyn Bryn Dinas in north-eastern Powys, based on the radiocarbon dates. The dates are, however, potentially biased by the specific context from which they are taken. Samples from rampart cores are likely to include material that is derived from earlier occupation. Therefore, while these dates demonstrate contemporary activity upon the hilltop, they do not necessarily date the construction of the ramparts. The intentional deposition of Ewart Park metalwork in the ramparts at Beeston (Needham 1993b, 48) could suggest that they were constructed later than earlier phases of occupation represented by the radiocarbon dates.

Indeed, the structural evidence at Beeston reflects a sequence of activity which pre-dates the deposition of Ewart Park metalwork. The earliest stone rampart phases are considered to have been preceded by a timber palisade gully with possible post settings (Ellis 1993, 21-25). Evidence for a palisade has also been recorded at Dinorben, pre-dating the earliest Late Bronze Age rampart (Savory 1971, 253). At the Breiddin a discontinuous gully with post sockets produced radiocarbon dates (BM-879 and HAR-1616) which fall into the Late Bronze Age (Musson 1991, 28). This feature is described as having an unclear stratigraphic relationship with the rampart (ibid.), but could also be suggested to be a palisade trench. Therefore it could be suggested that further sites in the study area, with palisade trenches pre-dating ramparts, were also occupied in the Late Bronze Age.

At Maiden Castle, Cheshire, a foundation trench was interpreted as evidence for a timber palisade, onto which a stone revetted rampart was superimposed (Forde Johnston 1962, 43-44). At Eddisbury, Cheshire, similar evidence was found of a timber palisade pre-dating rampart construction (Varley 1950, 34). Excavations at Old Oswestry, in Shropshire, by Varley in the 1930s also identified possible palisade trenches (Hughes 1994, 55). At Titterstone Clee, Shropshire, a palisade feature was also recorded during excavations (O'Neil 1934, 17), although it was not interpreted as belonging to an earlier phase. At Caynham Camp, Shropshire, there is a possibility of a palisade represented by carbonised wood and a burnt horizon (Gelling 1959, 146), which pre-dated what appears to be a timber-laced rampart. Excavations at Ffridd Faldwen, Powys, produced evidence for a double timber palisade (Guilbert 1981, 20), preceding the rampart. At Sutton Walls, Herefordshire, pre-rampart 'hollows' and a posthole suggest the possibility of a timber palisade (Kenyon 1953, 10). At Moel Hiraddug, Flintshire, a possible early stone bank was recorded with an oval hole beneath (Brassil et al. 1982, 28). This feature has been considered in terms of a palisade, but is inconclusive (ibid. 82). At Crickley Hill, Gloucestershire, there is also the possibility that the rampart was pre-dated by the postholes of a palisade (Dixon 1994, 177). Therefore there is significant evidence to suggest that the initial phases of enclosure upon a number of hilltops involved the construction of lines of upright timbers. The fact that these have been shown to either pre-date Late Bronze Age ramparts, or provide Late Bronze Age radiocarbon dates at more recently excavated sites, can be used to suggest that these sites were also enclosed in the Late Bronze Age.

Ceramic assemblages from excavated hillforts in the Welsh Marches can also be used to suggest that hilltops were occupied in the Late Bronze Age. The dating of ceramic forms originally placed in the Iron Age on sites in southern England, was revised in the light of subsequent excavations (Barrett 1980). Bowls, jars and cups are considered to belong in a Late Bronze Age post-Deverel-Rimbury phase, with plain wares being typologically earlier (ibid. 302-306). It is not suggested that ceramic forms from the south of England necessarily equate with those from the Welsh Marches. However, it is possible that ceramics from early excavations at hillfort sites in the Welsh Marches may also belong to the Late Bronze Age, rather than the Iron Age.

The largest Late Bronze Age ceramic assemblage in the Welsh Marches was excavated at the Breiddin, Powys (Musson 1991). The forms of vessels include predominantly plain ware jars of barrel, conical or situlate form (ibid. 119). At Beeston Castle, Cheshire, the pottery assemblage was dominated by largely undecorated coarse barrel-shaped jars, together with slack-shouldered jars and some finer wares which may have included small cups (Royle and Woodward 1993, 69). Comparisons with the assemblages at the Breiddin, Powys, Sharpstones Hill and the Wrekin in Shropshire have been made (ibid. 77), suggesting contemporary Late Bronze Age occupation. At Sutton Walls, Herefordshire, the pre-rampart horizon is also described as having produced plain wares, although the form of the vessels is unclear (Kenyon 1953, 26).

The pottery from Llwyn Bryn-dinas, Powys, is also comparable to that found on other sites in the Welsh Marches, with an assemblage containing sherds with finger tipped decoration on cordons and the everted rims of jars (Musson et al. 1992, 270). The fabrics here are also compared with the Late Bronze Age assemblage from the Breiddin, Powys (ibid.), and their contexts at Llwyn Bryn-dinas are contemporary with the first rampart, dated by radiocarbon to the Late Bronze Age (ibid.).

At Caynham Camp, Shropshire, the description of a sherd of pottery as having finger- tip decoration and a "degenerate" situlate profile (Gelling 1959, 148), could also be compared with "slack shouldered or situla type necked jars" regarded as potentially Late Bronze Age in date at the Wrekin (Morris 1984, 79). This could suggest contemporary Late Bronze Age occupation at hillfort sites in Shropshire. The pottery assemblage from Caynham Camp has also been compared with that from the Bronze Age cremation cemetery at Bromfield, Shropshire (Gelling and Peacock 1968, 96; Stanford 1982, 313). Pottery from Bromfield has also produced radiocarbon dates. Charcoal in which a comparable pot (ibid.) was buried is associated with a radiocarbon date (Birm-62) which calibrates to between 1050 – 760 BC at 95.4% confidence and 920-800 BC at 68.2% confidence. These dates are later than those obtained from hilltop sites in the study area. However, they still fall within Needham's period 7 of the Bronze Age, considered to be contemporary with plain post-Deverel-Rimbury pottery types from southern England (Needham 1996, 136).

The pottery at Crickley Hill, Gloucestershire, with bi-partite jars and finger tip decoration, has been compared with that from the Breiddin (Dixon 1994, 216), while Ann Woodward has compared it to the Late Bronze Age assemblage at Shorncote Quarry, Gloucestershire (Woodward 1999, 83). The forms that predominate at Shorncote Quarry are ovoid and shouldered jars in course fabrics (Morris 1994a, 40). Unlike the assemblages from the north of the study area at the Breiddin and Beeston, there appears to be a greater degree of decoration in the form of finger tipping and cordons (ibid. 39). The pottery from Shenberrow Hill Camp, Gloucestershire (Fell 1961), with finger-tip decoration at the shoulders, is also comparable with the Late Bronze Age assemblage from Shorncote Quarry. It is possible that these assemblages have more in common with styles recorded in the Thames Valley and the south of England (Morris 1994a, 41) than assemblages from the northern Marches. No Late Bronze Age radiocarbon dates have been recorded in association with the Shorncote Quarry pottery assemblage or hilltop sites in Gloucestershire, therefore direct comparisons with sites in the northern Marches cannot be made, but it remains possible that they are contemporary.

Radiocarbon dates from structural sequences, together with the relative dating of artefact assemblages, can be used to suggest Late Bronze Age occupation at a number of hilltop sites in the Welsh Marches. However, it is the nature and duration of this occupation that needs to be explored further, in order to assess the degree to which these sites represent dislocation with previous settlement patterns.

The function of Late Bronze Age enclosures

It is generally assumed that phases of enclosure dating to the Late Bronze Age represent defensive sites which are precursors to Iron Age hillforts. This has, however, been recently questioned. Hamilton and Manley (1997, 99) have questioned the practicality of defence for a number of Late Bronze Age enclosures in Sussex, and have suggested that they operated in terms of 'looking out' and controlling or co-ordinating activities in the surrounding landscape (ibid. 101).

It could be argued that the position of Late Bronze Age enclosures would have exploited the natural defensive qualities of the hill to their full extent. However, it was suggested by Varley for example, that the earliest univallate enclosure at Eddisbury, Cheshire, did not exploit the full defensive potential of the hill (Varley 1964, 87). At Rams Hill, Berkshire, a late second millennium BC (Needham and Ambers 1994) palisaded enclosure was excavated and can be seen to lie within, and be considerably smaller than, the Iron Age hillfort which is later constructed on the site (Bradley et al. 1975, 6). This demonstrates that it is not necessarily possible to equate the size of early enclosures upon hilltops with the extent of Iron Age hillforts. The problem is compounded by the fact that only a limited

Woodward 1993, 66; Musson 1991, 119). This reflects that activity on the sites, whether sustained or intermittent, drew on the immediate resources of the locality. However, the nature of the relationship between these hilltop sites and that immediate locality, is unclear. Whether the use of local resources represented obligatory relationships with those settled in a hinterland is unclear, but possible. Indeed, an examination of the relationship between hill top enclosures and Late Bronze Age metalwork suggests that they were associated with high status materials, which may suggest that their occupants may have lain at the top of a social hierarchy.

The production and consumption of metalwork at these sites may also suggest that they were a focus for the exchange of objects during the Late Bronze Age. Both the consumption and exchange of metalwork at defended hilltop sites may have served to elevate or reaffirm their status, within communities or between groups. It is therefore necessary to examine the production, exchange and deposition of metalwork in the Late Bronze Age and to interpret relationships with Late Bronze Age sites, as a means of illuminating their function within a wider social context.

Production, exchange and deposition of metalwork in the Late Bronze Age

Metallurgical analysis has shown that Wilburton Late Bronze Age artefacts were composed of copper whose source lay in central Europe, and objects with similar compositions can be found in the Rhineland and southern England (Northover 1982, 59). Comparable metalwork compositions have been demonstrated between northern France and southern England in the later Ewart Park phase, suggesting again that metal was being imported (ibid. 63-67). It has been argued that the recycling of metal imported from Europe was a characteristic feature in Britain in the Late Bronze Age (Northover 1980, 234-235).

Radiocarbon dates from Bronze Age copper mines in Wales cluster at the beginning of the second millennium BC, but do not appear to extend beyond the Middle Bronze Age (Ambers 1990, 59-63; Timberlake 2001, 180). Late Bronze Age radiocarbon dates have, however, been obtained from the Great Orme mines in north Wales (ibid.) suggesting that this may have been an important ore source for the period in Britain. Nevertheless, it is possible that the supply of metal ore may have been restricted in this period when compared to the early second millennium BC, and it is possible that recycling of material played a more prominent role. This could also suggest that metalwork had a significant economic value in the period.

If metalwork was being imported into regions such as the

proportion of any hillfort's defences has been excavated and the form of Late Bronze Age occupation is not therefore fully understood. Therefore the defensive qualities of these enclosures cannot be interpreted fully. However, the fact that their location was made even more inaccessible by the construction of ramparts or palisades, does suggest that defence was a primary consideration in their construction. It can be suggested that activities within these sites were restricted to a component of society, whether or not the sites acted in terms of looking out and surveying landscapes, as focal points or defended settlements.

Large ceramic assemblages from more recently excavated sites (Musson 1991, 118-123 Royle and Woodward 1993, 63-78) suggest that they were occupied either permanently or recurrently during the Late Bronze Age. If the sites had a primarily defensive function, then it would be important that they remained occupied by at least a component of a group on a permanent basis, otherwise their defences could be easily breached. However, if enclosures were constructed to delimit a sacred space, then taboos may have existed which were strong enough to prevent access by excluded individuals. This would not, however, explain the need for substantial palisades and ramparts, unless such sacred spaces were themselves the subject of dispute and conflict. Furthermore, any association between hilltop enclosures and sacred spaces is not necessarily incompatible with their occupation, particularly if this was by a limited number of individuals representing elite members of society.

The function of these sites is not illuminated greatly by structural evidence from their interiors, which is often truncated by later activity. Where structures have been identified which appear to relate to domestic occupation, their date is often unreliable. Stanford attempted to date four post structures to the Late Bronze Age at the Wrekin. However, his method of back-dating features by estimating the duration in use of timbers and the number of occasions on which they were replaced, appears to be tenuous (Stanford 1984, 69). Furthermore, where Late Bronze Age dates have been obtained from features, the form of associated structures is unclear (Ellis 1993, 22). At the Breiddin, Powys, a number of postholes and pits behind the Late Bronze Age rampart are suggested to be contemporary, including four-post structures (Musson 1991, 28-33). However, their dating and stratigraphic relationship appears to be uncertain. Furthermore, a recent re-evaluation of palaeo-environmental data at the Breiddin has suggested that the site was not occupied on a permanent basis in this period (Buckland et al. 2001). Therefore the nature of any settlement activity on hilltop sites remains ambiguous, despite evidence for substantial defensive circuits, and the use of ceramics.

The ceramic assemblages at Beeston Castle and the Breiddin are considered to have been locally produced (Royle and

Welsh Marches to be recycled, then exchange systems were important in order to maintain a supply which could be offset by losses, both accidental and intentional (Needham 1998, 292-295). The exchange of metalwork can take place within mechanisms which reinforce and perpetuate political power (Barrett and Needham 1988, 127). Such interpretations are influenced by Rowlands' theory of Late Bronze Age society, which was constructed through analogies with historical texts and ethnographic parallels (Rowlands 1980, 18-28). Bronze Age society is interpreted as being highly competitive and alliances and hierarchies were maintained through the exchange of prestigious objects (ibid. 33-36).

Specific social reconstructions based upon historical or ethnographic analogies have, however, been questioned regarding their usefulness in the reconstruction of exchange mechanisms (Needham 1993, 164). The distribution of artefacts in the landscape is seen by Needham in terms of displacement, which recognises that artefact distributions are the product of a number of processes during their life cycle, but that the social processes underlying them cannot be specifically identified from final depositional contexts (ibid. 162).

It is, however, the deposition of metalwork that is represented in the archaeological record rather than its exchange. It is possible that metalwork, particularly in hoards, was deposited in times of stress or dislocation, and never recovered. This could be seen in terms of 'accidental loss', whereby metalwork was not retrieved "due to some accident of body or memory" (Needham 1998, 292).

However, these deposits may not have been intended for recovery. Instead they have been seen as the product of 'competitive display' (Bradley 1990, 136) and conspicuous consumption (Barrett and Needham 1988, 135), through which the status of individuals or groups could be actively enhanced. A large proportion of this metalwork is composed of weapons (Bradley 1990, 97) which could be interpreted as prestige items, imbued with special significance relating to conflicts. This is reflected in the archaeological record by large hoards of spearheads, sword fragments and weapons accessories, totalling hundreds of individual objects, such as those found at Wilburton Fen (Evans 1885) and Isleham (Britton 1960) in Cambridgeshire.

The deposition of high status material in rivers or bogs could increase the prestige of those undertaking such an act by emphasising their wealth and power. This would also remove objects from circulation and therefore give a competitive advantage over rivals in that these items could no longer be obtained (Bradley 1990, 138). Such interpretations again appear to be influenced by Rowlands' theory of a highly stratified society (Rowlands 1980). However the composition of hoards and the development of weapons in the Late Bronze Age supports interpretations

of a society where conflict was prevalent and was tied to social prestige and competition.

The development of weapon types which have less functional advantages, such as large barbed spearheads, can be seen to emphasise the relationship between display and weaponry in the period (Burgess et al. 1972, 226-228) further suggesting that conflict and prestige were directly related. The non-functional nature of thin bronze shields (Osgood 1998, 8) and the ritual killing of objects (ibid. 11), could suggest that activities replicating war, or 'surrogate warfare' (ibid. 23) took place in order to emphasise the status of individuals or groups.

Hoards traditionally accepted as reflecting a utilitarian trade in scrap material intended for recycling may also have been deposited intentionally within the context of ritual (Bradley 1998, xix). The process of metalworking itself could have been seen in terms of "arcane and dangerous procedures" (ibid.), which could have conferred status upon the smith. This status may have been represented in the formal deposition of objects related to metalworking and recycling.

Therefore the deposition of metalwork in the landscape, particularly weapons or prestigious objects, has to be seen as belonging within a closely controlled system of production, exchange and deposition. Objects and groups of objects may have had a particular social significance in the Late Bronze Age. They could have been imbued with special significance if related to significant events such as warfare, or may have been used to affirm the status of individuals or groups. Therefore it is necessary to examine the types of object deposited in specific landscape contexts and their association with settlement sites. This may allow a fuller understanding of the role of hilltop enclosures.

Late Bronze Age metalwork and enclosed settlement sites

Excavations at Flag Fen and Fengate in Cambridgeshire serve to show that the ritual deposition of metalwork, particularly weapons, in wet places was not necessarily divorced from settlement in the Late Bronze Age. Agricultural settlement can be seen to be contiguous with a timber alignment and platform extending into marshland, which was the focus of votive deposition (Pryor 1992a). The recent discovery of a Late Bronze Age shield at South Cadbury hillfort, Somerset (Tabor 1999, 252-253; Coles et al. 1999) together with evidence for a contemporary settlement phase (Barrett et al. 2000, 88) can also be seen to represent a link between defended sites and the potentially ritual deposition of objects associated with conflict.

The Parc-y-meirch hoard of the Ewart Park phase is associated with the Late Bronze Age enclosure at

Dinorben, Denbighshire. This hoard of horse harness-fittings is considered to have continental affinities (Savory 1980, 59-60). The composition of the metal also suggests a central European origin (Northover 1980, 235). This hoard would therefore appear to have been involved in a complex network of exchange during its life cycle, finally being deposited at a site lying at a considerable distance from its original source. If settlement on the hilltop was contemporary, then it can be suggested that the site was one of high status, having received a rare and important group of objects. Kristiansen has emphasised the potential significance of crossing cultural boundaries, that distant places could be related to sacred perceptions and that travel to such places could confer status upon individuals (Kristiansen 1998, 337). Possession of a hoard of material with perceived foreign or exotic origins may therefore have been prestigious, even if it had been obtained indirectly from its source of production. The hoard may also have represented military prowess, if horse harness can be related to the trappings of warfare. Its deposition may have represented a form of 'surrogate warfare' (Osgood 1998, 23) whereby display and deposition of war regalia substituted the act of conflict itself. The deposition and consumption of this hoard may therefore have endowed those engaged in such an act with status. It can be argued that any such act of display was undertaken by those either resident at the hilltop site, or who had exclusive access to it, and was designed to confirm or elevate their position within a social hierarchy. Such an act may have been undertaken in the presence of individuals attached to that group, in order to emphasise obligations, or to express prestige in the face of rivals.

The association of a hoard of spearheads found near the Wrekin, Shropshire, can be compared with the hoard found at Dinorben and could also be significant in terms of expressions of status at a contemporary defended settlement. At least 150 spearheads were discovered in 1834 at Willow Moor (Burgess et. al. 1972, 242-243). The fact that the hoard contained a barbed spearhead and a Ewart Park sword (ibid.) makes it contemporary with other hoards in the region belonging to Burgess' 'Broadward Complex', after the hoard found in southern Shropshire (ibid. 211-235). Further weapon finds were originally discovered in 1790 at Willow Moor (ibid. 243) and could either belong to the same hoard (Chitty 1928, 42) or suggest a further deposit. The spearheads are said to have contained "vestiges of wooden shafts" (ibid. 39) which indicates that they were deposited in a wet context. This is characteristic of Broadward Complex depositions (Burgess 1972, 222). As with Dinorben and the Parc-y-meirch hoard, this deposition can be seen to represent an intentional consumption of significant objects. The fact that the hoard was deposited into a potentially irretrievable wet context emphasises this. The fact that the objects consumed represent objects used in warfare may have further symbolic associations and again suggest that their

deposition was used to express status. The deposition of a hoard of weapons at the foot of the Wrekin supports suggestions that the site was either a defended settlement associated with conflict, or that symbolic objects were used as a means of conferring status and significance to an enclosed hilltop site.

The Guilsfield hoard, Powys, contains both tools and weapons which can be dated to the Wilburton phase of metalworking (Savory 1980, 117). The tools consist of eleven palstaves of late (ibid.) or transitional type, a socketed axe comparable with Irish 'bag-shaped' examples (Savory 1980, 49) and two socketed gauges. The weapons and accessories include thirteen leaf-shaped spearheads (or fragments), with at least three Wilburton leaf-shaped swords (Savory, 1980, 118) and several sword chapes and spear ferrules. This hoard is not in association with any dated Late Bronze Age settlement site, yet its close proximity at c.100m from Crowther's Camp Iron Age hillfort (ibid.) strongly suggests that this is possible. The fact that the distribution of Wilburton metalwork types concentrate primarily in the south-east of England (Burgess 1968, 9) may suggest that the hoard was of significance in the region, and as with the Parc-y-meirch hoard at Dinorben, its value was reflected through its deliberate consumption. The Guilsfield hoard may, therefore, represent a further example of the relationship between a potentially defended site, warfare and prestige in the Late Bronze Age.

The Guilsfield hoard also demonstrates that this area of the Welsh Marches was engaged in wide exchange mechanisms. The fact that Wilburton objects concentrate in the south and east of England (ibid.) suggests that the Guilsfield hoard reflects the product of exchange processes with groups in these areas. The presence of an Irish bag shaped axe is further evidence to support wide exchange mechanisms. It is possible that defended enclosures in the region played a role in such exchange processes. This could be manifested in the deposition of metalwork at these sites, which was designed to reiterate their position in the distribution and control of resources through acts of display and consumption.

Further evidence to suggest the extent of this practice across the study area can be demonstrated at Nottingham Hill, Gloucestershire. Here tools and weapons were associated in a Ewart Park phase hoard together with evidence for settlement in the period (Hall and Gingell, 1974, 306-309). The presence of single spearhead finds in close proximity to Maiden Castle, Bickerton, Cheshire and Llanymynech hillfort, Powys (Fig. 21) may reflect a similar association between defended enclosures, conflict and metalwork deposition, and suggest further contemporary settlement phases at these sites.

Hoards of tools, unlike those containing weapons, show less of an association with hillfort sites. The Tomen y Cefn

Lle Oer hoard, Llanfylin, Powys, is around 6km from the nearest known site of Late Bronze Age settlement at Llwyn Bryn Dinas and similarly, the Plas yn Cefn hoard of socketed axes is around 6km from Dinorben, Denbighshire. This does not preclude their association with unidentified settlement sites, but does serve to underline the strong association between weapons and defended enclosures in the region. A number of individual socketed axe finds have been recorded in the vicinity of Dinas Bran hillfort near Llangollen, Denbighshire (Fig. 21), which may suggest a Late Bronze Age phase at the site and associated activity in the surrounding landscape.

A number of single tool finds have also been recorded in the vicinity of known Late Bronze Age defended sites (Fig. 19). The majority of these finds belong to the Ewart Park phase, contemporary with metalwork assemblages at hilltop sites such as the Breiddin, Powys, Beeston Castle, Cheshire and Nottingham Hill, Gloucestershire. However, their distance from hillfort sites may reflect alternative settlement foci in the landscape. For example, a Ewart Park socketed axe was found c.2.5km from Titterstone Clee, Shropshire. Similarly a ribbed socketed axe from Bickerton, Cheshire, has been recorded c.2.5km away from the site at Maiden Castle. At a similar distance is a socketed axe around 2.5km from Sharpstones Hill, Shropshire and two socketed axes from Monmouthshire at Shirenewtown and Wentwood resevoir, c.2km and 3km away respectively from Llanmelin Wood Camp. At a lesser distance is a socketed axe at Little Wenlock 1km away from the Wrekin in Shropshire.

The relationship between the distribution of single finds in the landscape and enclosed sites, which witnessed the consumption of potentially high status objects, clearly needs to be examined further. It is possible that single objects were redistributed from defended enclosures and ultimately deposited either at contemporary settlement nodes elsewhere, or other significant places.

There is evidence from a number of hillfort sites to suggest that their occupants were engaged in metalworking in the Late Bronze Age. This could be further evidence to suggest that enclosures played a role in the distribution of metalwork in the period. The traditional concept of the itinerant smith, originally proposed by Gordon Childe in the 1950s, has recently been contested, and this has been used to emphasise the relationship between metalworking and settlement in the Bronze Age (Bradley 1990, 27).

At Beeston Castle, Cheshire, crucibles and evidence of high temperature hearths (Ellis 1993, 24), together with Late Bronze Age pottery, came from later contexts and are therefore residual, but nevertheless are considered to represent metalworking here in the Bronze Age. Needham argues that although the metalworking refactories are not diagnostic they are "in keeping with a Bronze Age rather

than later date" (Needham 1993, 47). The fact that copper ore sources exist at the foot of Beeston itself and elsewhere in the adjacent Peckforton Hills, is further evidence to support the idea of metalworking here (Ellis 1993, 13). The fact that two Ewart Park socketed axes were found at the same stratigraphic horizon within the earliest rampart, and are considered to have been a deliberate deposition (Needham 1993, 48), could reflect the significance of metalwork to the site. The objects could have been placed into the rampart as a symbolic act, reflecting activities within.

The Breiddin, Powys, also has evidence for metalworking. Crucibles with copper slag are considered to belong to the Bronze rather than Iron Age (Tylecote and Biek 1991, 147). A mould fragment for a pin from a Bronze Age context and others for the casting of knives or spearheads, albeit unstratified, may also be testimony to metalworking in this period (ibid. 149). Therefore it is possible that not only metalworking existed in the Late Bronze Age at these two sites, but that the objects manufactured differed and that each site may have had a specialist role in metal production (Needham 1993b, 47).

There are hints that metalworking could have been taking place at further hillfort sites in the region also, although the evidence is tentative. At the Wrekin, Shropshire, there is a suggestion of metalworking at the site, with possible bronze casting residue coming from a residual context (Stanford 1984, 69). Also significant is the possibility of metalworking at Sutton Walls, Herefordshire. A small crucible with traces of bronze is recorded, although its stratigraphic position and date is again unclear (Kenyon 1953, 27).

In the light of the potential restrictions to the supply of metal ore in the Late Bronze Age (Northover 1982, 59-67) and the fact that the recycling of metalwork was increasingly common (Northover 1980, 234), the role of defended hilltop sites in the period may have been pivotal to the exchange and production of metal objects in the Welsh Marches. However, there is evidence to suggest that enclosed and defended sites may not have exclusively controlled the production of metalwork in the Late Bronze Age. Therefore, it is necessary to examine the evidence for further settlement sites in alternative landscape contexts in the period, and to place the distribution of artefacts with non-hillfort associations into context. This in turn may enable enclosed sites to be understood within a wider pattern of settlement.

Unenclosed settlements in the study area

If defended hilltop enclosures were the focus of political power and prestige in the Late Bronze Age then it can be argued that settlements occupying lower positions in

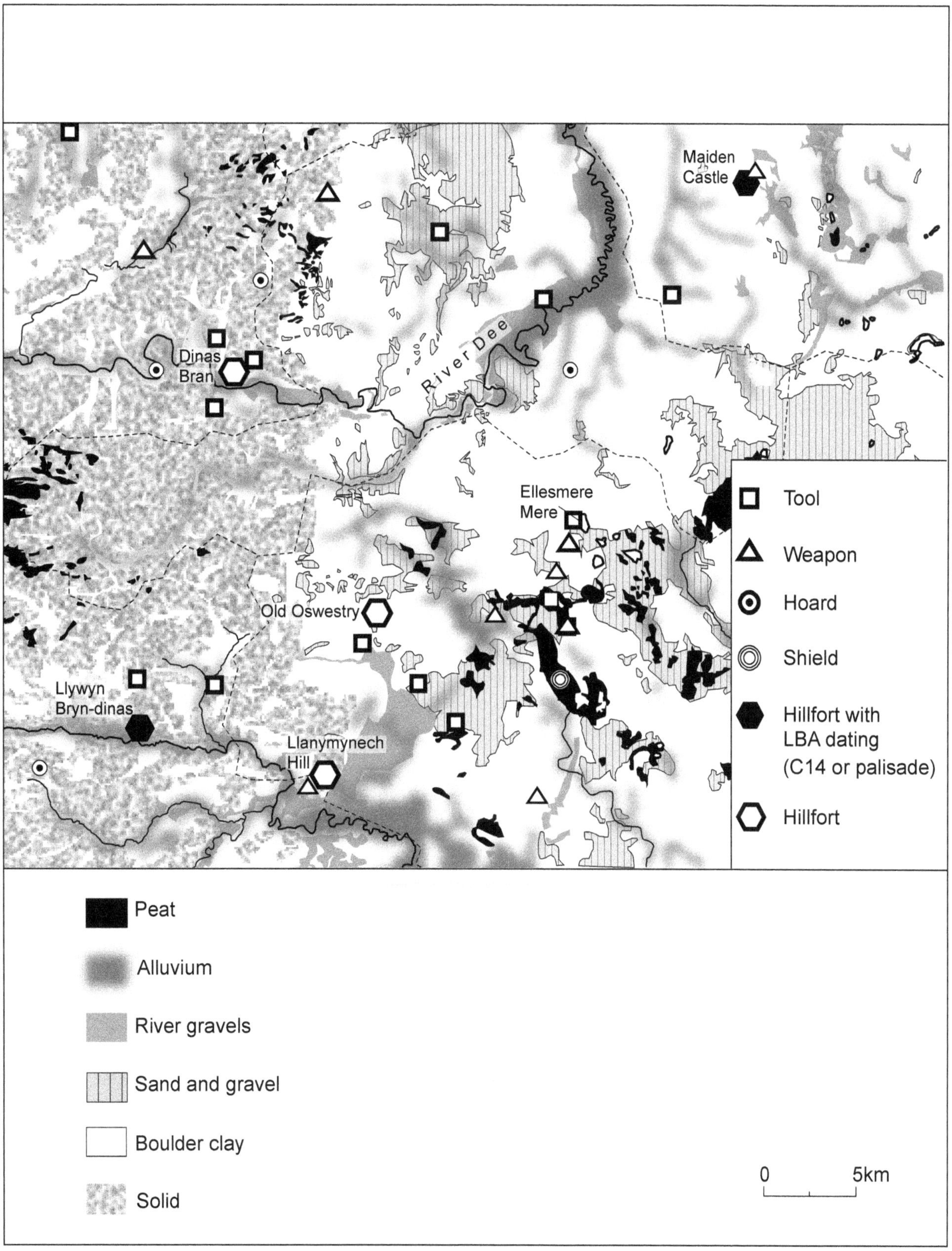
Maiden Castle
River Dee
Dinas Bran
Ellesmere Mere
Old Oswestry
Llywyn Bryn-dinas
Llanymynech Hill
Tool
Weapon
Hoard
Shield
Hillfort with LBA dating (C14 or palisade)
Hillfort
Peat
Alluvium
River gravels
Sand and gravel
Boulder clay
Solid
0
5km

Fig.21 Late Bronze Age metalwork and drift geology in north-west Shropshire, South-west Cheshire and north-east Wales (see Fig.8)

the social hierarchy existed in other landscape contexts. Agricultural practice may also have dictated the location of settlement elsewhere, and mechanisms of exchange may also have influenced the location of further settlement nodes. Therefore the existence of enclosed and defended sites in the Late Bronze Age in the Welsh Marches is unlikely to have been an exclusive settlement form. Continuity in the mode of settlement may have characterised the region in this period, alongside the development of defended sites.

Continuity between the Early and Middle Bronze Age through the ceramic assemblage and radiocarbon dates has been demonstrated at Oversley Farm, Cheshire (Garner 2001, 49-53). This continuity can arguably be extended into the Late Bronze Age (Fig. 7; ibid. 53). A radiocarbon date (Beta-127178) from a pit at the site, in association with a saddle quern and grinding stone and possibly a structure (ibid. 53-54) calibrates between 900 and 760 BC at 68.2% confidence. This date therefore represents settlement activity in Needham's Period 7 of the Bronze Age, contemporary with Ewart Park metalwork (Needham 1996, 136). The presence of Ewart Park metalwork at Beeston Castle, Cheshire (Needham 1993b, 44) suggests that these unenclosed and enclosed sites may have had contemporary phases of occupation.

At Shorncote Quarry, Gloucestershire, evidence for metalworking has been recorded at a Late Bronze Age unenclosed site (Morris 1994b, 44-45). The clay mould fragments found on the site are for the production of a socketed axe of Ewart Park type (ibid.). This discovery has been highlighted as significant (ibid. 45), since it demonstrates that enclosed sites such as the Breiddin or Beeston Castle in the north of the study area, did not necessarily have sole control over the production of metal objects. This brings into question the degree of prestige associated with the production of metalwork at enclosed and unenclosed sites. The fact that significant hoards in proximity to hilltop sites are composed of weapons rather than tools may suggest that the production of axes was regarded as utilitarian and may not have held the same significance as objects associated with conflict. Therefore the significance of metalworking at a site may have varied depending upon the type of objects that were being produced. This could suggest that unenclosed sites were involved in the production of objects that were less highly regarded and that therefore their status was lower than the defended sites. However, there is no evidence to suggest that weapons were necessarily being produced at Beeston Castle, and the only evidence from the Breiddin to suggest the form of objects produced, suggests that these were personal ornaments (Tylecote and Biek 1991, 149). These objects may not have been accorded the same significance as hoards of weapons. Therefore it can be argued that it is the use of objects and their life cycle within a social context that accords them significance in the Late Bronze Age. It is possible that their production was not necessarily

associated with status or the need for defence.

It can be argued that defended hilltop sites in the Welsh Marches represent a dislocation with earlier patterns of settlement. The construction of these sites may have been a response to a need to reassert power in the face of instability. However, the limited evidence from the study area does not allow for a radical shift in the location of lowland unenclosed settlements. Instead, the context of these sites suggests continuity with earlier periods.

The settlement evidence at Thornwell Farm, Monmouthshire, is comparable in its location to both Early and Middle Bronze Age settlement in the study area. The Early Bronze Age sites at Oversley Farm and Arthill Heath Farm in Cheshire (Fig.6), and the Middle Bronze Age sites at Rhuddlan in Denbighshire (Fig. 15) and Glanfeinion in Powys (Fig. 14), all lie in lowland or valley contexts above the floodplain and within 500m of rivers. Thornwell Farm also lies in a lowland context at 40m OD but on ground above, and 0.3 km from, the River Wye (Fig. 15). Early and Middle Bronze Age ceramics, found in residual contexts on the site (Hughes 1996, 89), could also suggest that this location acted as a continued focus for settlement throughout the Bronze Age, in a similar fashion to Oversley Farm in Cheshire.

The size of the Late Bronze Age structure at Thornwell Farm is c.12.5m in diameter, considerably larger than other Bronze Age structures recorded in the study area. The Middle Bronze Age round-house at Glanfeinion, Powys, is c. 7m diameter (Britnell et al. 1997, 180). The oval Early Bronze Age structures c. 6x4m at Oversley Farm (Garner 2001, 47) and circular structures c.5-8m in diameter at Arthill Heath Farm in Cheshire (Nevell 1988, 7-9), are also smaller than the Late Bronze Age example at Thornwell Farm. The size of the structure at Thornwell has been suggested to reflect potential change in the nature of residency in the Late Bronze Age and perhaps the coalescence of members of extended family groups (Hughes 1996, 93). The fact that the entrance to the structure is considered to face south-east (ibid. 93) can be compared with the Middle Bronze Age structure at Glanfeinion, Powys (Britnell et al. 1997, 196) and Middle Bronze Age structures on settlement sites in southern England (Brück 1999b, 155). Therefore some continuity in elements of domestic architecture can also be discerned here.

The proximity of barrows to the Thornwell Farm settlement (Hughes 1996, 89) may be further evidence to suggest continuity in the occupation of a specific locale. A similar relationship can be seen at Shorncote Quarry, Gloucestershire, between Late Bronze Age settlement and earlier funerary activity (Hearne and Heaton 1994, 17-19). Although Early Bronze Age structures have not been recorded in close association with barrows in the study area, it has been suggested that Middle Bronze Age settlement activity at Rhuddlan, Denbighshire, may have focussed upon an existing funerary monument. It is possible therefore that the Late Bronze Age settlement at Thornwell represents a conscious association with an earlier monument, perhaps to legitimise claims to land tenure.

At Shorncote Quarry the relatively extensive nature of the settlement evidence, including five round-houses and a lack of inter-cutting features, has been suggested to represent a number of short-lived phases of occupation (Hearne and Heaton 1994, 52). However, on Middle Bronze Age settlement sites in the south of England it has been suggested that the reorganisation of space, with round-houses frequently being re-built on different parts of the site, represents change across generations and the social organisation of extended family groups (Brück 1999b, 149). Therefore it could be suggested that occupation at Shorncote Quarry does not necessarily indicate episodic activity, but rather longevity in occupation, characterised by a conscious organisation of space through time. A degree of formal spatial organisation has been suggested in the pairing of two structures at Shorncote Quarry (Hearne and Heaton 1994, 49). Therefore a shift in the settlement pattern at the site, which has been suggested to move from west to east across time, may not necessarily represent re-occupation of the site, but re-organisation.

The quantity of burnt stone recovered from features on the site, with up to 148kg from a single pit (ibid. 26), suggests repeated processes involving the heating of water. Heated stones immersed in water have been interpreted as representing the fulling of textiles at burnt mound sites (Jeffrey 1991), and such a process may also be applicable here. A clay loomweight from one of the roundhouses supports the suggestion of textile production (Hearne and Heaton1994, 32). The large quantity of burnt stone is also a feature of the Early Bronze Age settlement phase at Oversley Farm, Cheshire, again suggesting similarities in the economy of lowland settlement locales throughout the Bronze Age, and across the study area.

The evidence for the agricultural economy at Shorncote Quarry and Thornwell Farm is also comparable with the evidence for the mixed cereal cultivation and animal husbandry evidenced at Early and Middle Bronze Age sites in the Welsh Marches. Shorncote Quarry has evidence for the cultivation of wheat and barley (Hearne and Heaton 1994, 52). At Thornwell Farm sandstone geology to the east of the site supports a clay loam suitable for arable agriculture (Moffett 1996, 88). A rubbing stone from a Late Bronze Age context attests the possible processing of grain, if used in conjunction with a saddle quern on the site (Roe 1996, 45). The animal bone assemblage comprises cow, sheep/ goat and pig (Pinter-Bellows 1996, 84). This is again comparable with settlement sites elsewhere in the region

which have demonstrably earlier origins (e.g. Garner 2001, 51-53; Britnell et al. 1997, 184-186).

Therefore there is enough evidence to suggest that the few Late Bronze Age settlement sites recorded in the study area represent continuity with earlier patterns of settlement, particularly through their location. However, there is a suggestion that upland settlement may have witnessed re-organisation in the Late Bronze Age. Evidence for agriculture in the Late Bronze Age has been recorded in an upland context around 400m OD upon the Denbigh Moors, Denbighshire (Manley 1990). At Graig Fechan (Fig. 19), excavation revealed a circular enclosure in stone with a conjoined circular hut. Radiocarbon samples from the interior of the hut gave dates of 1151-1149 or 1130-925 BC (ibid. 523) Samples from within the wall of the hut produced dates of 990-955 or 945-840 BC (ibid.)

The radiocarbon dates from Graig Fechan could suggest more than one phase of activity at the enclosure during the Late Bronze Age. Environmental evidence from pollen samples has been given to suggest "a mixture of rough grazing land and light scrub woodland" (ibid. 524). No evidence for cereal cultivation was collected, and Manley sees a system of transhumance operating here, with the field systems providing upland grazing in the summer months (ibid). Such an interpretation would suggest frequent re-occupation.

The fact that the morphology of the field systems of Mynydd Poeth and Ffridd Brynhelen differs, may suggest that they were not laid out at the same time. Equally such differences could suggest functional variations within the agricultural landscape or even differences in land tenure. A lack of direct dating evidence from the field walls in this landscape does, however, leave their relationship with the Graig Fechan enclosure open to debate. Nevertheless, a Late Bronze Age phase of occupation in an upland context is not open to doubt. If such activity represents the same degree of continuity in the location of settlement that can be witnessed in lowland contexts, then this suggests that artefact distributions in upland contexts recorded for earlier periods reflect similar phases of occupation. To what extent such occupation was formalised by the construction of field walls in the Late Bronze Age is unknown, but has been argued for comparable landscapes elsewhere (e.g. Barnatt 2000, 5). Such a move may reflect a desire to formalise rights to land holding, supporting the concept that an association between Late Bronze Age settlement sites and earlier barrows in lowland contexts reflect a similar desire to assert claims to the tenure of specific locations.

Altitude above Ordnance Datum	Early Bronze Age	Middle Bronze Age	Late Bronze Age
≤122m	30	83	82
122-244m	14	33	43
244-427m	14	30	16
≥427m	5	3	2

Fig.22 The altitude of Bronze Age metal finds in the study area

The distribution of metal objects in the wider landscape of the study area

The presence of unenclosed settlement sites in lowland contexts in the study area and evidence for organised pastoral agriculture in the uplands, demonstrates that settlement loci existed beyond defended hilltops in the Late Bronze Age. It has been argued that hilltop sites show an association with hoards of weapons. Therefore it is possible that other nodes of settlement in the study area have an association with metal objects. An examination of the distribution of metalwork in the Welsh Marches, within the limits of a map of recovery (Needham 1993a, 164) may be able to illuminate a wider settlement pattern.

The fact that the number of metalwork finds from above the 244m contour in the Late Bronze Age is virtually halved when compared to Middle Bronze Age metalwork distributions (Fig. 22) could suggest that there is a genuine contraction in upland activity. This could suggest that climatic deterioration was a genuine factor in the period and that it precipitated a dislocation in the pattern of upland settlement and land-use, as suggested by Burgess (1985, 202). The enclosed settlement and associated field systems on the Denbigh Moors, Denbighshire (Manley 1990), may at least reflect a reorganisation or formalisation of land holding in the face of economic and/or social pressures during the Late Bronze Age.

Settlement in a lowland context has been argued to represent continuity with earlier settlement patterns, and this can be reinforced by the distribution of metalwork. It has been argued that an association existed with at least a proportion of settlement locales in the Early and Middle Bronze Age and rivers in the study area. This has been reiterated by the location of a Late Bronze Age round-house in close association with the River Wye, at Thornwell Farm in Monmouthshire. Evidence from Runnymede Bridge, Surrey, suggests that settlement adjacent to rivers could have played a key role in the exchange of metalwork

(Needham and Longley 1980). Evidence for a timber wharf at the site against which river traffic could moor (ibid. 418), together with continental metalwork and metalworking based on scrap material (ibid. 420), suggests that the site may have been an important exchange centre.

Such a wealth of artefactual material has not been recorded from riverside sites in the Welsh Marches study area, which appear to show a preference for positions above floodplains, rather than the closer physical relationship recorded between settlement and river at Runnymede Bridge. Nevertheless, it is possible that sites in the Welsh Marches were related to nodes of exchange on major rivers in the region. The hoard of metalwork from a ditch terminal at Petters Sports Field also in Surrey (O'connell 1986), has been interpreted as scrap intended to be recycled (Needham 1986, 59-60). The fact that this site is within half a kilometre of the Thames and Runnymede Bridge, demonstrates that close associations between exchange centres and other forms of settlement may have existed. The evidence for metalworking at the two sites suggests they were related within wider networks of exchange.

Therefore, using Runnymede Bridge and Petters Sports Field as precedents, metalwork in the Welsh Marches study area that has been recorded in close proximity to rivers, may suggest the location of associated settlement sites. The Eardington hoard, Bridgenorth, Shropshire, is a relatively well-recorded example of a hoard found close to the River Severn (Dodd 1960). A late Bronze Age Ewart Park hoard consisting of a socketed gauge, socketed chisel and two late palstaves, are described as having been found together within a gravel river terrace above the River Severn and between it and a small tributary (ibid. 213-217). The suitability for settlement of the gravels and riverine location was suggested by Dodd (ibid. 215). The location of the site can also be compared to that of the recorded Early and Middle Bronze Age settlement locales in the study area. It is possible therefore that this hoard represents a Late Bronze Age settlement locale at which metalwork was deposited in a similar fashion to that at Petters Sports Field. However, unlike the Surrey sites there is no evidence for metalworking here which could be used to suggest the production and exchange of objects. Therefore without excavated features it cannot be demonstrated that this hoard represents the location of a node of settlement associated with exchange on the Severn.

Several other metal finds have been recorded in close proximity to the Severn, and may reflect associated settlement activity along a major communication route in the study area. A socketed knife recorded from Llandinam, Powys has been recorded c. 250m from the Severn. The find has a provenance apparently only accurate to within 1km. However the location of the find is only 500m from the recorded Middle Bronze Age round-house at Glanfeinion, Llandinam, Powys (Fig. 14). Therefore it is possible that the provenance of this find represents continued settlement activity in this area of the Severn Valley.

A Late Bronze Age socketed axe has been recorded at Highnam, Gloucestershire, around 500m from the River Severn, but again its provenance appears to be only accurate to within 1km. A hoard has also been recorded near the Severn at Buttington Hall, Cletterwood, Powys, containing a spearhead, chisel and late palstave, c.1km from the Severn. Similarly a socketed axe from Hen Domen, Powys appears to have been found 600m from the Severn. However, without associated structures, it cannot be demonstrated that these finds reflect nodes of settlement along the river. The deposition of these objects may reflect locations important for exchange, although again this cannot be specifically identified in the archaeological record.

A Ewart Park phase socketed axe has been recorded c.1.25km from the River Severn in Shrewsbury on river gravels, comparable to the location of the Eardington Hoard. However the fact that it had preserved wood in the socket suggests that it was deposited in a wet context, which could suggest a votive deposition. Indeed, several metal objects have been attributed to the River Severn, including socketed axes from Shrewsbury, Shropshire, Highnam, Gloucestershire, and Holt, Worcestershire. Therefore it is possible that the river itself was a focus of deposition. To what extent these depositions are related to settlement sites in their proximity is unknown.

At Buildwas Bridge, Shropshire, a concentration of metalwork from the River Severn has been recorded. It may be possible to suggest the location of a riverine settlement here, although the link between metal deposition and occupation cannot be demonstrated. A Ewart Park socketed axe, leaf-shaped sword and palstave were recorded in 1795, together with a dugout canoe (Chitty 1928, 127). The fact the objects appear to have been dredged from the river itself suggests that these items

were deposited as part of a deliberate votive act, although an association between the components of this 'hoard' cannot be demonstrated. Therefore whether this represents evidence for a site engaged in the exchange of metalwork adjacent to a major river, akin to Runnymede Bridge, is questionable. The fact that further leaf shaped swords have been recorded downstream from Buildwas at Ironbridge, and Diglis, Worcestershire, appears to support the concept that the river was actually the focus of votive deposition.

The use of rivers in the exchange of metalwork, and their role as arterial route-ways, could suggest that they were a focus for conflict, in that they facilitated a greater frequency of contact with other individuals or groups. Such contacts may have given rise to disputes regarding the control of exchange networks. Ritual display designed to emphasise status, through the deposition of prestige metalwork (Bradley 1990, 39), could account for the deposition of weapons hoards and significant objects at such points of contact.

The Broadward hoard could belong to a tradition of ritual deposition in the Welsh Marches, and is located within half a kilometre of the River Clun in Shropshire. This hoard contains forty spearheads or fragments, including twenty distinctive barbed spearheads (Burgess et al 1972, 213). The presence of the remains of wooden shafts in some of these (ibid. 213), suggests their preservation in anaerobic wet conditions. Indeed Burgess has emphasised the relationship between barbed spearheads and wet contexts, and states that "of the 34 individual provenances, 22 are river, lake or bog sites..." (ibid. 222). It has also been suggested that the form of these spearheads and their thin casting would make them unsuitable for practical use as weapons, and that they were likely to have been used as ceremonial display items (ibid. 226-227). Similarly the Congleton hoard, Cheshire is located less than half a kilometre away from the River Dane. This hoard also belongs to Burgess' 'Broadward complex' (ibid. 236). The Bloody Roman's Field hoard from Lydham, Shropshire, also contains spearheads and is again within half a kilometre of the River Onny. The National Monument Record records that " numerous Bronze Age spearheads" were found here in 1862. Although the date and character of this hoard are unclear, it would appear to be comparable in terms of context to those at Broadward and Congleton and the hoards associated with the Wrekin, Shropshire, at Willow Moor.

It appears that Late Bronze Age metalwork finds recorded in close association with rivers in the study area, actually represent the deliberate consumption of objects by deposition in wet contexts, particularly in the case of weapons hoards. These acts could be designed to affirm status in the face of rival groups, encountered through processes of exchange taking place along river systems. The fact that the depositions were taking place away from the actual river itself may suggest they had an association with settlement locales. Intentional depositions may have been designed to emphasise claims to territory or social status as an integral part of processes of exchange with outside groups. This is reinforced by the recorded association between hilltop enclosures and significant metalwork hoards in the study area. The degree of separation between settlements and locations chosen for the deposition of significant metal objects, in contexts removed from hilltop enclosures is, however, unknown.

If an area of drift geology is examined in north-west Shropshire, Wrexham and south-west Cheshire, the context of metal depositions in the Late Bronze Age can be illuminated further (Fig. 21). The drift geology of this area is composed largely of boulder clay, with substantial areas and isolated pockets of glacial sand and gravel, overlain by river terrace gravels and large expanses of alluvium along the main rivers. Significantly large areas of peat concentrate around the Oswestry, Ellesmere and Wem districts of Shropshire.

Several finds of tools lie upon glacial sand and gravel deposits, including Late Bronze Age socketed axes from Wrexham, Oswestry and West Felton. A socketed axe has also been recorded upon river terrace gravels at Sesswick, Wrexham. The fact that Early, Middle and Late Bronze Age structures have been recorded from gravel contexts in the study area could suggest that these finds were deposited in the vicinity of other such settlement locales. However, there are a slightly greater number of finds from the boulder clay, including two Ewart Park socketed axes from Ellesmere, Shropshire, and a socketed axe from Oswestry. Further north a Ewart Park socketed axe or late palstave fragment lies upon boulder clay at Cuddington, Cheshire, as does a possible hoard of two socketed axes from Ruabon, Wrexham. It can be noted also that these two finds lie close to river tributaries, which may suggest that they were actually deposited in wet locations. A Late Bronze Age hoard recorded at Llantisilio, Denbighshire, appears to have been recovered from an alluvial context near to the River Dee, suggesting that it may also have been deposited into water in prehistory.

A Ewart Park sword from Val Hill, Ellesmere (Leah et al 1998, 187) and a leaf shaped socketed spearhead from Ruyton, Oswestry, have both been recorded from a boulder clay context. A socketed knife, which could conceivably have been used as a weapon or a tool, was also found on boulder clay at Cockshutt, Shropshire. It can be argued, however, that the wetlands played a more important part in influencing the deposition of weapons and associated objects in this period. A Late Bronze Age shield was found at Baggy Moor, Hordley (Leah et al.1998, 188) and it is perhaps significant that the tools recorded on boulder clay from the Oswestry and Ellesmere area form part of a concentration of finds close to large expanses of peat and

meres (Fig. 20). The area is characterised by a frequent patchwork of peat deposits (ibid. 28) and therefore it is possible that a number of finds in this area were originally deposited in wet contexts. Two tool finds are from the peat deposits themselves, a socketed axe with a preserved wooden haft from Ellesmere (ibid. 193) and a socketed axe from Baggy Moor, Hordley (ibid.188).

The fact that a number of weapons have been found in such close proximity could suggest that this area represents a focus for intentional depositions. Two further finds recorded from sand and gravel contexts include a Ewart Park sword from Tetchill, Ellesmere, and a Ewart Park sword from Whittington, Shropshire. The SMR (02797) describes the latter as having a "slight twist to the handle and the point bent." This is comparable with apparently deliberately broken weapons from wet contexts elsewhere. A Ewart Park sword, also bent, was found from the post alignment at Flag Fen, Cambridgeshire (Coombs 1992, 511). This feature extends from the enclosed agricultural system of droveways on the dryland fen edge, into the marsh or wet deposits to the east and towards the Flag Fen 'platform', and is considered to have attained symbolic significance (Pryor 1992, 527-528). Both ritual deposition and settlement in the Late Bronze Age have been recorded together at Flag Fen and Fengate (ibid.). This serves to show that settlement and agriculture, and the ritual deposition of metalwork into bogs can have a direct relationship.

The fact that weapons and tools were deposited in and around the wetlands of the Ellesmere area does not therefore necessarily indicate that it was one of votive ritual divorced from contemporary settlement. Wooden piles recorded from White Mere together with "timbers and clay platforms beneath the peat" at Pikes End in the Ellesmere region (Leah et. al. 1998, 188) could, potentially, provide parallels with Flag Fen, Cambridgeshire. It is also possible that field systems identified from aerial photographs around Baggy Moor, Ellesmere could be contemporary (Leah et al 1998, 195), although this could not be proven without excavation.

A Late Bronze Age bucket was recorded by William Stukeley in the eighteenth century (Briggs 1977, 90), from Cuddington, Cheshire (Fig. 19). It has been suggested that this was from a wet location, since comparable finds have been recorded from other mosses in this region (ibid. 91). This suggests therefore that deposition into bogs may have been a widespread phenomenon in the study area.

However, it is notable that no Late Bronze Age finds appear to have been recorded in the peats on the uplands to the west (Fig. 21). It could therefore be suggested that the archaeological record in the lowlands represents a fieldwork bias. Indeed, the distribution of metal finds could be affected by modern land use. It could be argued that areas of modern arable cultivation are likely to produce a greater number of finds in the disturbed soil. Therefore the land mapped between 1932 and 1935 by The Land Utilisation Survey of Britain has been examined in the same area as the drift geology. It can be seen that there is a greater degree of arable land between Oswestry, Ellesmere and Wem and to the south towards Shrewsbury. The area of land to the north, which is essentially an expanse of boulder clay through which the River Dee flows, is more greatly characterised by 'meadowland and permanent grass'. Therefore it could be suggested that Bronze Age finds are likely to be recorded from areas under more intensive cultivation in modern times. The area around the town of Wrexham shows a relatively greater intensity of arable agriculture. However, although metalwork has been recorded here, it does not display the same concentration as is visible in the Oswestry and Ellesmere area, and there are no weapons finds, unless the socketed knife from Minera is included. This suggests that the distribution of metalwork does not equate directly with the pattern of modern land use. Similarly, although the valley of the Dee around Llangollen has a significant proportion of the land given over to arable cultivation in the earlier part of the twentieth century, the majority of the finds here appear to be associated with areas of 'heath, moorland, commons and rough pasture'. It is also possible that peat cutting in the Ellesmere area is similarly responsible for a disproportionate number of finds. However, the composition of the assemblage in this area, with a significant number of weapons, suggests that it was a genuine focus of specific activity in prehistory. It can be suggested therefore that modern land use has not significantly distorted the pattern of Late Bronze Age metalwork deposition in the archaeological record.

The emergence of centres of prestige within a settled landscape

The clearest indication of dislocation in the Late Bronze Age is represented by the widespread deposition of metalwork in hoards and in wet contexts. The fact that these depositions were not intended to be retrieved suggests that any scarcity of resources in the period was actively used to enhance prestige. The fact that enclosed settlement sites on hilltops can be seen to have attracted the deposition of potentially high status metalwork hoards, suggests that prestige was associated with fixed settlement sites. The fact that a number of these hoards are composed of weapons reflects the fact that these sites were defended and that their status was to some extent governed by conflict. The fact that specific enclosed points in the landscape became a focus for the expression of prestige, may also reflect a centralisation and crystallisation of power in the Late Bronze Age.

The fact that the deposition of potentially significant metal objects also took place at other points of the landscape,

suggests that the relationship between enclosed hilltop sites and ritual expressions of status was not exclusive. However, the deposition of objects in irretrievable contexts as votive acts, or acts of conspicuous consumption, was not necessarily divorced from settlement locales. The relationship between settlement and the deposition of metalwork into lowland bog contexts is unclear since associated sites have not been recorded in the study area. It is possible that settlement existed in close proximity to depositions recorded in river valleys and that these represent a relationship with nodes of exchange. However, the status apparent in the construction of enclosures on hilltops has not been mirrored by the identification of enclosed and defended sites in other contexts. This suggests that settlement beyond these sites and any associated exchange mechanisms, may not necessarily have been economically autonomous. The ritual deposition of significant objects into bogs may represent an extension of the power held at defended hilltop sites, through demonstrations of prestige at significant locations within the wider landscape.

Continuity in the location of settlement in the study area can be witnessed through a limited number of excavated sites and this may suggest that dislocation in the Late Bronze Age did not affect a wider settlement pattern. It can be suggested therefore that the construction of defended enclosures represents a separating-out of the pattern of settlement into a hierarchical order, rather than a widespread upheaval in the location of residency. It could be argued that the construction of hilltop enclosures was a response to a constriction in the supply of resources, and a desire to control or defend them. It could equally be argued that settlement locales in differing landscape contexts adapted to a changing environmental and perhaps economic climate, as suggested by Young (2000, 75-77). The evidence for enclosed settlement in an upland agricultural context in Denbighshire could relate to a reorganisation of space in the Late Bronze Age, and a desire to formalise patterns of land tenure, rather than a radical settlement shift. The possibility that unenclosed lowland settlement locales consciously referred to earlier monuments in their siting may reflect a more subtle means of reinforcing an attachment to place, although the context of these sites does not appear to have differed greatly from those established in the Early and Middle Bronze Age.

The small number of settlement sites recorded in the Welsh Marches limits our understanding of landscape contexts chosen for settlement. The fact that all known unenclosed settlement sites of the Early, Middle and Late Bronze Age have been recorded from lowland or valley contexts, restricts any interpretation that upland marginal areas were abandoned in the Late Bronze Age, as argued by Burgess (1985). Therefore it can be concluded that the only exception to at least a prevailing lowland pattern of settlement, was the construction of defended hilltop enclosures. This may reflect changes in relationships between settlement locales and a clearer definition of social hierarchy, but it cannot be suggested that this represents widespread upheaval and population shift in the Welsh Marches during the Late Bronze Age.

6. Conclusions: interpreting Bronze Age settlement in the Welsh Marches

The evidence for Bronze Age settlement sites in the Welsh Marches is clearly limited. The restricted extent of recorded settlement in the region has meant that the pattern of residency beyond individual excavated sites can only be inferred. The settlement pattern has therefore been extrapolated by examining the distribution and context of contemporary sites, monuments and artefacts in the study area. From the evidence available there is a strong suggestion of considerable longevity in the occupation of specific locales and environmental contexts. It can be argued that residential mobility operated within a network of fixed settlement locales from the Early Bronze Age. There is nothing to suggest dislocation in this pattern of settlement until the Late Bronze Age and the construction of defended enclosures.

A lack of recorded settlement sites with clearly defined domestic architecture and an associated domestic artefact package, has been used to infer a pattern of residential mobility for the Early Bronze Age in southern England (Brück 1999a). However, structures dating to the Early Bronze Age, though rare, have been recorded in the Welsh Marches study area, in association with the residues of domestic and agricultural production and consumption. Moreover, the evidence for the accumulation of midden deposits (Garner 2001, 47 and forthcoming), and the reconstruction of buildings (Nevell 1988, 9) suggests a degree of permanency in the occupation of specific places in the Early Bronze Age, though this does not necessarily exclude them from systems of residential mobility.

Funerary monuments have been seen as playing an integral part in patterns of residential mobility in Early Bronze Age southern England (Brück 1999a, 68-69). The few Early Bronze Age settlement locales recorded in the Welsh Marches, however, do not appear to have a close association with round barrows. Therefore ceremonial activity at these monuments may have taken place at a distance from the domestic sphere, requiring the movement of people to an alternative location. However, the relative location of barrows to known settlement locales does not suggest that such movement, over perhaps 3-4km, was so great as to warrant the abandonment of a previously occupied location. The association of flint debitage with barrows and ceremonial monuments may reflect temporary domestic activity, but does not necessarily suggest that the mode of Early Bronze Age settlement was inherently transient. Such movement may indeed have been episodic, but could also have made repeated reference to an existing and established settlement locale elsewhere in the landscape. Such settlements may have remained occupied by a component of a group while others engaged in alternative activity elsewhere. It is possible that permanently occupied locales witnessed movement that may have been selective on grounds of age or gender and that they were never entirely abandoned.

The limited evidence for Middle Bronze Age settlement locales in the study area is comparable with the location of structures recorded for the late third and early second millennium BC. These share an association with well-drained contexts in close proximity to rivers. There is evidence for the partial rebuilding of structures (Britnell et al. 1997, 180) suggesting a degree of permanency in the location of settlement and also that Early Bronze Age settlement locales may have continued to be occupied into the Middle Bronze Age (Garner 2001, 52-53). The similarity in the location of recorded Early and Middle Bronze Age settlement locales also suggests that agricultural practice continued unchanged during the second millennium BC. Direct evidence for agriculture is limited in the Welsh Marches, but where this has been recorded at Early and Middle Bronze Age sites, it suggests the cultivation of cereals and the presence of domestic cattle and sheep or goat (Garner 2001, 51-53; Britnell et al. 1997, 184-188).

Continuity can be seen in the occupation of lowland contexts between the Early and Middle Bronze Age. However, it is the upland zones that are the least well-understood areas for Early and Middle Bronze Age settlement in the Welsh Marches. The presence of funerary monuments and metalwork depositions is testimony to at least episodes of settlement, particularly in contexts at a distance from recorded settlement locales at lower altitudes, or river valley contexts. However, no settlement structures have been recorded above river valleys dating to the Early or Middle Bronze Age. Evidence from beneath barrows can perhaps be dismissed as relating to specific ceremonial events. It has been argued therefore that such locations were settled temporarily as part of a system of transhumance, where lands perhaps held in common between communities, were used for grazing livestock in the summer.

This interpretation assumes that such contexts were unsuitable for more permanent nodes of settlement and were economically marginal, which may not necessarily be the case. Excavations in highland Scotland, for example, have demonstrated the existence of long-lived settlement locales for the Early and Middle Bronze Age (McCullagh and Tipping 1998). However, the fact that locations away from well-drained gravel deposits, particularly in river valleys, have failed to produce the same level of settlement evidence from both lowland and upland contexts, may be evidence to support a real distinction between economically favourable and marginal contexts in the Bronze Age.

Such a distinction may not necessarily have been purely agricultural, since the location of a settlement next to a major river may have facilitated more frequent exchange with outside groups. This may have been advantageous both economically in terms of acquiring technology or raw materials, and perhaps socially where the exchange of commodities could be used to maintain positions within a hierarchical society (Rowlands 1980, 33).

If contrasting landscape zones were economically marginal in prehistory, then their occupation may have been seasonal or episodic. The repeated activity recorded at burnt mounds (O'Kelly 1954, 121-123) is perhaps the most convincing indication of the episodic re-occupation of specific places during the Bronze Age. The date of these sites from Shropshire (Hannaford 1999, 73) and the West Midlands (Hodder 1990, 106-107), suggests their use in the Middle Bronze Age although dating elsewhere has suggested that they may have been in use throughout the Bronze Age (Kelly 1992). Nevertheless their use could suggest that a degree of residential mobility existed in the Welsh Marches in the mid-late second millennium BC. However, as with the relationship between barrows and Early Bronze Age sites, the use of burnt mounds does not necessarily preclude the existence of fixed nodes of residency in the landscape.

The location of burnt mounds adjacent to constant supplies of water clearly contrasts with that for settlement sites, which have a relationship with water sources, but appear to have a preference for well-drained locations. The context of burnt mounds in waterlogged locations may therefore have been intentionally situated away from more permanently settled areas of domestic activity (Barfield 1991, 60).

If burnt mounds are regarded as cooking sites, then they could be associated with episodic hunting activity (O'Kelly 1954, 138). However, cooking meat does not require boiling water with hot stones. If burnt mounds were used as a means of cooking, it is possible that the method of cooking was intentionally different from that carried out elsewhere. This difference may have served to mark the separation of the site from more permanently settled domestic residencies. It is possible that the actual use of a mound for cooking, was secondary to its primary function. These sites could be seen as primarily fulfilling a social role, legitimised through a symbolic association with water, in locations intentionally removed from the domestic sphere. The use of the sites as saunas (Barfield and Hodder 1987) may have performed a medicinal or spiritual role (ibid. 373-374) and may have been restricted to only a component of a social group. It is possible therefore that burnt mounds functioned in terms of creating bonds between individuals, perhaps as a means of establishing a specific position or role within a social group. This activity may have been legitimised through its isolation and association with a traditional activity, whether cooking meat after hunting expeditions or using a symbolic water source for sauna baths.

It is unlikely that burnt mounds had a purely utilitarian function, in terms of fulling textiles for example (Jeffrey 1991), since there is no reason why this could not have taken place at more permanently occupied settlements, which are frequently associated with burnt stones and the products of textile production such as loom weights. It can be argued therefore that burnt mounds represent settlement mobility, perhaps restricted to only a component of a social group. The use of burnt mounds may have coincided with the use of areas of the landscape for grazing animals in the summer months. Alongside activities at burnt mounds more permanently settled domestic sites continued to be occupied. Those who remained at these settlement locales may have been involved in craft production, exchange or the tending of crops.

It can be argued therefore that a system of residency that allowed mobility as part of agricultural cycles and social and ceremonial events, but that also maintained more permanent nodes of residency elsewhere, existed between the Early and Middle Bronze Age in the study area. This is at odds with recent interpretations of changing settlement patterns in southern England (Brück 2000). There is no apparent shift towards enclosed or nucleated settlement forms during any Early to Middle Bronze Age transition in the region from the limited evidence available. It is possible that the association with funerary monuments became closer from the Middle Bronze Age reflecting associations recorded in southern England (Bradley 1981, 100). The Middle Bronze Age settlement at Rhuddlan, Denbighshire, and Late Bronze Age settlement sites at Shorncote Quarry, Gloucestershire, and Thornwell Farm, Monmouthshire, appear to be located in close proximity to earlier funerary monuments. This could reflect a subtle discontinuity with earlier settlement patterns and may reflect a desire to reinstate an ancestral association with a specific place, perhaps to legitimise and assert tenure over land. This may suggest disruption with patterns of land-tenure established in the Early Bronze Age. However, this association does not appear to be universal in the limited settlement record. Furthermore, the environmental context of unenclosed settlement locales remains comparable with earlier patterns of residency, suggesting a general continuity in settlement and agricultural practice during the Early, Middle and Late Bronze Age.

It is not until the late second millennium BC that any significant signs of dislocation in patterns of settlement appear to emerge. The weight of dating evidence suggests that enclosures on hilltops were constructed in this period, which represents a radical departure from the location and form of earlier settlement locales.

The desire for defence at these sites is demonstrated by timber palisades or ramparts dating to the Late Bronze Age and the association of a number of sites with hoards of weaponry. However, not all excavated hilltop sites have produced evidence for Late Bronze Age activity, and it is not necessarily possible to equate the location of all Iron Age hillforts with Late Bronze Age defensive sites. It is possible that this represents only a limited desire in specific local contexts to create defended spaces, or that settlement on hilltops was restricted to limited groups of individuals in the Late Bronze Age. This could suggest that their occupants represent groups at the apex of a hierarchical society.

The presence of Late Bronze Age ceramics and evidence for metalworking could suggest occupation at defended enclosures in association with specialist activities. However, the presence of metalworking on unenclosed lowland sites such as Shorncote Quarry, Gloucestershire (Morris 1994b, 44-45), suggests that the production of metalwork was not exclusively associated with defended hilltops. Furthermore, there is no evidence to suggest that metalworking at defended sites was restricted to the production of high status objects such as weapons. The presence of settlement sites beyond the study area, which appear to have been associated with the exchange of metalwork along river systems (Needham and Longley 1980), also suggests that defended hilltops may not have had an exclusive relationship with the exchange of objects, if similar riverine sites existed in the Welsh Marches. Therefore control of the production and exchange of metalwork was not necessarily the primary motivation for the construction of defended sites. However, the consumption by deposition of metal objects that had attained significance during their life cycle, may have been used as a means of enhancing the prestige of those resident at defended enclosures.

Evidence for the presence of Bronze Age barrows has been recorded at Sharpstones Hill, Shropshire, the Breiddin, Powys, and Beeston Castle, Cheshire (Barker et al. 1991;

Musson 1991; Ellis 1993). Early Bronze Age metalwork hoards have also been recorded at Moel Arthur, Flintshire (Forde-Johnston 1964) and Titterstone Clee, Shropshire (Chitty 1926, 235-236). It therefore appears that the enclosure of hilltops in the Late Bronze Age represents a shift from a previously funerary or ceremonially focussed location, to one of domestic occupation. However, the association of these defensive sites in the Late Bronze Age with hoards of prestigious metal objects could suggest that they retained their ritual significance, if these depositions are seen in terms of conspicuous display or votive acts. The previous association of these hills with funerary and ritual events may have been used to augment their status as defended and powerful settlements. Ceremonial tradition associated with these sites may have continued within the context of conflict and competition in the Late Bronze Age. The existing ritual status of a hilltop location may also have actively influenced its transformation into an enclosed site. However, a defended enclosure would also need to have been constructed in a location that could actively engage in systems of exchange and production within a wider settled landscape.

The association of a number of sites with hoards of metalwork in the form of weapons or weapon accessories, coupled with evidence for palisades and ramparts, indicates that the sites were the focus of conflict, and were therefore politically significant. Their significance would therefore indicate that they were occupied on a permanent basis, or otherwise the basis of their security and power would be compromised. To what extent these permanently occupied sites represent a population shift from existing settlements in the surrounding landscape is unknown. However, it is possible that this population shift represented only limited numbers and this may be supported by recent Palaeo-environmental evidence from such hilltop sites (Buckland et al. 2001).

The fact that unenclosed sites in comparable locations to Early and Middle Bronze Age settlements have been dated to the Late Bronze Age in the study area also suggests that settlement dislocation in the period was not widespread or universal. It appears that unenclosed sites were occupied alongside the emergence of defended enclosures. It is possible therefore that defended sites held influence over communities in surrounding landscapes. However, a mutually beneficial relationship between the two must have existed in order that enclosed sites were not isolated from agricultural production and economic interactions. This perhaps invokes a feudal type arrangement between high status defended sites and surrounding communities, although this is not possible to demonstrate archaeologically. It can be suggested that defended enclosures were associated with status, which was maintained physically through the construction of defences and politically and socially through the consumption or exchange of significant objects. However, the basis of political, social or economic prestige held by the occupants of these enclosures is difficult to reconstruct, beyond a possible association with success in warfare. Furthermore, the extent of fluidity within social and political hierarchies is unknown, but the necessity for defended enclosures and associated ceremonial activities designed to enhance or maintain prestige, suggests that political and social hierarchies in the period were frequently contested.

It is possible to suggest that forms of settlement in more marginal locations were also changing in the Late Bronze Age, representing further dislocation with earlier patterns of settlement. The enclosure dated to the Late Bronze Age on the Denbigh Moors, Denbighshire, appears to be associated with nearby field systems (Manley 1990). The creation of enclosures and field systems has not been dated in the study area to earlier periods and it could be suggested that by the late second millennium it was necessary to clearly define tenure over landscapes that were of agricultural value. The fact that field systems have not been associated with lowland settlement sites in the study area could suggest that those dependant upon upland farming began to witness a constriction in land suitable for agriculture, requiring a more clearly defined tenure over land. This may suggest a less communal approach to farming the uplands, where areas of livestock grazing became more closely controlled.

The dating of the Denbigh Moors enclosure to the Late Bronze Age (Manley 1990, 523) does not necessarily support Burgess' interpretation of widespread settlement shift away from upland contexts (1985, 202), although a drop in the number of metal objects recorded at higher altitudes in the study area could support this. It could instead be argued that more marginal upland contexts were reorganised in the Late Bronze Age and adapted to environmentally less productive locations (Young 2000, 77).

It could be argued that such reorganisation was also precipitated by increased competition in the period (Rowlands 1980, 33), and that agricultural production was linked to social and economic prestige. However, widespread reorganisation in the settlement pattern is not clearly visible in a lowland context in the study area. There is no evidence from the Welsh Marches to suggest agricultural intensification in the more agriculturally favourable contexts, as argued for settlement in southern England (Barrett and Bradley 1980, 9; Yates 2001). This in turn suggests that dislocation in the upland settlement pattern was not widespread, since a movement away from upland contexts may have resulted in increased pressure upon lowland resources and a need to reorganise patterns of land holding.

The limited evidence for settlement in the Welsh Marches study area has highlighted the potential for continuity in the settlement pattern throughout the Bronze Age. Any settlement dislocation is undermined by evidence for the continued occupation of contexts which may have been favoured for settlement since the Neolithic. There is also evidence to suggest from excavated sites in the study area that specific places were consistently occupied or re-occupied throughout the Bronze Age. Therefore any evidence for mobility that may be discerned from the distribution of monuments and artefacts in the landscape or activities at burnt mounds, can be seen within a residency pattern that made repeated reference to specific settlement locales. It can be argued that these locales were occupied on a year-round basis by at least a proportion of a social group, in order to maintain land tenure, tend crops or engage in processes of exchange.

The construction of enclosed sites on hilltops can be seen to represent the only significant dislocation in the pattern of settlement recorded in the Welsh Marches during the Bronze Age. It is not until the late Middle Bronze Age around the thirteenth century BC, which marks the earliest potential construction of hilltop sites, that any distinction with earlier patterns of settlement can be argued. Therefore it is perhaps more suitable to distinguish the period as an earlier and later Bronze Age as proposed by Barrett and Bradley (1980, 9) since no radical distinction can be seen in terms of an Early and Middle Bronze Age transition, at least in terms of settlement.

Clearly, changes in patterns and forms of settlement in the Welsh Marches during the Bronze Age remain ambiguous, despite the fact that certain inferences can be made from the available evidence. An understanding of the context of the limited number of recorded settlement locales in the region is important if further sites are to be identified by fieldwork in the future. The study of metalwork and monument distributions has been the only means of extrapolating this settlement pattern in a study area with a paucity of recorded settlement sites. This method has highlighted potential settlement contexts and the variety of activities that may have been undertaken within a settled landscape. The identification of general contexts where settlement sites may be expected to be found for the period is all that can be achieved through the available evidence and it is not possible to be more specific.

Metalwork has been recorded in comparable contexts to recorded domestic structures and this may be used to suggest similar settlement foci elsewhere. However, it is not possible to equate the location of recorded metal objects directly with the location of settlement for the Early and Middle Bronze Age. No metal objects have been recorded from lowland unenclosed settlement locales in the region and a number of factors may have influenced distribution patterns. However, the fact that metalwork has been recorded from enclosed hilltop sites in the study area and Middle and Late Bronze Age settlement sites elsewhere in Britain (e.g. Drewett 1982; O'Connell 1986), supports the validity of examining metalwork distributions as an indicator of settlement context.

The identification of further settlement structures is still likely to depend on their chance discovery through projects which sample large areas of landscape. It cannot, however, be maintained that all Early Bronze Age settlement activity is necessarily in association with funerary and ceremonial monuments, since this is not borne out by the location of recorded settlement locales or the distribution of metalwork. A clearer understanding of the nature of domestic activity in the vicinity of monuments is certainly necessary, and this can perhaps be achieved by a shift in emphasis from the excavation of monuments to their surrounding contexts.

There is a particular need to understand patterns of settlement in upland contexts more fully. It is possible that uplands were settled in the Early and Middle Bronze Age but that their specific location cannot be identified, due to the fact that activity was not fixed to specific settlement nodes and that land tenure was perhaps more co-operative (Young 2000, 75) and less clearly defined materially, than in later periods. However, a lack of domestic structures from upland contexts unduly influences interpretations of the pattern of settlement, which is more easily regarded as seasonal or episodic as a result.

A fuller understanding of settlement in the uplands may be able to establish more clearly the extent to which settlement in river valleys reflects a genuine preference in prehistory and the extent to which residency patterns change between the Early, Middle and Late Bronze Age. The dating of upland field systems to the Late Bronze Age also needs to be confirmed, in order to suggest with confidence a reorganisation in systems of land holding in the Late Bronze Age. The fact that these locations are marginal in a modern context perhaps undermines the likelihood of the chance discovery of settlement locales by large-scale development programmes. If the location of upland settlement locales reflects the same degree of longevity suggested for those in lowland contexts, then it is perhaps only by the study of later enclosed and more visible settlement and agriculture that earlier episodes of residency may be identified.

A lack of enclosures identified in a lowland context in the study area has directly influenced the interpretation of continuity between the Early and Middle Bronze Age, which contrasts with the development of more nucleated settlement forms in southern England (Brück 1999b; Brück 2000). However, the number of settlement sites recorded is few, and the context of settlement has been restricted by significantly truncated features or limited excavations (e.g. Quinell and Blockley. 1994; Britnell et al. 1997, 194). It is possible therefore that enclosed sites dating to the Middle Bronze Age exist in the study area

and remain unidentified. The lack of definition of such enclosures has been highlighted in southern England (Barrett et al. 1991,183), suggesting that they may not be easily recognisable in the landscape. However, a recent survey of crop marks in a lowland context in the Llyn peninsula, Gwynedd, has identified an enclosed Middle Bronze Age settlement (Ward and Smith 2001, 14-38). This underlines the potential for enclosures identified by aerial photography in the Welsh Marches (Whimster 1989) to belong to the Bronze Age.

It is also necessary to examine more fully the role of dated Late Bronze Age hilltop enclosures in the Welsh Marches within a wider landscape context. The relationship between these sites and unenclosed settlements in surrounding landscapes remains unclear, beyond the fact that other settlement forms existed in the period. The identification of settlement locales in contexts surrounding enclosed hilltop sites is therefore necessary in order to illuminate the economic and social relationship between different settlement forms. Again, the identification of unenclosed settlements through specific archaeological methodology is problematic, and it may only be possible to predict the general location of possible settlement locales beyond hillfort sites through demonstrating an association with field systems, or by a closer examination of the context of artefact concentrations.

Despite a relative lack of recorded settlement sites in the Welsh Marches, the distribution of a wide range of artefacts and monuments recorded for this study has highlighted the variety of landscape contexts that may have been settled during the Bronze Age. The study has also reiterated the number of Early Bronze Age funerary monuments present across the landscape and the distinction apparent with the later second millennium BC where the deposition of metalwork predominates in the archaeological record. The widespread presence of monuments and artefacts in the study area highlights the fact that settlement sites existed within the context of a variety of social and economic interactions during the period.

An emphasis has been placed on the potential continuity of occupation at specific settlement locales and in more general landscape contexts. This runs counter to long-standing interpretations of Early Bronze Age residency patterns, though the presence of fixed settlement nodes does not necessarily exclude the existence of settlement mobility. Continuity between the Early and Middle Bronze Age settlement pattern has also been suggested, which again contrasts with the emphasis placed on a transition in the form of settlement in southern England for this period. It is clearly possible that changes in settlement form have not been identified in the study area, and that more widespread change may have preceded and continued alongside the construction of defended enclosures in the Late Bronze Age. Nevertheless, the evidence for longevity in the occupation of settlement sites and continuity in the pattern of settlement can serve to contribute to debate upon the subject. Continued debate is necessary if further Bronze Age settlement sites are to be identified in the Welsh Marches and their social and economic context is to be more fully understood.

Bibliography

Abercromby, J. 1912. *A Study of the Bronze Age Pottery of Great Britain and Ireland and its Associated Grave Goods,* Oxford: Clarendon Press.

Ambers, J. 1990. 'Radiocarbon, calibration and early mining: some British Museum radiocarbon dates for Welsh copper mines', in P. Crew and S. Crew (eds), 1990, 59-63.

Bamford, H.M. 1982. *Beaker Domestic Sites in the Fen Edge and East Anglia.* East Anglian Archaeology Report 16, Norfolk: Norfolk Archaeological Unit.

Barclay, A and Glass, H. 1995. 'Excavations of Neolithic and Bronze Age ring-ditches, Shorncote Quarry, Somerford Keynes, Gloucestershire', *Transactions of the Bristol and Gloucestershire Archaeological Society* 113, 21-60.

Barfield, L.1981. 'The Flints', In G.Webster, 1981, 'The excavation of a Romano-British rural establishment at Barnsley Park, Gloucestershire', *Transactions of the Bristol and Gloucestershire Archaeological Society* 99, 37-45.

Barfield, L.H. 1991. 'Hot stones: hot food or hot baths?', in M.A Hodder and L.H. Barfield (eds), 1991, *Burnt mounds and hot stone technology. Papers from the second international burnt mound conference, Sandwell, 12th-14th October 1990,* Sandwell: Sandwell Metropolitan Borough Council, 59-67

Barfield, L.H. and Hodder,M. 1987. 'Burnt mounds as saunas and the prehistory of bathing', *Antiquity* 61, 370-379.

Barker, P.A.,Haldon,R., and Jenks, W.E. 1991. 'Excavations on Sharpstones Hill near Shrewsbury, 1965-71', in M.O.H. Carver and M. Humler, 1991, 15-57.

Barnatt, J. 2000. ' To each their own: later prehistoric farming communities and their monuments in the Peak', *Derbyshire Archaeological Journal* 120, 1-86.

Barrett, J. 1976. 'Deverel-Rimbury: problems of chronology and interpretation', in C. Burgess and R. Miket (eds), 1976, *Settlement and economy in the third and second millennia BC,* Oxford: British Archaeological Reports, British series 33, 289-307.

Barrett, J. 1980. ' The pottery of the later Bronze Age in lowland England',*Proceedings of the Prehistoric Society* 46, 297-319.

Barrett, J. and Bradley, R. (eds) 1980. *Settlement and Society in the British later Bronze Age,* Oxford: British Archaeological Reports, British series 83 i

Barrett, J. and Bradley, R. 1980. 'Preface: the ploughshare and the sword', in J.Barrett and R. Bradley (eds), 1980, 9-13.

Barrett, J.C. and Needham, S.P. 1988. 'Production, circulation and exchange: problems in the interpretation of Bronze Age bronzework', in J.C. Barrett and I.A. Kinnes (eds), 1988. *The Archaeology of Context in the Neolithic and Bronze Age: recent trends,* Sheffield: Department of Archaeology and Prehistory, University of Sheffield, 127-140.

Barrett, J, Bradley, R and Green, M.1991. *Landscape Monuments and Society; the prehistory of Cranborne Chase,* Cambridge: Cambridge University Press.

Barrett, J.C., Freeman, P.W.M., Woodward, A. 2000. *Cadbury Castle Somerset, the later prehistoric and early historic archaeology,* London: English Heritage Archaeological Report 20.

Benson, D.G., Evans, J.G., Williams,G.H., Darvill, T and David, A. 1990. 'Excavations at Stackpole Warren, Dyfed', *Proceedings of the Prehistoric Society* 56, 179-245.

Berridge, P. 1994. 'Bronze Age pottery'. In Quinell and Blockley (eds) 1994, *Excavations at Rhuddlan, Clwyd: 1969-1973. Mesolithic to Medieval,* York: Council for British Archaeology Research

Report 95,

Bradley, P. 1999. ' The flint scatters from the Walton Basin' in A. Gibson 1999, 52-79.

Bradley, R.1981.'Various Styles of Urn, Cemeteries and Settlement in southern England c.1400-1000 bc', in R. Chapman, I. Kinnes and K. Randsborg (eds), 1981, *The Archaeology of Death,* Cambridge: Cambridge University Press, 93-104.

Bradley, R. 1990. *The Passage of Arms: an Archaeological Analysis of prehistoric hoards and votive deposits,* Cambridge: Cambridge University Press.

Bradley, R.1998. *The Passage of Arms: an Archaeological Analysis of Prehistoric Hoards and Votive Deposits,* Oxford: Oxbow Books.

Bradley, R. 2000. *An Archaeology of Natural Places,* London: Routledge.

Bradley, R and Ellison, A. 1975 *Rams Hill: a Bronze Age defended enclosure and its Landscape,* Oxford: British Archaeological Reports, British series 19.

Bradley, R, Entwistle, R and Raymond, F. 1994. *Prehistoric Land Divisions on Salisbury Plain, The work of the Wessex Linear Ditches Project,* London: English Heritage.

Brandon, A. 1989. *Geology of the Country Between Hereford and Leominster,* British Geological Survey, London: Her Majesty's Stationery Office.

Brassil,K.S., Guilbert,G.C., Livens, R.G., Stead, W.H. and Bevan-Evans, M. 1982. 'Rescue excavations at Moel Hiraddug between 1960 and 1980', *Journal of the Flintshire Historical Society* 30, 13-88.

Briggs, S. 1977. 'A Roman camp kettle of copper', *Antiquaries Journal* 57, 90-91.

Brindley,A.L.and Lanting, J. 1990. 'Radiocarbon dates for the Mount Gabriel copper mines', in P. Crew and S. Crew (eds) 1990, 64.

Britton, D. 1960. 'The Isleham Hoard, Cambridgeshire', *Antiquity* 34, 279-282.

Britnell, W.J, Silvester,R.J, Gibson, A.M, Caseldine, A.E, Hunter, K.L, Johnson, S, Hamilton-Dyer, S, and Vince, A. 1997. 'A Middle Bronze Age round-house at Glanfeinion, near Llandinam, Powys', *Proceedings of the Prehistoric Society* 63,179-197.

Brossler, A. 2001 'Reading Business Park the results of phases 1 and 2' in J. Brück (ed.) 2001, 129-138.

Brück, J and Goodman, M. 1999 *Making places in the prehistoric world: themes in settlement archaeology,* London: UCL press.

Brück, J. 1999a. 'What's in a settlement? Domestic practice and residential mobility in Early Bronze Age Southern England', in J. Brück, J and M. Goodman (eds), 1999, 52-75.

Brück, J. 1999b. 'Houses, Lifecycles and Deposition on Middle Bronze Age Settlements in Southern England', *Proceedings of the Prehistoric Society* 65, 145-166.

Brück, J. 2000. 'Settlement, Landscape and Social Identity: The Early-Middle Bronze Age Transition in Wessex, Sussex and the Thames Valley', *Oxford Journal of Archaeology* 19, 273-300.

Brück, J. (ed.) 2001. *Bronze Age Landscapes; tradition and transformation,* Oxford: Oxbow Books.

Buckland, P.C., Parker-Pearson, M., Wigley,A. and Girling, M.A. 2001. 'Is there anybody out there? A reconsideration of the environmental evidence from the Breiddin Hillfort, Powys, Wales', *Antiquaries Journal* 81, 51-76.

Burgess, C.B.1968. 'The Later Bronze Age in the British Isles and North Western France', *Archaeological Journal* 125, 1-45

Burgess, C. 1979. 'The Background of Early Metalworking in Ireland and Britain', in M. Ryan (ed),1978, *The Origins of Metallurgy in Atlantic Europe Proceedings of the Fifth Atlantic Colloquium,* Dublin: Dublin Stationery Office, 207-214.

Burgess, C. 1985 ' Population, climate and upland settlement', in D. Spratt and C.B. Burgess (eds), 1985, 195-230.

Burgess, C. 1995. 'Bronze Age Settlements and Domestic Pottery in Northern Britain: Some Suggestions'. In I. Kinnes and G. Varndell', *Unbaked Urns of Rudeley Shape Essays on British and Irish Pottery for Ian Longworth,* Oxford: Oxbow Monograph 55, 145-158.

Burgess, C., Coombs, D. and Gareth-Davies, D. 1972. 'The Broadward complex and barbed spearheads', in F. Lynch and C. Burgess (eds), 1972, 211-283.

Burgess, C and Cowen, J.D.1972. 'The Ebnal Hoard and Early Bronze Age Metal-working Traditions', in F. Lynch and C. Burgess (eds), 167-181.

Burgess, C. and Shennan, S. 1976. 'The Beaker phenomenon: some suggestions', in C. Burgess and R. Miket (eds), *Settlement and Economy in the Third and Second Millennia BC,* B.A.R., British series 33, 309-323.

Burstow, G.P. and Holleyman, G.A. 1957. 'Late Bronze Age Settlement on Itford Hill, Sussex.', *Proceedings of the Prehistoric Society ,* 167-212.

Carman, J.1999. 'Settling on sites: constraining concepts', in J. Brück and M. Goodman (eds), 1999, 20-29.

Carver, M.O.H. and Humler,M.R. 1991. 'Excavations at Rock Green, Ludlow', in M.O.H. Carver (ed), Prehistory in Lowland Shropshire, *Transactions of the Shropshire Archaeological and Historical Society* 67, 84-97.

Cherry, S. 1990. 'The Finds From Fulachta Fiadh' in V. Buckley (ed), *Burnt Offerings, International Contributions to Burnt Mound Archaeology,* Dublin: Wordwell, 49-54.

Childe, V.G. 1930. *The Bronze Age,* Cambridge: Cambridge University Press.

Chitty, L.F.1926. 'Notes on Prehistoric Implements', *Transactions of the Shropshire Archaeological Society* 10, 233-246.

Chitty, L.F. 1928. 'Dug-out canoes from Shropshire', *Transactions of the Shropshire Archaeological Society,* 44, 113-133.

Clarke, D.L. 1970. *Beaker Pottery of Great Britain and Ireland,* Cambridge: Cambridge University Press

Coates, G. 2002. *A Prehistoric and Romano-British Landscape: excavations at Whitemoor Haye Quarry, Staffordshire, 1997-1999,* Oxford: British Archaeological Reports, British Series 340

Coles, J.M., Leach, P., Minnitt, S.C., Tabor, R., and Wilson, A.S. 1999. ' A later Bronze Age shield from South Cadbury, Somerset, England', *Antiquity* 73, 33-48.

Coombs, D.G. 1971. ' Mam Tor: a Bronze Age hillfort?', *Current Archaeology* 3, 100-102.

Coombs, D.G. 1991. 'Bronze Objects', in C.R. Musson, 1991, *The Breiddin Hillfort: a later prehistoric settlement in the Welsh Marches,* London: CBA Research Report 76, 132-139

Coombs, D. 1992. 'Flag Fen Platform and Fengate Power Station Post Alignment – The Metalwork', *Antiquity* 66, 504-517.

Cowell, R. 2000. 'The Neolithic and Bronze Age in the Lowlands of North West England'. In J. Harding and R. Johnston (eds), 2000, *Northern Pasts Interpretations of the Later Prehistory of Northern England and Southern Scotland,* Oxford: British Archaeological Reports, British series 302, 111-130

Crawford, O.G.S. 1912. 'The distribution of Early Bronze Age settlements in Britain', *The Geographical Journal* 40, 184-203.

Crew, P. and Crew, S. 1990. *Early Mining in the British Isles, Plas Tan y Bwlch Occasional Paper 1,* Maentwrog: Snowdonia National Park.

Cunliffe, B. 1995. *Danebury: an Iron Age hillfort in Hampshire. Vol.6 A hillfort community in perspective,* York: Council for British Archaeology research report 102.

Darvill, T.C. and Timby, J. 1986. 'Excavations at Saintbridge, Gloucester, 1981', *Transactions of the Bristol and Gloucester Archaeological Society* 104, 49-60.

Darvill,T.C. and Grinsell, L.V.1989.'Gloucestershire Barrows: supplement 1961-1988.', *Transactions of the Bristol and Gloucestershire Archaeological Society* 107, 39-105.

Davey, P.J.1976. 'The distribution of Bronze Age metalwork from Lancashire and Cheshire', *Journal of the Chester Archaeological Society* 59, 1-13.

Davies, J.R., Fletcher, C.J.N., Waters, R.A., Wilson, D., Woodhall, D.G., and Zalasiewicz, J.A. 1997. *Geology of the Country around Llanilar and*

Rhayader, British Geological Survey, London: The Stationery Office.

Dixon,P.1994. *Crickley Hill, the Hillfort Defences,* Nottingham: Crickley Hill Trust and the University of Nottingham.

Dodd. 1960. 'The Eardington bronze hoard', *Transactions of the Shropshire Archaeological Society* 56, 213-217.

Doody, M 2000. 'Bronze Age Houses in Ireland'. In A. Desmond, G. Johnson, M. McCarthy, J. Sheehan, and E. Shee Twohig, *New agendas in Irish Prehistory: papers in commemoration of Liz Anderson,* 135-159. Bray, Wordwell

Dorling, P., Chambers, F.M., Gibson, A., Green H.S., Lageard, J.A., and Elliot,L.1990. ' Field Survey, Excavation and Pollen Analysis at Mynydd y Drum, Ystradgynlais, Powys, 1983 and 1987', *Bulletin of the Board of Celtic Studies* 37, 215-246.

Drewett, P. 1980. 'Black Patch and the Later Bronze Age in Sussex', in J.Barrett and R. Bradley (eds), *Settlement and Society in the British Later Bronze Age,* Oxford: British Archaeological Reports, British series 83 i, 127-140.

Drewett, P.1982. 'Later Downland Economy and Excavations at Black Patch, East Sussex', *Proceedings of the Prehistoric Society 48,* 321-400.

Drewett, P and Hamilton, S. 1999. 'Marking time and making space: excavations and landscape studies at the Caburn Hillfort East Sussex, 1996-8', *Sussex Archaeological Collections* 137, 7-37.

Ehrenberg, M.R.1991.   'Some Aspects of the Distribution of Burnt Mounds', in L. Barfield and M. Hodder (eds), 1991, *Burnt Mounds and Hot Stone Technology,* Papers from the Second International Burnt Mound Conference Sandwell 12th-14th October 1990, Sandwell: Sandwell Metropolitan Borough Council, 41-58.

Ellis, P (ed.).1993. *Beeston Castle, Cheshire, Excavations by Laurance Keen and Peter Hough, 1968-85,* London: English Heritage Archaeological Report 23.

Ellison, A. 1972. ' The Bronze Age Pottery' in E.W. Holden,1972, 104-113

Ellison, A. 1980a. ' Deverel-Rimbury Urn Cemeteries: The evidence for social organisation', in Barrett and Bradley (eds) 1980, 115-126.

Ellison, A.1980b. 'Settlements and Regional Exchange: A Case Study', in J. Barrett and R. Bradley (eds) 1980, 127-140.

Elsdon,S. 1994. 'The Iron Age pottery', in P.Dixon, 1994, *Crickley Hill, The Hillfort Defences,* 203-208.

Enright, D. 1999. 'A Bronze Age Pin from Siddington, Gloucestershire', in *Transactions of the Bristol and Gloucestershire Archaeological Society* 117, 151-166.

Eogan, G. 1967. 'The Associated Finds of Gold Bar Torcs', *Journal of the Royal Society of Antiquaries of Ireland* 97, 129-175.

Evans, J. 1881. *The Ancient Bronze Implements, Weapons and Ornaments of Great Britain and Ireland,* London: Longmans, Green & co.

Evans, J. 1885. 'On a hoard of bronze objects found in Wilburton Fen Near Ely', *Archaeologia* 48, 106-114.

Evans, C and Knight, D. 2000. 'A Fenland delta: Later Prehistoric Land-Use in the Lower Ouse Reaches.' In M. Dawson (ed), 2000, *Prehistoric, Roman and Post-Roman Landscapes of the Great Ouse Valley,* York: Council for British Archaeology Research Report 119, 89-106.

Fell,C.I. 1961. 'Shenberrow Hill Camp, Stanton, Gloucestershire', *Transactions of the Bristol and Gloucestershire Archaeological Society* 80, 16-41.

Firman, R.J. 1994. 'Crickley Hill: The Geological Setting and its Archaeological Relevance', in P. Dixon, 1994, 11-24.

Fleming, A. 1971. 'Territorial patterns in Bronze Age Wessex', *Proceedings of the Prehistoric Society* 37, 138-166.

Forde-Johnston, J. 1962. 'The Iron Age Hillforts of Lancashire and Cheshire', *Transactions of the Lancashire and Cheshire Antiquarian Society* 72 , 9-46.

Forde-Johnston, J. 1962.'Earl's Hill, Pontesbury and Related Hillforts in England and Wales', *Archaeological Journal* 109, 66-91.

Forde-Johnston, J. 1964. 'A Hoard of Flat Axes from Moel Arthur, Flintshire.' *Flintshire Historical Society Transactions* 21, 99-100.

Garner, D. 2001. ' The Bronze Age of Manchester Airport: Runway 2', in Brück (ed.) 2001, 41-56.

Gelling Peter,S. 1959. 'Excavations at Caynham Camp, near Ludlow', *Transactions of the Shropshire Archaeological Society* 56, .145-148.

Gelling, P.S. and Peacock, D.P.S.1968.'The pottery from Caynham Camp, near Ludlow', *Transactions of the Shropshire Archaeological Society* 58, 96-100.

Guilbert, G. 1976. 'Moel y Gaer (Rhosesmor) Flintshire, 1972-1973: An Area Excavation of the Interior', in D.W. Harding (ed), 1976, 303-317.

Guilbert, G. 1979. 'Dinorben 1977-1978' *Current Archaeology* 6, 182-188.

Guilbert,G. 1980. 'Dinorben C14 dates', *Current Archaeology* 6, 336-338

Guilbert, G. 1981. 'Ffridd Faldwyn', *Archaeological Journal* 138, 20-22.

Gibson, A.1982. *'Beaker domestic sites. A study of the domestic Pottery of the late third and early second Millennia bc in the British Isles'*, Oxford: British Archaeological Reports, British series 107.

Gibson, A.1992. 'Approaches to the Later Neolithic and Bronze Age Settlement of Britain', in C. Mordant and A. Richard (eds),1992, L' Habitat et L' Occupation Du Sol L'Age Du Bronze en Europe. Documents Prehitoriques 4. Paris: Editions du Comite des travaux historiques et Scientifiques, 41-48.

Gibson, A. 1997. 'Pottery' in W.J. Britnell et al. 1997, 188-193.

Gibson, A. 1999. *The Walton Basin Project: Excavation and Survey in a Prehistoric Landscape 1993-7,* York: Council for British Archaeology Research Report 118.

Green, G.W.1992. *British Regional Geology, Bristol and Gloucester Region,* British Geological Survey, London: Her Majesty's Stationery Office.

Grinsell, L.V.1993. 'Herefordshire Barrows.', *Transactions of the Woolhope Naturalists Field Club* 47, 299-317.

Hains, B.A.1991. *Applied Geological Mapping in the Wrexham Area: Geology and Land-Use Planning,* Nottingham: British Geological Survey.

Hall, M and Gingell, C. 1974. ' Nottingham Hill, Gloucestershire, 1972', *Antiquity* 48, 306-309.

Hamilton, S and Manley, J. 1997, 'Points of View: prominent enclosures in 1st millennium BC Sussex', *Sussex Archaeological Collections* 135, 93-112.

Hannaford, H. 1999. ' A Bronze Age burnt mound at Rodway, Telford', *Transactions of the Shropshire Archaeological and Historical Society* 74, 67-74.

Harding, D.W. 1976 *Hillforts: Later Prehistoric Earhworks in Britain and Ireland,* London: Academic Press.

Harris, B.E. and Thacker, A.T. (eds). 1987 A History of County of Chester, Volume 1, *The Victoria History of the Counties of England,* Oxford: Oxford University Press.

Hearne, M. and Heaton, M.J. 1994. 'Excavations at a Late Bronze Age Settlement in the Upper Thames Valley at Shorncote Quarry near Cirencester, 1992', *Transactions of The Bristol and Gloucestershire Archaeological Society,* 112, 17-57.

Hebblethwaite, S.M. 1987. 'Physique', in B.E. Harris and A.T. Thacker (eds). 1-35.

Herz, N and Garrison, E.G.1998. *Geological Methods for Archaeology,* Oxford: Oxford University Press

Higham, N.J. and Cane, T.1999. 'The Tatton Park Project, Part 1: Prehistoric to Sub-Roman Settlement and Land Use', *Journal of The Chester*

Archaeological Society 74, 1-61.

Hodder, M.A. 1990. 'Burnt Mounds in the English West Midlands',in V. Buckley (ed), 1990, *Burnt Offerings: International Contributions to Burnt Mound Archaeology,* Dublin: Wordwell, 106-111.

Holden, E.W.1972. 'A Bronze Age Cemetery Barrow on Itford Hill, Beddingham, Sussex.', *Sussex Archaeological Collections* 110, 70-117.

Holleyman, G.A. and Curwen, E.C. 1935. 'Late Bronze Age lynchet settlements on Plumpton Plain, Sussex', *Proceedings of the Prehistoric Society* 1, 16-38.

Hughes, G. 1994. 'Old Oswestry Hillfort: Excavations by W.J.Varley 1939-1940', *Archaeologia Cambrensis*, 143, 46-91.

Hughes, G. 1996. *The Excavation of a Late Prehistoric and Romano-British Settlement at Thornwell Farm, Chepstow, Gwent, 1992,* Oxford: British Archaeological Reports, British series 244.

Hume, C.R. and Jones,G.W. 1960 'Excavations on Nesscliff Hill', *Transactions of the Shropshire Archaeological Society* 41, 129-132.

Hurst, J.D. 1988. 'A Bronze Age vessel from near Leintwardine', *Transactions of the Woolhope Naturalists Field Club*

James, H.J. 1986. 'Excavations of Burnt Mounds at Carne, near Fishguard, 1979 and 1981', *Bulletin of the Board of Celtic Studies* 33, 245-265.

Jeffrey, P. 1991. 'Burnt Mounds, Fulling and Early Textiles', in M.A Hodder and L.H. Barfield (eds), 1991, *Burnt Mounds and Hot Stone Technology: Papers from the Second International Burnt Mound Conference, Sandwell, 12th-14th October 1990,* Sandwell: Sandwell Metropolitan Borough Council, 97-107.

Jenckins, D.A. 1991. 'The Environment: past and present', in J. Manley, S. Grenter, F. Gale (eds), 1991, 13-25.

Jobey, G. 1985. 'The unenclosed settlements of the Tyne-Forth: a summary' in D. Spratt and C. Burgess (eds), 1985, 177-194.

Kelly, R.S. 1992. 'The Excavation of a Burnt Mound at Graeanog, Clynnog, Gwynedd in 1983', *Archaeologia Cambrensis* 141, 74-96.

Kenyon, K.M. 1942. 'Excavations on The Wrekin, Shropshire, 1939' *Archaeological Journal* 99, 99-109.

Kenyon, K.M. 1953. 'Excavations at Sutton Walls, Herefordshire 1948-1951', *Archaeological Journal* 110, 1-87.

Kitchen, W. 2001. ' Tenure and territoriality in the British Bronze Age: a question of varying social and geographic scales?' in J. Brück (ed.) 2001, 110-120.

Kristiansen, K.1998. 'A Theoretical Strategy for the Interpretation of Exchange and Interaction in a Bronze Age Context.', In C. Mordant, M. Pernot and V. Rychner (eds),1998, *L'Atelier du Bronzier en Europe 3, Production,Circulation et Consommation du Bronze,* Paris: CTHS, 333-343.

Lewis, A. 1990. 'Underground Exploration of the Great Orme Copper Mines', in P.Crew and S.Crew (eds), 1990, 5-10.

Lewis, A.1998   'The Bronze Age mines of the Great Orme and Other Sites in the British Isles and Ireland', In C. Mordant, M. Pernot and V. Rychner (eds), *L'Atelier du Bronzier en Europe 2,* Paris:CTHS, 45-58.

Leah, M.D, Wells, C.E, Appleby,C and Huckerby,E.1997. *The Wetlands of Cheshire,* North West Wetlands Survey 4, Lancaster: Lancaster University Archaeological Unit.

Leah, M.D.,Wells, C.E., Stamper, P., Huckerby, E., and Welch, C. 1998. *The Wetlands of Shropshire and Staffordshire,* North West Wetlands Survey 5, Lancaster: Lancaster University Archaeological Unit.

Longley, D.M.T.1987. 'Prehistory', in B.E. Harris and A.T. Thacker (eds), 36-114.

Longworth, I.H. 1961. 'The origins and development of the primary series in the Collared Urn tradition in England and Wales', *Proceedings of the Prehistoric Society* 27, 263-306.

Lynch, F. 1991. *Prehistoric Anglesey,* Llangefni: Anglesey Antiquarian Society, 2nd edn.

Lynch, F.1993. *Excavations in the Brenig Valley: A Mesolithic and Bronze Age Landscape in North Wales,* Cardiff: Cambrian Archaeological Monographs 5.

Lynch, F. and Burgess, C (eds) 1972. *Prehistoric Man in Wales and the West,* Bath: Adams and Dart

Lynch, F and Gibson, A.M. 1991. 'Neolithic and Early Bronze Age pottery', in C. Musson 1991, 116-118.

McCullagh, R.P.J and Tipping,R. 1998. *The* Lairg Project 1988-1996. The Evolution of an Archaeological Landscape in Northern Scotland, Edinburgh: Star Monograph 3.

Mc Omish, D.S.and Smith, N.A 1996. 'Welshbury hillfort', *Transactions of the Bristol and Gloucester Archaeological Society* 114, 55-64.

Malim,T. 2000. 'The ritual landscape of the Neolithic and Bronze Age along the Middle and Lower Ouse Valley', in Dawson (ed.), 2000, *Prehistoric, Roman and Post-Roman Landscapes of the Great Ouse Valley,* York: Council for British Archaeology Research Report 119, 57-88

Manley, J. 1990. 'A Late Bronze Age landscape on the Denbigh Moors, north-east Wales', *Antiquity* 64, 514-526.

Manley, J., Grenter, S and Gale, F. 1991. *The Archaeology of Clwyd,* Mold: Clwyd Archaeology Service.

Marshall, A. 1985. 'Neolithic and Earlier Bronze Age Settlement in the Northern Cotswolds: a preliminary outline based on the distribution of surface scatters and funerary areas', *Transactions of the Bristol and Gloucestershire Archaeological Society* 103, 23-54.

Megaw, J.V.S. and Simpson, D.D.A.1988. *Introduction to British Prehistory, fourth edition,* Leicester: Leicester University Press.

Moffett, L 1996. 'The charred plant remains' in G.Hughes 1996, 85-86.

Moore, J. and Jennings, D. 1992. *Reading Business Park: a Bronze Age Landscape,* Oxford: Oxford University Committee for Archaeology, Thames

Valley Landscape Series 1.

Morgan, D.E.M. 1990. *Bronze Age Metalwork from Flintshire, Liverpool:* North West Archaeological Trust report 4.

Morris, E.L. 1984. 'The Prehistoric Pottery', in S.C.Stanford, 1984, 79.

Morris, E.L. 1994a. 'Pottery', in M. Hearne and M.J. Heaton 1994, 34-44.

Morris, E.L. 1994b 'Metalworking Debris' in M. Hearne and M.J. Heaton 1994, 44-45.

Morris, E.L. 1994c. ' The Prehistoric Pottery and Salt Containers', in G.Hughes,1994, 65-74.

Morris, M. 1992. ' The rise and fall of Bronze Age studies in England 1840-1960', *Antiquity* 66, 419-426.

Musson, C.R. 1976. 'Excavations at the Breiddin 1969-1973', in D.W. Harding (ed.), 1976, 293-299.

Musson, C.R. 1981 'Prehistoric and Romano-British settlements in northern Powys and western Shropshire, *Archaeological Journal* 138, 5-7.

Musson, C. 1991. *The Breiddin Hillfort, A Later Prehistoric Settlement in the Welsh Marches,* London: Council for British Archaeology Research Report 76.

Musson, C.R. and Northover, J.P. 1989 ' Llanymynech Hillfort, Powys and Shropshire: observations on construction work 1981', *Montgomeryshire Collections* 77, 17-26.

Musson, C. Britnell, W.J., Northover, J.P. and Salter, C.J. 1992. 'Excavations and metal-working at Llwyn Bryn-dinas Hillfort, Llangedwyn,Clwyd', *Proceedings of The Prehistoric Society* 58, 265-283.

Needham, S. 1986. 'The Metalwork' in O'Connell, 1986, 22-60.

Needham, S. 1990. 'The Penard – Wilburton Succession: new Metalwork finds from Croxton (Norfolk) and Thirsk (Yorkshire)', *Antiquaries Journal* 70, 253-270.

Needham, S. 1993a. 'Displacement and Exchange in Archaeological Methodology', in Chris Scarrre and Frances Healy (eds), 1993, *Trade and Exchange in Prehistoric Europe,*

Oxford: Oxbow Monograph 33, 161-169.

Needham, S. 1993b. 'The Beeston Castle Bronze Age metalwork and its significance' in Ellis (ed.) 1993, 41-50.

Needham,S. 1996. 'Chronology and periodisation in the British Bronze Age', *Acta Archaeologica* 67, 121-140.

Needham, S. 1998 'Modelling the Flow of Metal in the Bronze Age'. In Claude Mordant, Michel Pernot and Valentin Rychner (eds), 1998, L'Atelier du bronzier en Europe. Production, Circulation et consommation du bronze, 285-307.

Needham, S and Longley,D.1980. 'Runnymede Bridge, Egham: a Late Bronze Age Riverside Settlement', in J. Barrett and R. Bradley (eds), 1980, 397-436.

Needham, S and Ambers, J. 1994 'Redating Rams Hill and Reconsidering Bronze Age Enclosure' *Proceedings of the Prehistoric Society* 60, 225-243.

Needham, S. and Spence, T. 1997. 'Refuse and the formation of middens', *Antiquity* 71, 77-90.

Needham, S., Bank-Ramsey,C., Coombs, D.,Cartwright, C., and Pettit, P. 1997. 'An independent chronology for British Bronze Age metalwork. The results of the Oxford Radiocarbon Accelerator Programme', *Archaeological Journal* 154, 55-107.

Nevell, M.1988. 'Arthill Heath Farm. Trial Excavations on a Prehistoric Settlement 1987-88. Interim report', *Manchester Archaeological Bulletin*.3, 4-13.

Northover, J.P. 1980. 'The analysis of Welsh Bronze Age Metalwork', in H.N. Savory 1980, 229-243.

Northover, P. 1982. 'The exploration of the Long-distance Movement of Bronze in Bronze and Early Iron Age Europe', *Institute of Archaeology Bulletin* 19, 45-72.

O'Connell, M.   1986. *Petters Sports Field, Egham. Excavation of a Late Bronze Age/ Early Iron Age Site,* Surrey Archaeological Society, Research Volume 10.

O'Kelly, M. J. 1954 'Excavations and Experiments in Ancient Irish Cooking Places', *Journal of the Royal Society of Antiquaries of Ireland* 83, 105-155.

O'Kelly , M. J, Cleary, R.M. and Lehane, D.1983. *Newgrange Co.Meath, Ireland. The Late Neolithic/Beaker Period Settlement,* Oxford: British Archaeological Reports, International series 190.

O'Neil, B.H. St.John. 1934. 'Excavations at Titterstone Clee Hill Camp, Shropshire,1932' *Antiquaries Journal* 14, 13-32.

Osgood, R. 1998. *Warfare in the Late Bronze Age of North Europe,* Oxford: British Archaeological Reports, International Series 694.

Owen, G and Britnell, W. 1989. 'Pit Alignments at Four Crosses, Llandysilio, Powys', Montgomeryshire Collections 77, 27-40

Parry, C. 1999. 'Excavations at Camp Gardens, Stow-on-the-Wold, Gloucestershire' *Transactions of the Bristol and Gloucestershire Archaeological Society* 177, 75-87.

Piggot, S. 1949. *British Prehistory,* London: Oxford University Press.

Pinter-Bellows, S.1996. 'The animal bone', in G. Hughes 1996, 81-84.

Powell, T.G.E. 1953. ' The gold ornament from Mold, Flintshire, north Wales', *Proceedings of the Prehistoric Society* 19, 161-179.

Probert, L.A. 1976. 'Twyn y Gaer Hillfort, Gwent: an interim assessment', in G.C.Boon and J.M.Lewis (eds),1976, *Welsh Antiquity,* Cardiff: National Museum of Wales, 105-20.

Pryor, F. 1980 '*Excavation at Fengate, Peterborough, England: The Third Report,* Leicester; Toronto: Northhamptonshire Archaeological Society: Royal Ontario Museum Monograph 1.

Pryor, F. 1992a. 'Introduction to Current Research at Flag Fen, Peterborough.' *Antiquity* 66, 439-457.

Pryor, F. 1992b. 'Discussion: The Fengate/ Northey Landscape', *Antiquity* 66, 518-531.

Pryor, F. 1999. *Farmers in Prehistoric Britain,* Stroud: Tempus.

Quinell, H, and Blockley, M. 1994. *Excavations at Rhuddlan, Clwyd: 1969-1973. Mesolithic to Medieval,* York: Council for British Archaeology Research Report 95.

R.C.A.H.M.W. 1986. *An Inventory of the Ancient Monuments in Brecknock (Brycheiniog). The Prehistoric and Roman Monuments (Part ii) Hillforts and Roman Remains,* London: Her Majesty's Stationery Office.

Roe, F 1996. ' The prehistoric worked stone', in G. Hughes 1996, 45.

Rogers, I. 1995. 'Rhuddlan, Gwindy Street', *Archaeology in Wales 35,* 45.

Rowlands, M.J. 1980. ' Kinship, alliance and exchange in the European Bronze Age', in Barrett and Bradley (eds), 1980, 15-55.

Rowley, T. 1989. 'The Physical Environment', in G.C. Bough (ed) A History of Shropshire Volume 4 *Victoria History of the Counties of England,* Oxford: Oxford University Press, 5-20.

R.W.B. 1885. 'On a Bronze Dagger found at Bwlch y Ddeu Faen, Breconshire', *Archaeologia Cambrensis 2,* 156.

Royle, C. and Woodward, A. 1993. 'The prehistoric pottery', in Ellis (ed.) 1993, 63-78.

Saville,A. 1978. 'Excavations at Icomb Hill, Gloucestershire 1975', *Transactions of the Bristol and Gloucestershire Archaeological Society 96,* 27-31.

Savory, H.N. 1971 ' A Welsh Bronze Age Hillfort', *Antiquity 45,* 251-261.

Savory, H.N. 1976. *'Welsh Hillforts: A Reappraisal of Recent Research'* in D.W. Harding (ed.), 1976, *Hillforts: Later Prehistoric Earthworks in Britain and Ireland,* London: Academic Press, 237-292.

Savory, H.N. 1980 *Guide Catalogue of the Bronze Age Collections,* Cardiff : National Museum of Wales.

Savory, H.N. and Gardner,W. 1964 *'Dinorben: A Hill-fort Occupied in Early Iron Age and Roman times',* Cardiff: National Museum of Wales.

Schmidt, P.K. and Burgess, C.B. 1981. *The Axes of Scotland and Northern England,* Prahistorische

Bronzefunde 9.

Sharples, N.M. 1991. *Maiden Castle: Excavations and Field Survey 1985-6.* London: English Heritage Archaeological Report 19.

Simpson, D.D.A.1971. 'Beaker Houses and Settlements in Britain.', in D.D.A. Simpson (ed.), *Economy and Settlement in Neolithic and Early Bronze Age Britain and Europe,* Leicester: Leicester University Press, 131-152.

Smith, M. A. 1959. 'Some Somerset Hoards and their place in the Bronze Age of Southern Britain', *Proceedings of the Prehistoric Society,* 144-187.

Spratt, D. and Burgess, C.(eds) 1985. *Upland Settlement in Britain; the second millennium BC and after,* Oxford: British Archaeological Reports, British series 143.

Stanford, S. C.1982. 'Bromfield, Shropshire – Neolithic, Beaker and Bronze Age Sites, 1966-79', *Proceedings of the Prehistoric Society 48,* 279-320.

Stanford, S. C. 1984. 'The Wrekin Hillfort Excavations, 1973', *Archaeological Journal 141,* 61-90.

Stone, J. F .S. 1941. 'The Deverel-Rimbury settlement on Thorny Down, Winterbourne Gunner, S. Wilts.' , *Proceedings of the Prehistoric Society 7,* 114-133.

Tabor, R. 1999. ' South Cadbury: Milsom's Corner', *Current Archaeology 14,* 251-255.

Taylor, J.A. 1980. 'Environmental Changes in Wales during the Holocene Period',in J.A. Taylor (ed), 1980, *Culture and Environment in Prehistoric Wales,* Oxford: British Archaeological Reports, British series 76.

Timberlake, S. ' Mining and prospection for metals in Early Bronze Age Britain- making claims within the archaeological landscape', in J.Brück (ed.) 2001, 179-192.

Tylecote, R.F.and Biek, L. 1991.' Metal-working Evidence', in C.R.Musson, 1991, 147-149.

Varley, W.J. 1948. 'The Hill-forts of the Welsh Marches', *Archaeological Journal,* 105, 41-66.

Varley, W.J. 1950. 'Excavations of the Castle Ditch, Eddisbury 1935-38', *Transactions of* the Historic Society of Lancashire and Cheshire 102, 1-68.

Varley,W.J. 1964, *Cheshire Before the Romans,* Chester: Cheshire Community Council.

Ward, M and Smith, G. 2001. 'The Llyn crop marks project', *Studia Celtica* 35, 1-87.

Warren, P. T., Price, D., Nutt, M. J. C., Smith, E. G. 1984. *Geology of the Country around Rhyl and Denbigh, British Geological Survey,* London: Her Majesty's Stationery Office.

Warrilow,W, Owen, G and Britnell, W. 1986. 'Eight Ring-Ditches at Four- Crosses,Llandysilio, Powys 1981-85', Proceedings of the Prehistoric Society 52, 53-87.

Watson, M.D. 1991. 'Ring-Ditches of the Upper Severn Valley'. In M.O.H. Carver (ed.), Prehistory in Lowland Shropshire, *Transactions of the Shropshire Archaeological and Historical Society* 67, 9-14.

Webster, G. 1981. ' The Excavation of a Romano-British Rural Establishment at Barnsley Park, Gloucestershire, 1961-1979', *Transactions of the Bristol and Gloucestershire Archaeological Society* 99, 21-77.

Whimster, R.1989. The Emerging Past: Air Photography and the Buried Landscape. London: Royal Commission On the Historical Monuments of England.

Williams, G. 1990. 'Burnt Mounds in South-West Wales', in V. Buckley (ed.), *Burnt Offerings: International Contributions to Burnt Mound Archaeology,* Dublin: Wordwell, 129-140.

Williams, G.H, Taylor, J.A, Hunt, C, Heyworth, A, Benson,D.G.1987. 'A Burnt Mound at Felin Fulbrook, Tregaron, Ceredigion', *Bulletin of the Board of Celtic Studies* 34, 228-243.

Woodward, A. 1996. ' The prehistoric and native pottery', in G. Hughes 1996, 36-45.

Woodward, A. 1999. 'Pottery' in C. Parry 1999, 83.

Woodward, P.J. 1978. 'Flint Distribution, Ring-ditches and Bronze Age Settlement Patterns in the Great Ouse Valley: The Problem, a Field Survey Technique and Some Preliminary results', *Archaeological Journal* 135, 32-56.

Yates, D. 2001. 'Bronze Age agricultural intensification in the Thames Valley and Estuary', in J. Brück (ed.) 2001, 65-82.

Young, R. 2000. 'Continuity and Change: Marginality and Later Prehistoric Settlement in the Northern Uplands, in J. Harding and R. Johnston (eds), *Northern Pasts: interpretations of the later prehistory of Northern England and Southern Scotland,* Oxford: British Archaeological Reports British series 302, 71-80

Young, R and Simmonds,T. 1999. 'Debating Marginality: archaeologists on the edge?', in J. Brück and M. Goodman (eds), *Making Places in the Prehistoric World: themes in settlement archaeology,* London: UCL press, 198-211.

Appendix

Calibrated radiocarbon dates from
sites mentioned in the text

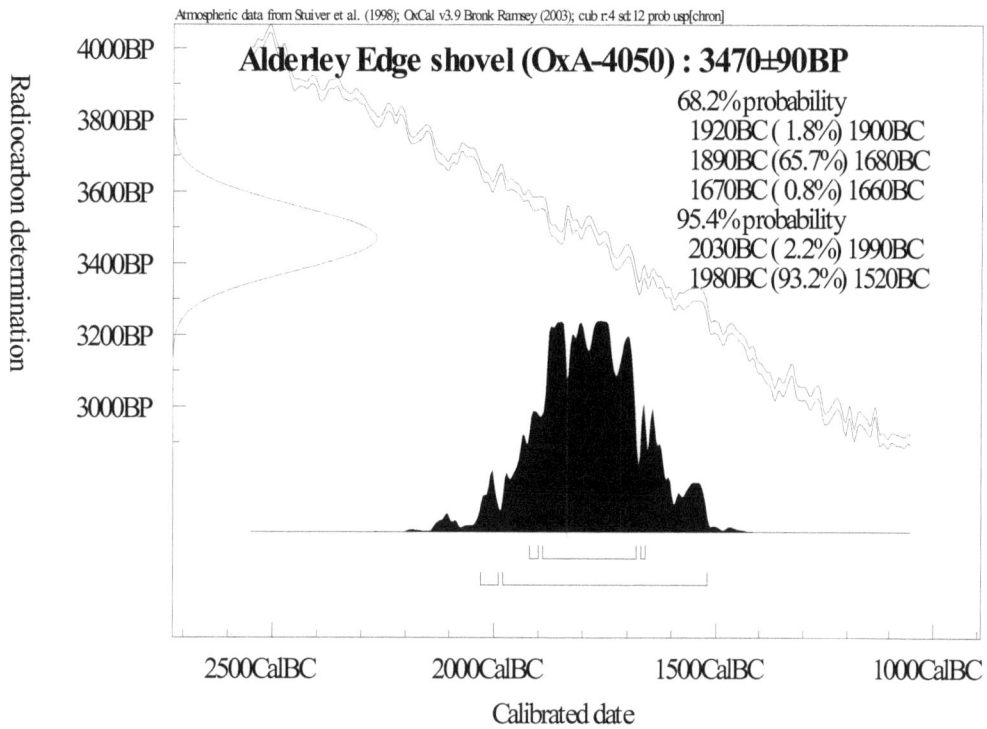

Atmospheric data from Stuiver et al. (1998); OxCal v3.9 Bronk Ramsey (2003); cub r:4 sd:12 prob usp[chron]

Alderley Edge shovel (OxA-4050) : 3470±90BP

68.2% probability
1920BC (1.8%) 1900BC
1890BC (65.7%) 1680BC
1670BC (0.8%) 1660BC
95.4% probability
2030BC (2.2%) 1990BC
1980BC (93.2%) 1520BC

Radiocarbon determination

4000BP
3800BP
3600BP
3400BP
3200BP
3000BP

2500CalBC   2000CalBC   1500CalBC   1000CalBC

Calibrated date

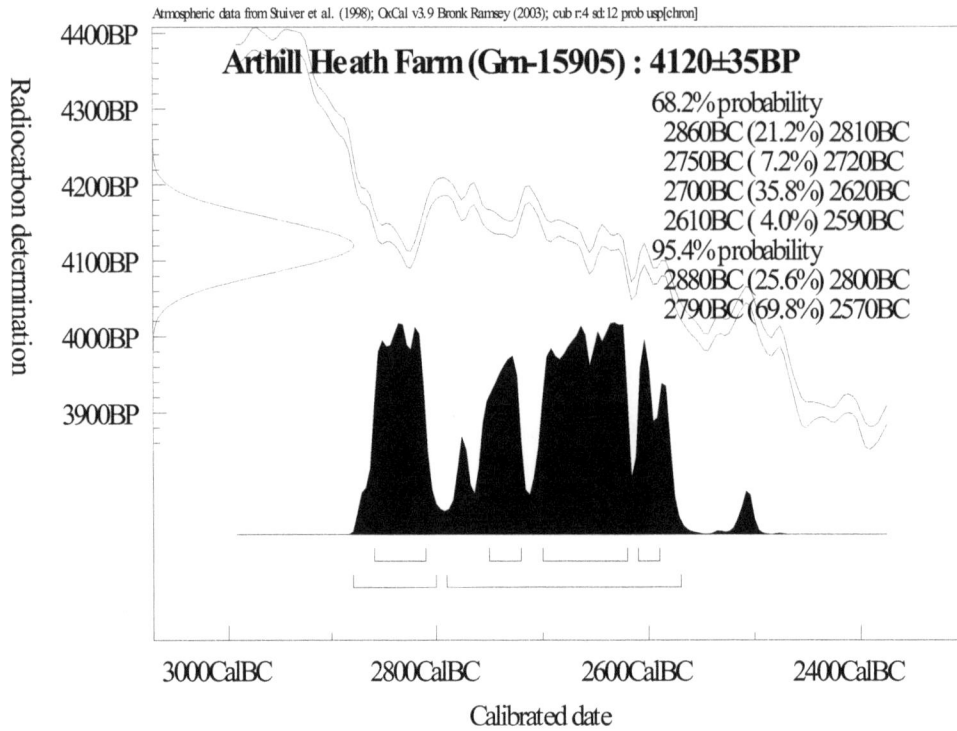

Atmospheric data from Stuiver et al. (1998); OxCal v3.9 Bronk Ramsey (2003); cub r:4 sd:12 prob usp[chron]

Arthill Heath Farm (Grn-15905) : 4120±35BP

68.2% probability
2860BC (21.2%) 2810BC
2750BC (7.2%) 2720BC
2700BC (35.8%) 2620BC
2610BC (4.0%) 2590BC
95.4% probability
2880BC (25.6%) 2800BC
2790BC (69.8%) 2570BC

Radiocarbon determination

Calibrated date

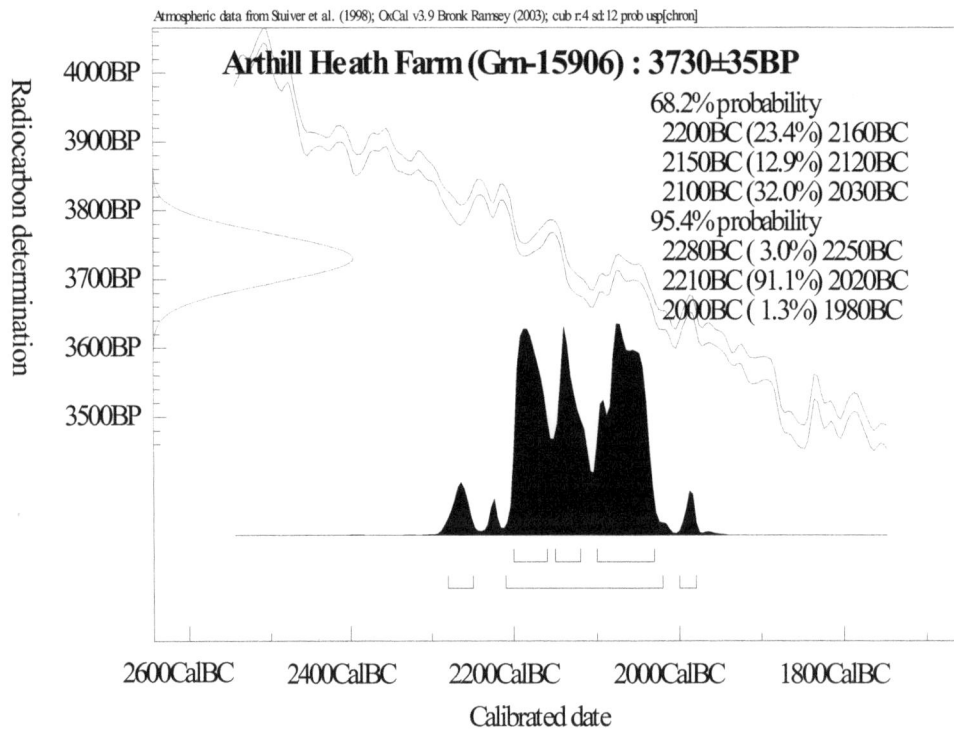

Atmospheric data from Stuiver et al. (1998); OxCal v3.9 Bronk Ramsey (2003); cub r:4 sd:12 prob usp[chron]

Arthill Heath Farm (Grn-15906) : 3730±35BP

68.2% probability
2200BC (23.4%) 2160BC
2150BC (12.9%) 2120BC
2100BC (32.0%) 2030BC
95.4% probability
2280BC (3.0%) 2250BC
2210BC (91.1%) 2020BC
2000BC (1.3%) 1980BC

Radiocarbon determination

Calibrated date

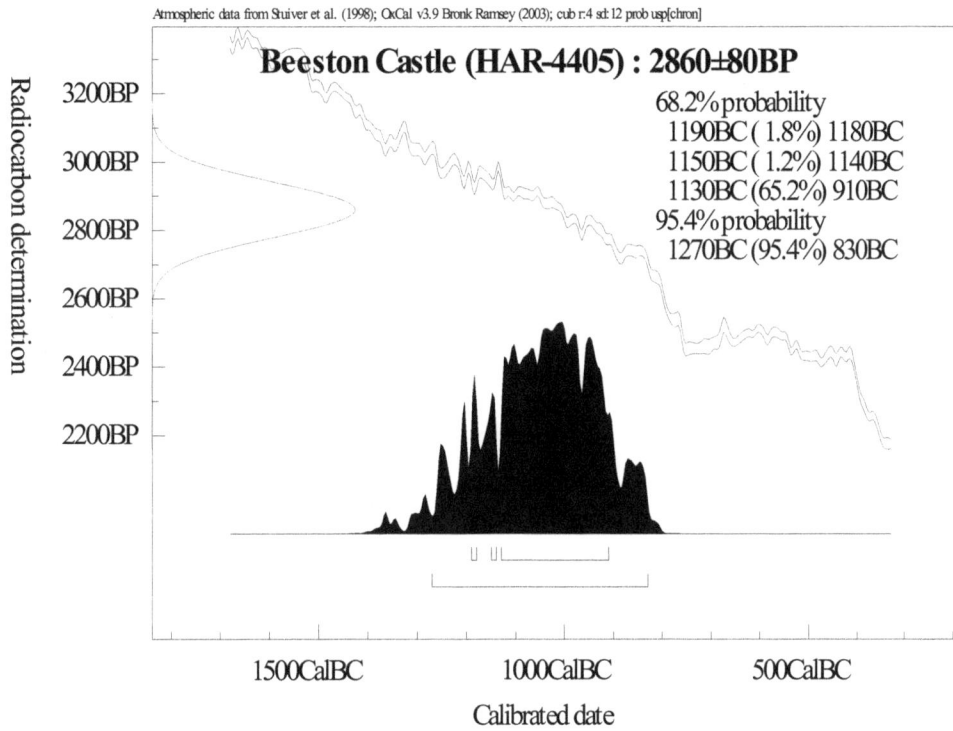

Atmospheric data from Stuiver et al. (1998); OxCal v3.9 Bronk Ramsey (2003); cub r:4 sd:12 prob usp[chron]

Beeston Castle (HAR-4405) : 2860±80BP

68.2% probability
1190BC (1.8%) 1180BC
1150BC (1.2%) 1140BC
1130BC (65.2%) 910BC
95.4% probability
1270BC (95.4%) 830BC

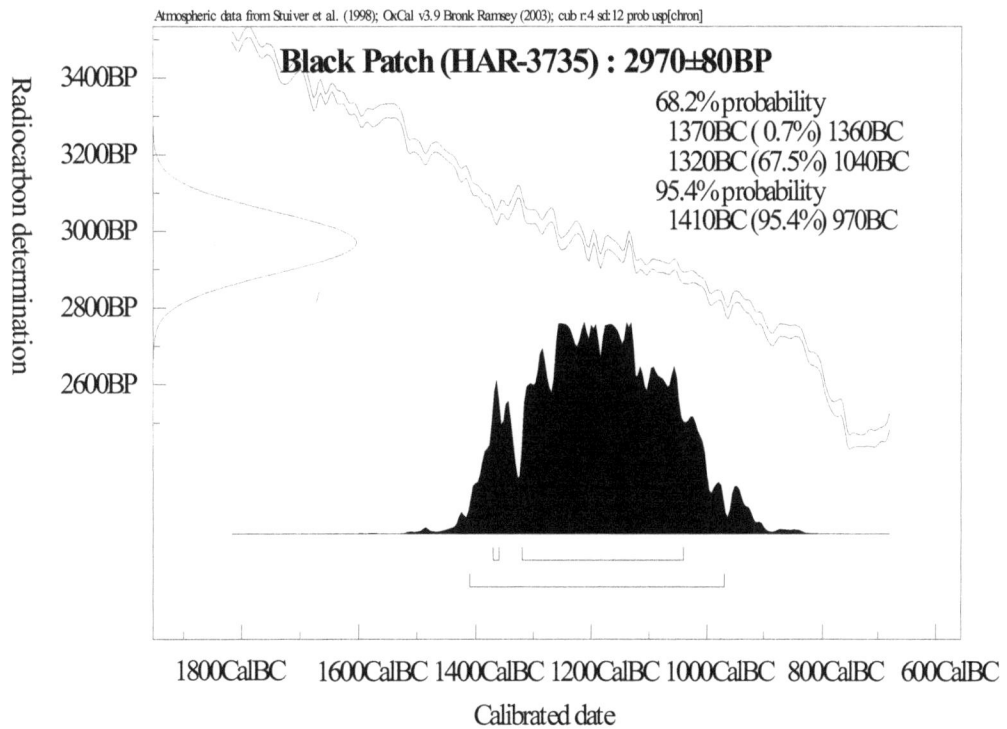

Atmospheric data from Stuiver et al. (1998); OxCal v3.9 Bronk Ramsey (2003); cub r:4 sd:12 prob usp[chron]

Black Patch (HAR-3735) : 2970±80BP

68.2% probability
1370BC (0.7%) 1360BC
1320BC (67.5%) 1040BC
95.4% probability
1410BC (95.4%) 970BC

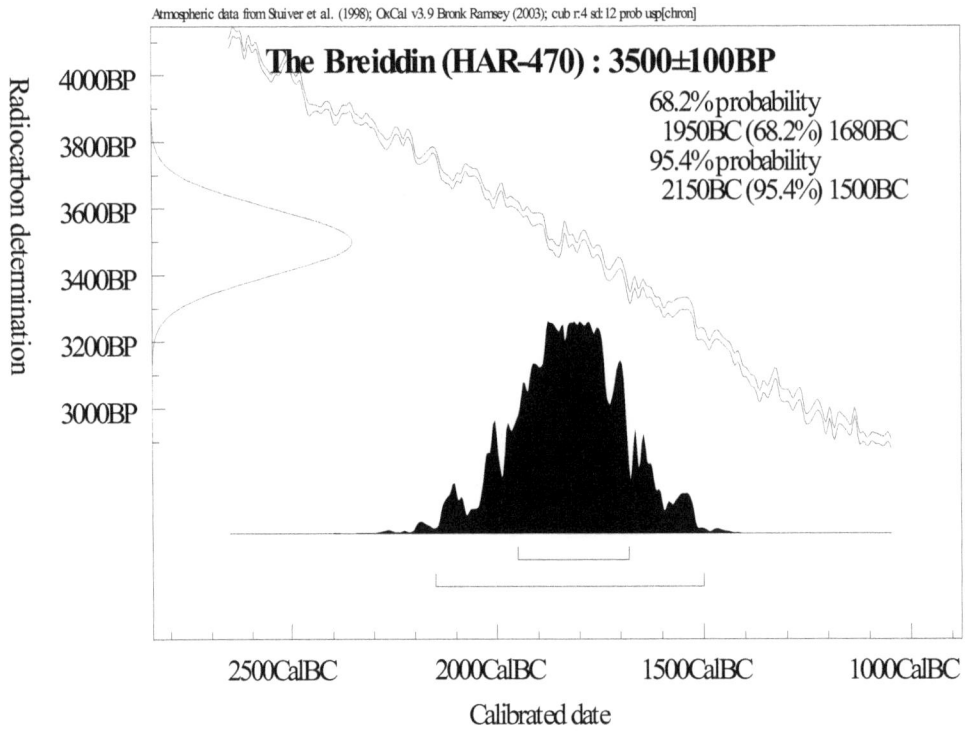

Atmospheric data from Stuiver et al. (1998); OxCal v3.9 Bronk Ramsey (2003); cub r:4 sd:12 prob usp[chron]

The Breiddin (HAR-470) : 3500±100BP

68.2% probability
1950BC (68.2%) 1680BC
95.4% probability
2150BC (95.4%) 1500BC

Radiocarbon determination

4000BP
3800BP
3600BP
3400BP
3200BP
3000BP

2500CalBC   2000CalBC   1500CalBC   1000CalBC

Calibrated date

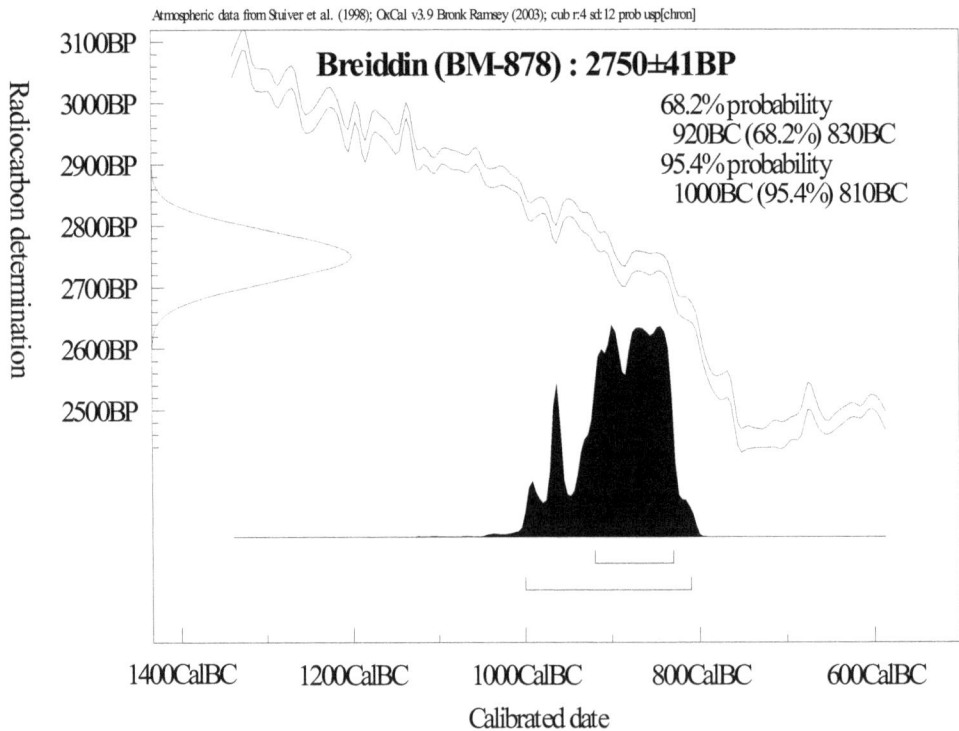

Atmospheric data from Stuiver et al. (1998); OxCal v3.9 Bronk Ramsey (2003); cub r:4 sd:12 prob usp[chron]

Breiddin (BM-878) : 2750±41BP

68.2% probability
920BC (68.2%) 830BC
95.4% probability
1000BC (95.4%) 810BC

Radiocarbon determination

3100BP
3000BP
2900BP
2800BP
2700BP
2600BP
2500BP

1400CalBC   1200CalBC   1000CalBC   800CalBC   600CalBC

Calibrated date

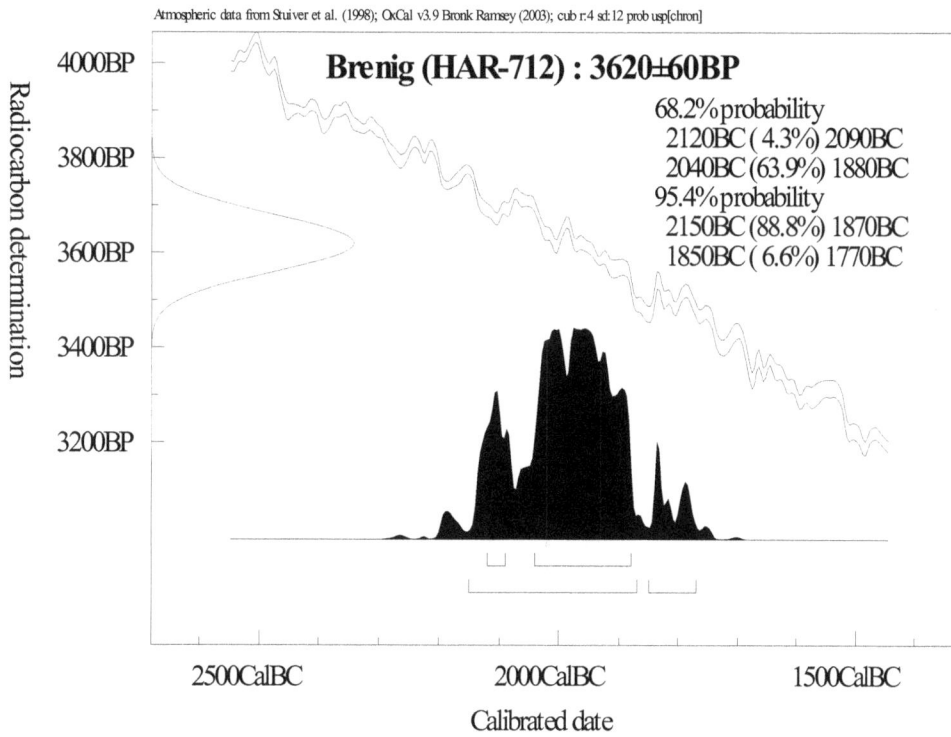

Brenig (HAR-712) : 3620±60BP

68.2% probability
2120BC (4.3%) 2090BC
2040BC (63.9%) 1880BC
95.4% probability
2150BC (88.8%) 1870BC
1850BC (6.6%) 1770BC

Radiocarbon determination

4000BP
3800BP
3600BP
3400BP
3200BP

2500CalBC   2000CalBC   1500CalBC

Calibrated date

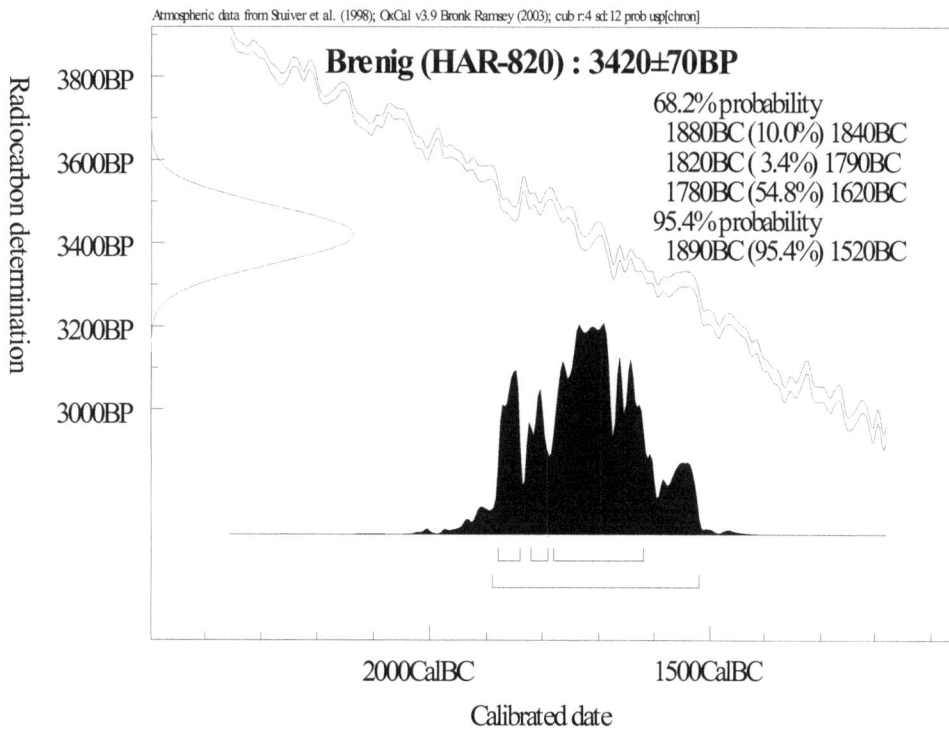

Brenig (HAR-820) : 3420±70BP

68.2% probability
1880BC (10.0%) 1840BC
1820BC (3.4%) 1790BC
1780BC (54.8%) 1620BC
95.4% probability
1890BC (95.4%) 1520BC

Radiocarbon determination

3800BP
3600BP
3400BP
3200BP
3000BP

2000CalBC   1500CalBC

Calibrated date

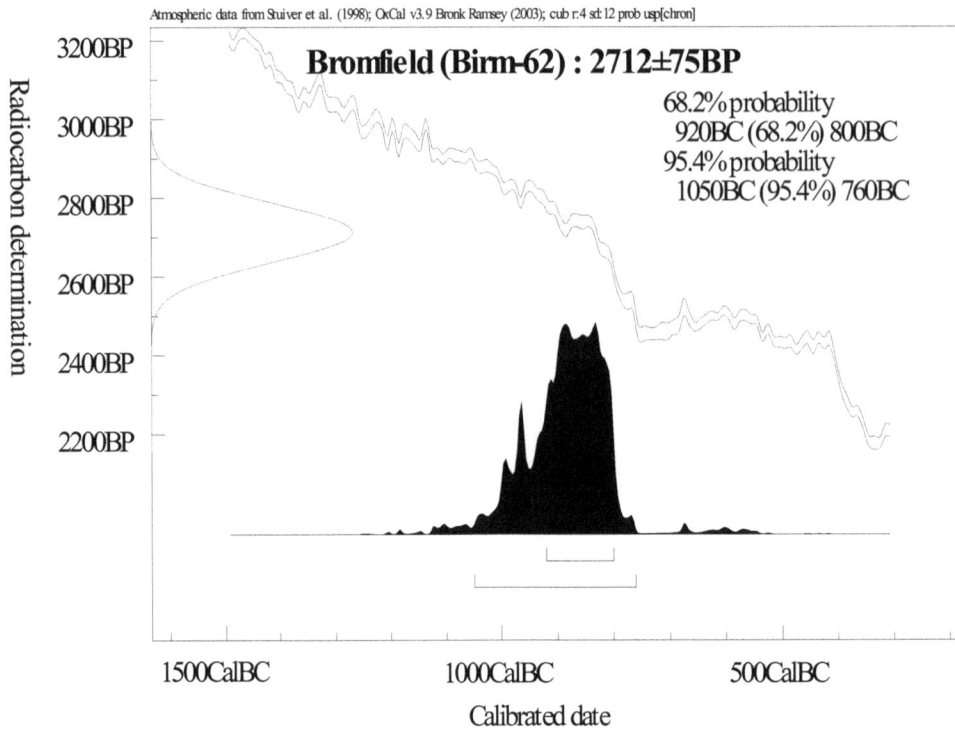

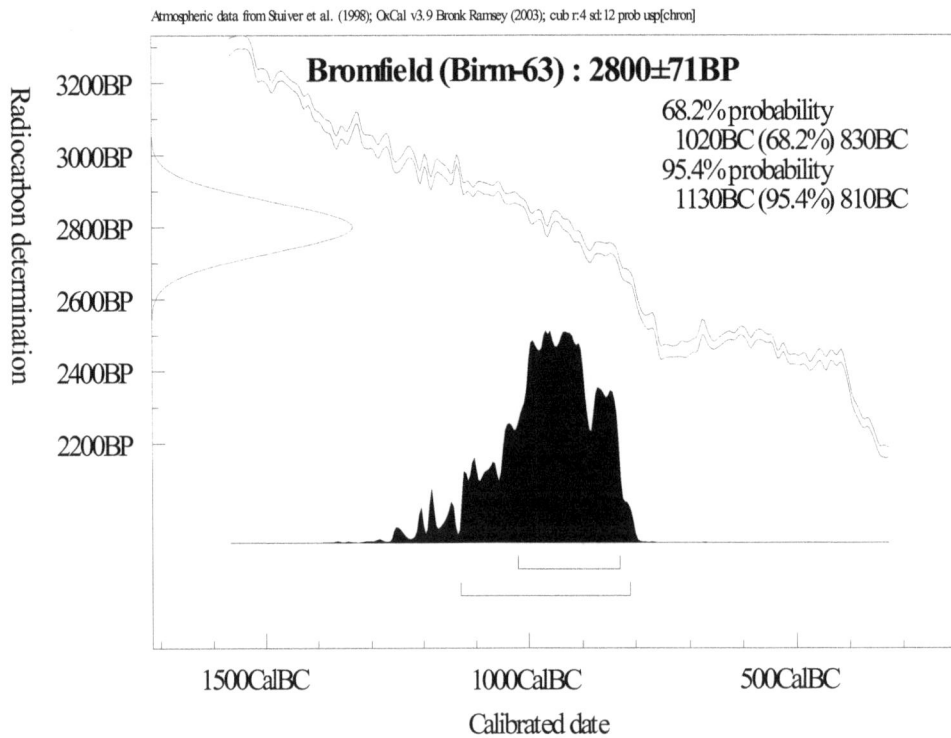

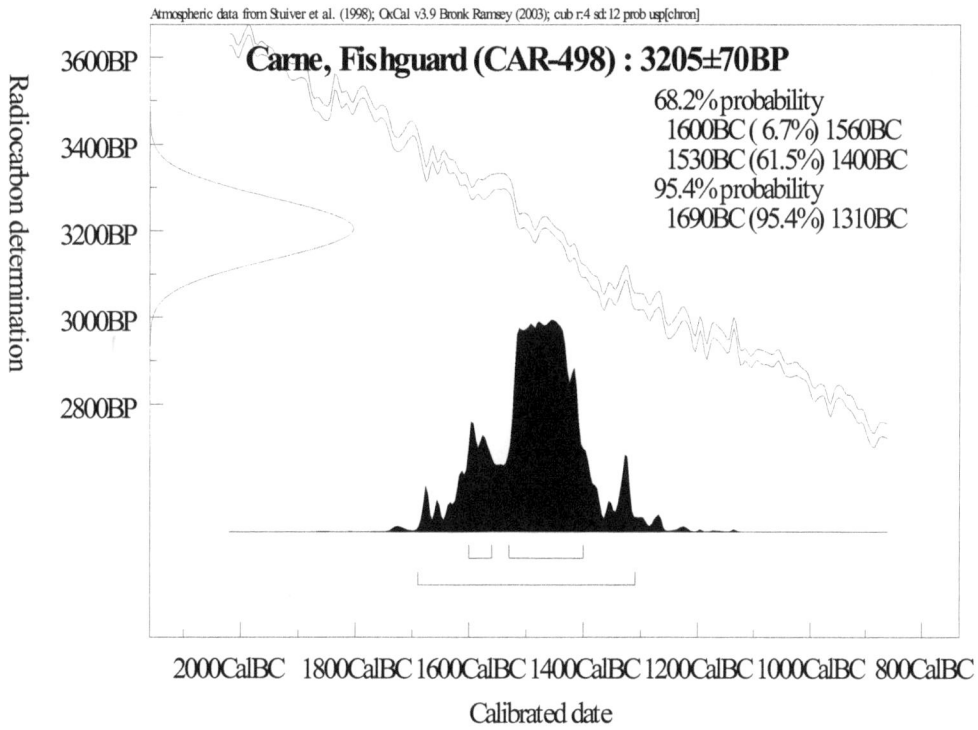

Atmospheric data from Stuiver et al. (1998); OxCal v3.9 Bronk Ramsey (2003); cub r:4 sd:12 prob usp[chron]

Carne, Fishguard (CAR-498) : 3205±70BP

68.2% probability
1600BC (6.7%) 1560BC
1530BC (61.5%) 1400BC
95.4% probability
1690BC (95.4%) 1310BC

Radiocarbon determination

3600BP
3400BP
3200BP
3000BP
2800BP

2000CalBC 1800CalBC 1600CalBC 1400CalBC 1200CalBC 1000CalBC 800CalBC

Calibrated date

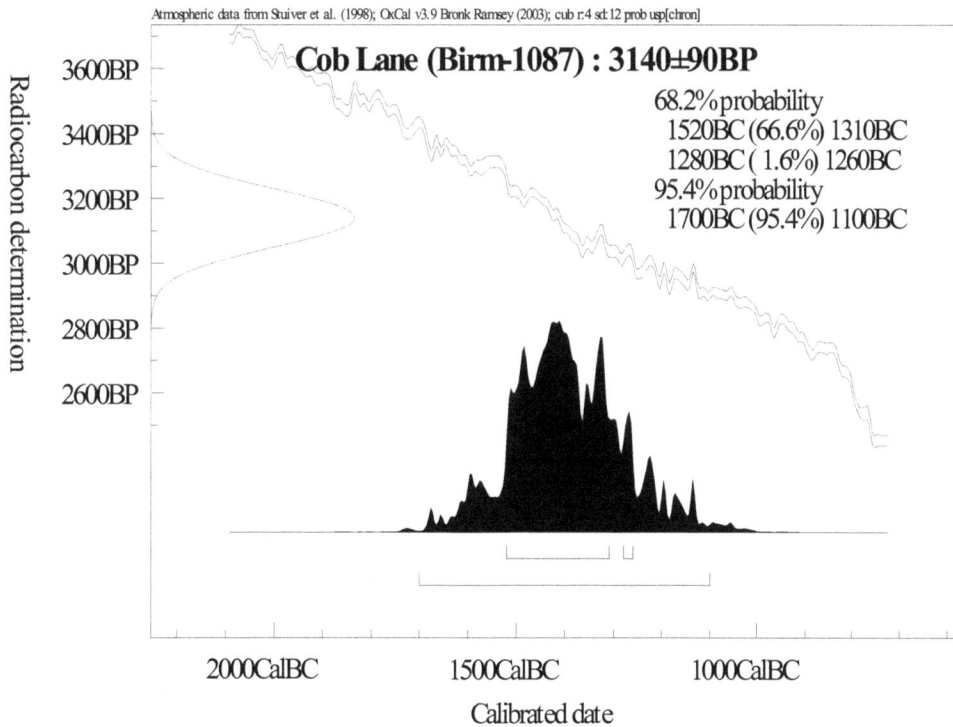

Atmospheric data from Stuiver et al. (1998); OxCal v3.9 Bronk Ramsey (2003); cub r:4 sd:12 prob usp[chron]

Cob Lane (Birm-1087) : 3140±90BP

68.2% probability
1520BC (66.6%) 1310BC
1280BC (1.6%) 1260BC
95.4% probability
1700BC (95.4%) 1100BC

Radiocarbon determination

3600BP
3400BP
3200BP
3000BP
2800BP
2600BP

2000CalBC 1500CalBC 1000CalBC

Calibrated date

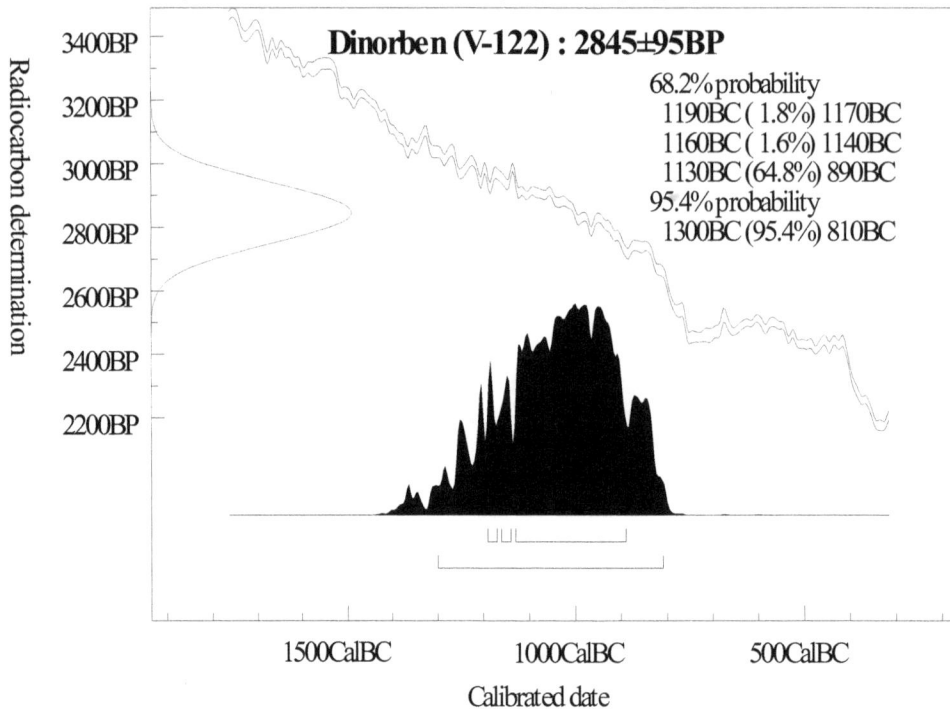

Atmospheric data from Stuiver et al. (1998); OxCal v3.9 Bronk Ramsey (2003); cub r:4 sd:12 prob usp[chron]

Dinorben (V-122) : 2845±95BP

68.2% probability
1190BC (1.8%) 1170BC
1160BC (1.6%) 1140BC
1130BC (64.8%) 890BC
95.4% probability
1300BC (95.4%) 810BC

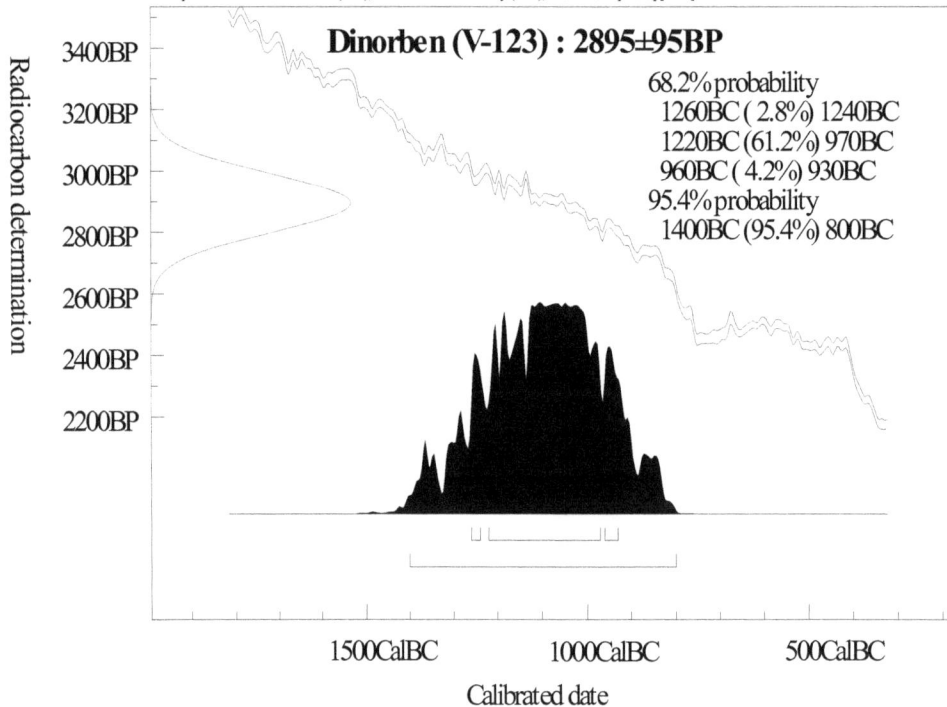

Atmospheric data from Stuiver et al. (1998); OxCal v3.9 Bronk Ramsey (2003); cub r:4 sd:12 prob usp[chron]

Dinorben (V-123) : 2895±95BP

68.2% probability
1260BC (2.8%) 1240BC
1220BC (61.2%) 970BC
960BC (4.2%) 930BC
95.4% probability
1400BC (95.4%) 800BC

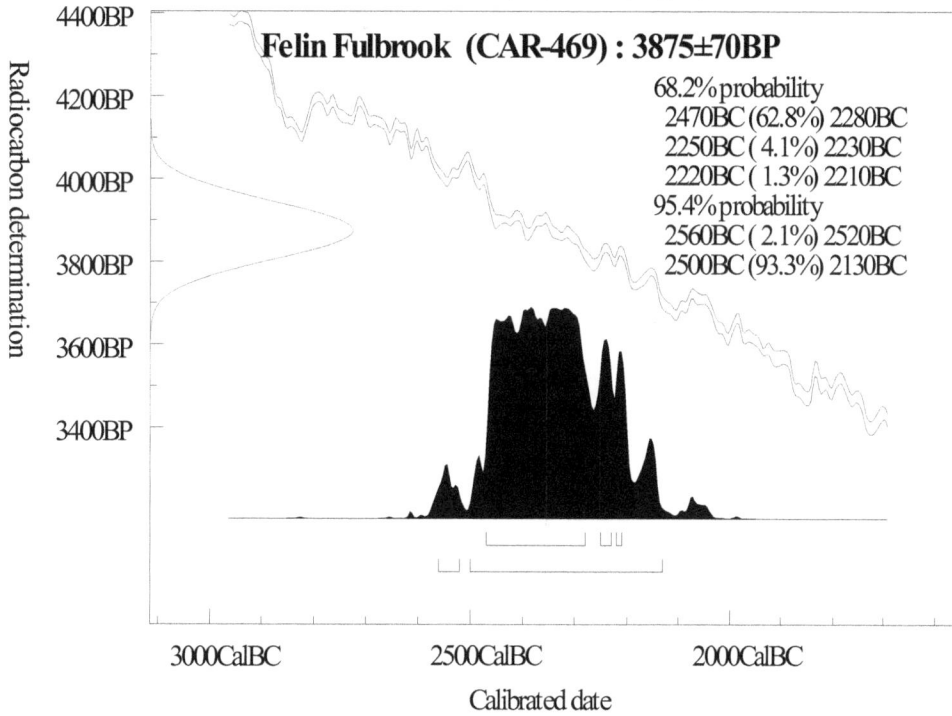

Felin Fulbrook (CAR-469) : 3875±70BP

68.2% probability
2470BC (62.8%) 2280BC
2250BC (4.1%) 2230BC
2220BC (1.3%) 2210BC
95.4% probability
2560BC (2.1%) 2520BC
2500BC (93.3%) 2130BC

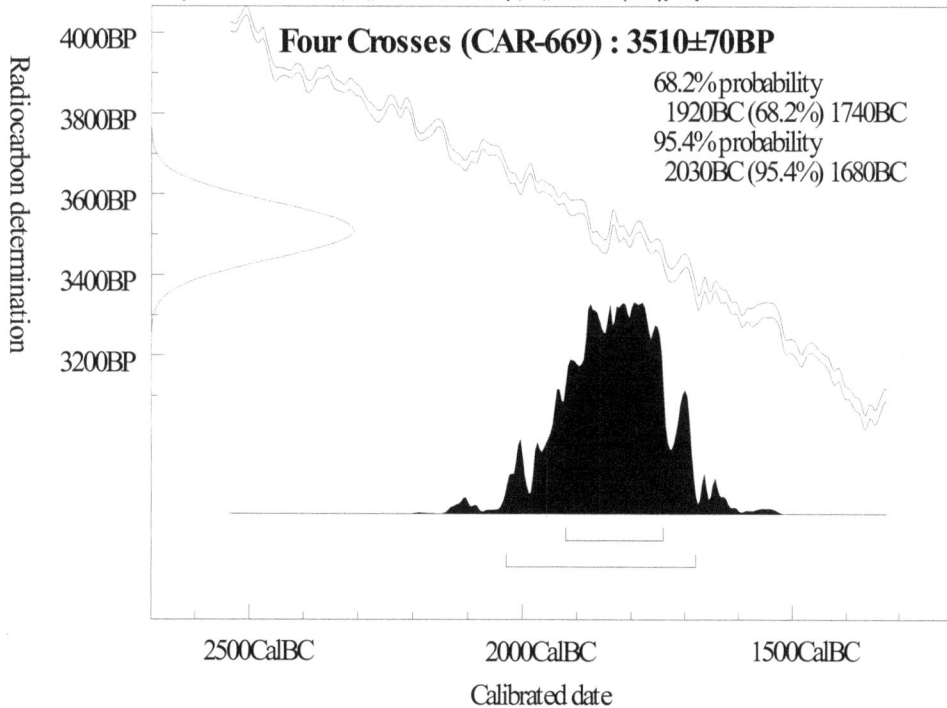

Four Crosses (CAR-669) : 3510±70BP

68.2% probability
1920BC (68.2%) 1740BC
95.4% probability
2030BC (95.4%) 1680BC

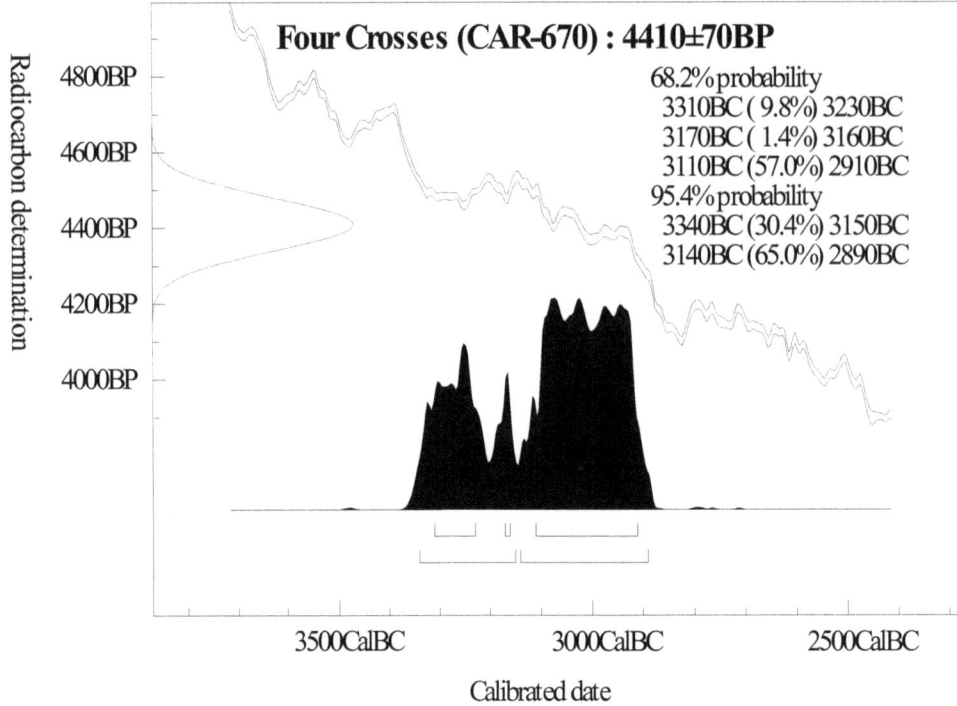

Atmospheric data from Stuiver et al. (1998); OxCal v3.9 Bronk Ramsey (2003); cub r:4 sd:12 prob usp[chron]

Four Crosses (CAR-670) : 4410±70BP

68.2% probability
3310BC (9.8%) 3230BC
3170BC (1.4%) 3160BC
3110BC (57.0%) 2910BC
95.4% probability
3340BC (30.4%) 3150BC
3140BC (65.0%) 2890BC

Radiocarbon determination

4800BP
4600BP
4400BP
4200BP
4000BP

3500CalBC   3000CalBC   2500CalBC

Calibrated date

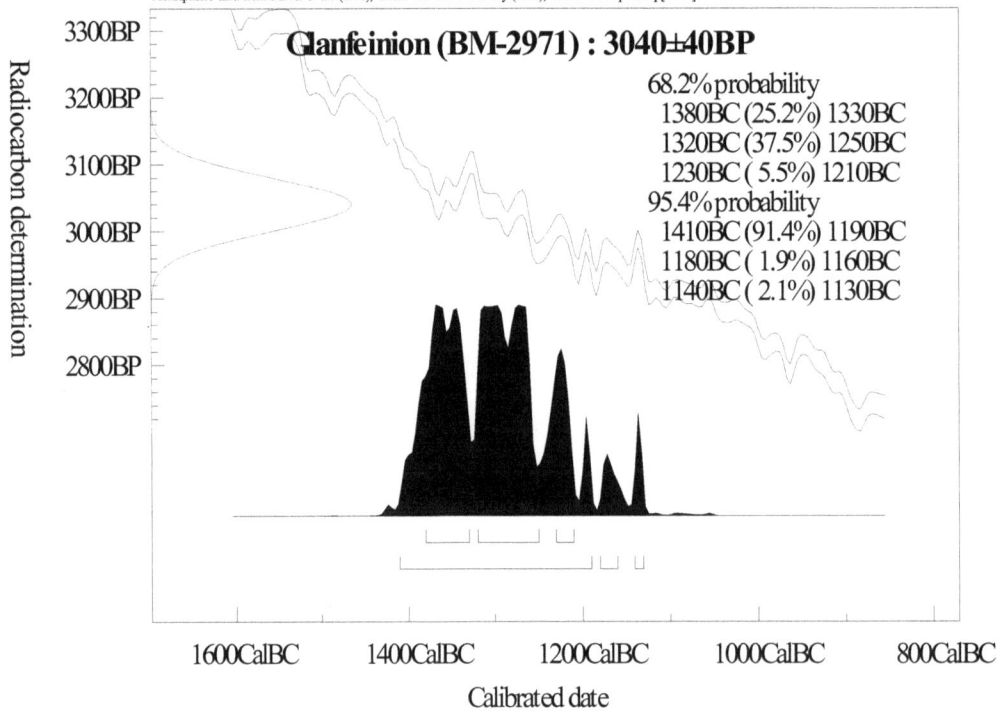

Atmospheric data from Stuiver et al. (1998); OxCal v3.9 Bronk Ramsey (2003); cub r:4 sd:12 prob usp[chron]

Glanfeinion (BM-2971) : 3040±40BP

68.2% probability
1380BC (25.2%) 1330BC
1320BC (37.5%) 1250BC
1230BC (5.5%) 1210BC
95.4% probability
1410BC (91.4%) 1190BC
1180BC (1.9%) 1160BC
1140BC (2.1%) 1130BC

Radiocarbon determination

3300BP
3200BP
3100BP
3000BP
2900BP
2800BP

1600CalBC   1400CalBC   1200CalBC   1000CalBC   800CalBC

Calibrated date

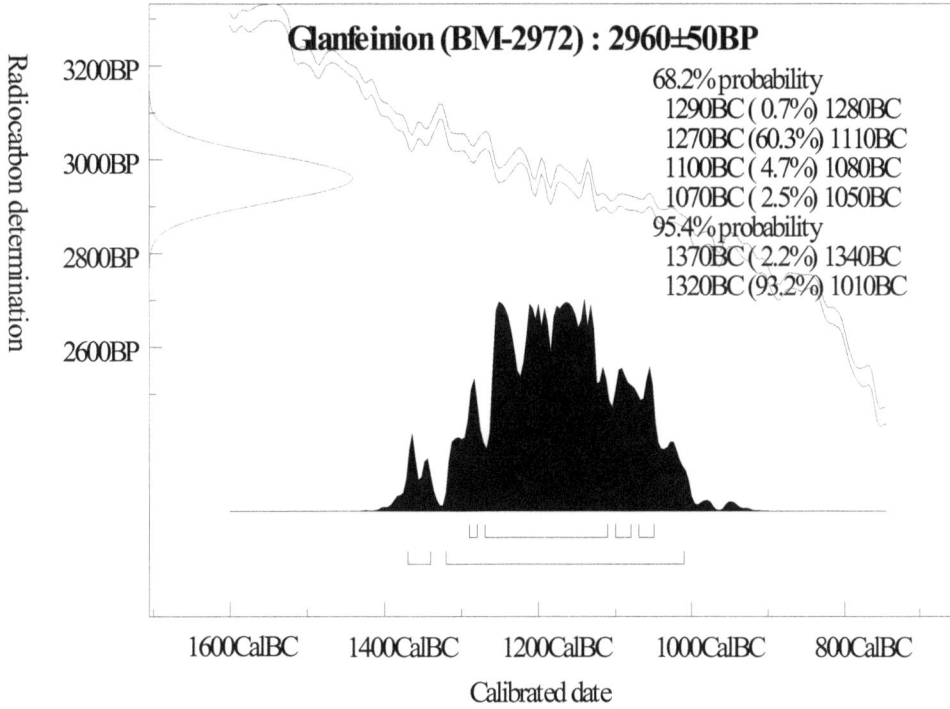

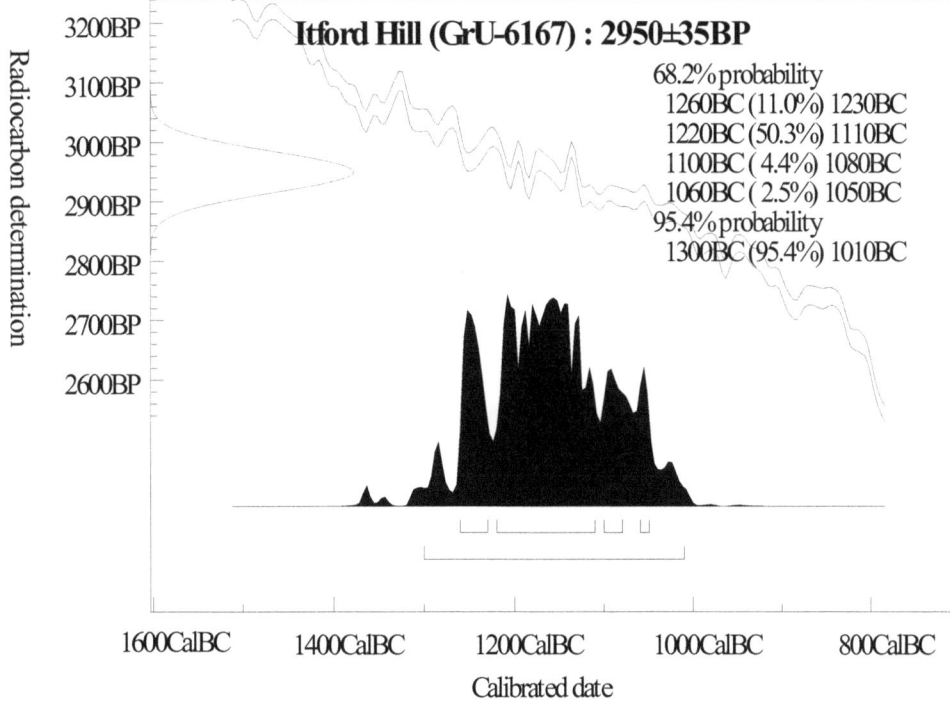

Glanfeinion (BM-2972) : 2960±50BP

68.2% probability
1290BC (0.7%) 1280BC
1270BC (60.3%) 1110BC
1100BC (4.7%) 1080BC
1070BC (2.5%) 1050BC
95.4% probability
1370BC (2.2%) 1340BC
1320BC (93.2%) 1010BC

Radiocarbon determination

3200BP
3000BP
2800BP
2600BP

1600CalBC   1400CalBC   1200CalBC   1000CalBC   800CalBC

Calibrated date

Itford Hill (GrU-6167) : 2950±35BP

68.2% probability
1260BC (11.0%) 1230BC
1220BC (50.3%) 1110BC
1100BC (4.4%) 1080BC
1060BC (2.5%) 1050BC
95.4% probability
1300BC (95.4%) 1010BC

Radiocarbon determination

3200BP
3100BP
3000BP
2900BP
2800BP
2700BP
2600BP

1600CalBC   1400CalBC   1200CalBC   1000CalBC   800CalBC

Calibrated date

91

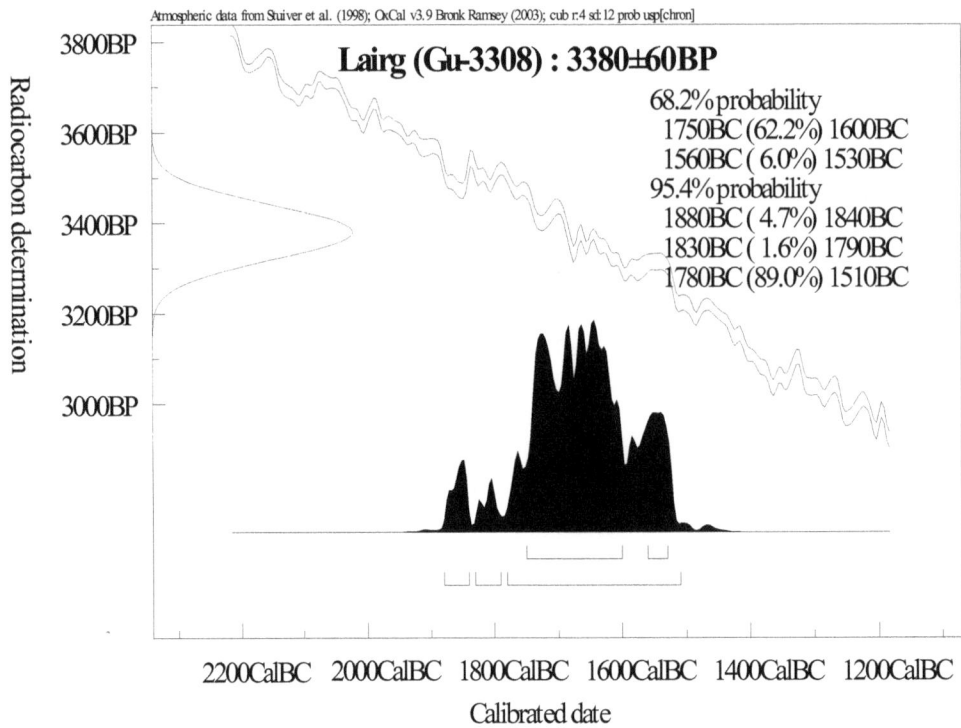

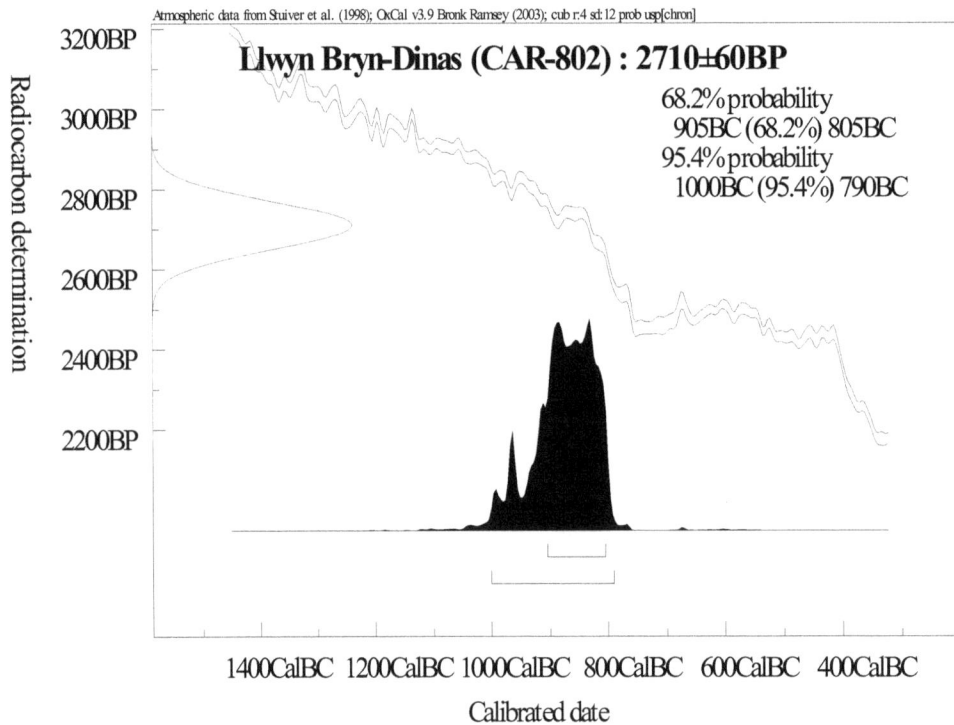

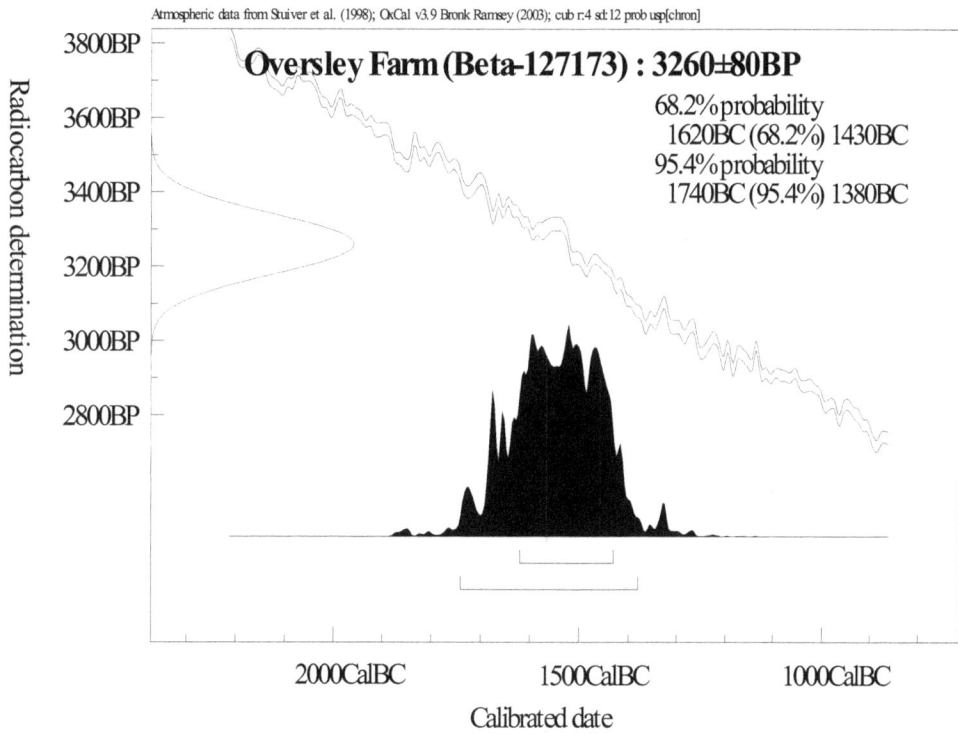

Atmospheric data from Stuiver et al. (1998); OxCal v3.9 Bronk Ramsey (2003); cub r:4 sd:12 prob usp[chron]

Oversley Farm (Beta-127173) : 3260±80BP

68.2% probability
1620BC (68.2%) 1430BC
95.4% probability
1740BC (95.4%) 1380BC

Radiocarbon determination

2000CalBC   1500CalBC   1000CalBC

Calibrated date

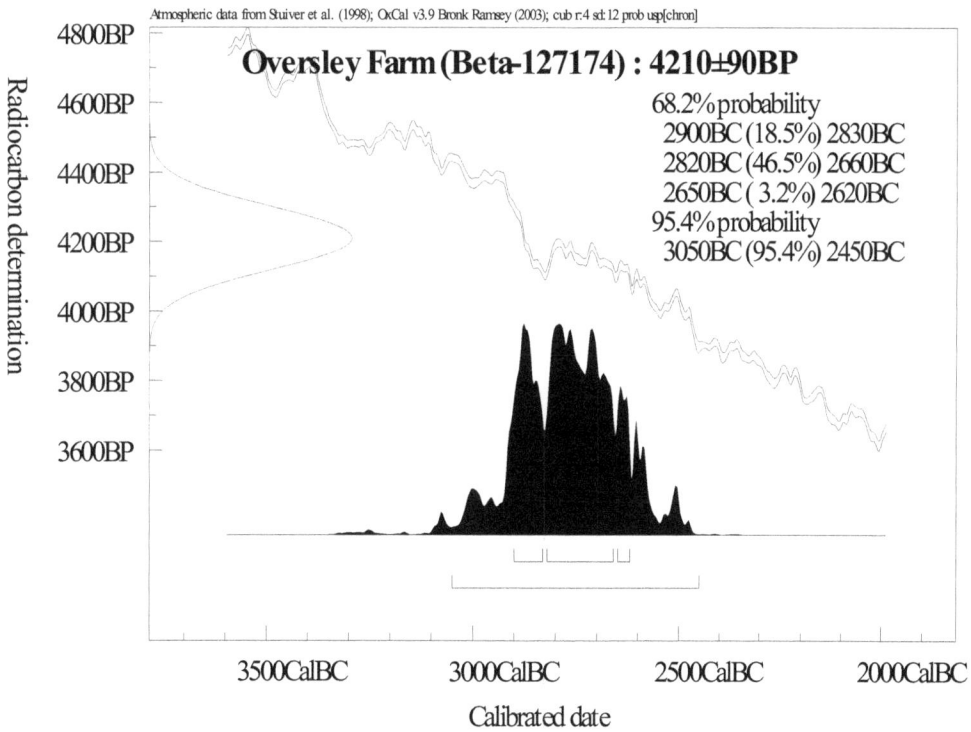

Atmospheric data from Stuiver et al. (1998); OxCal v3.9 Bronk Ramsey (2003); cub r:4 sd:12 prob usp[chron]

Oversley Farm (Beta-127174) : 4210±90BP

68.2% probability
2900BC (18.5%) 2830BC
2820BC (46.5%) 2660BC
2650BC (3.2%) 2620BC
95.4% probability
3050BC (95.4%) 2450BC

Radiocarbon determination

3500CalBC   3000CalBC   2500CalBC   2000CalBC

Calibrated date

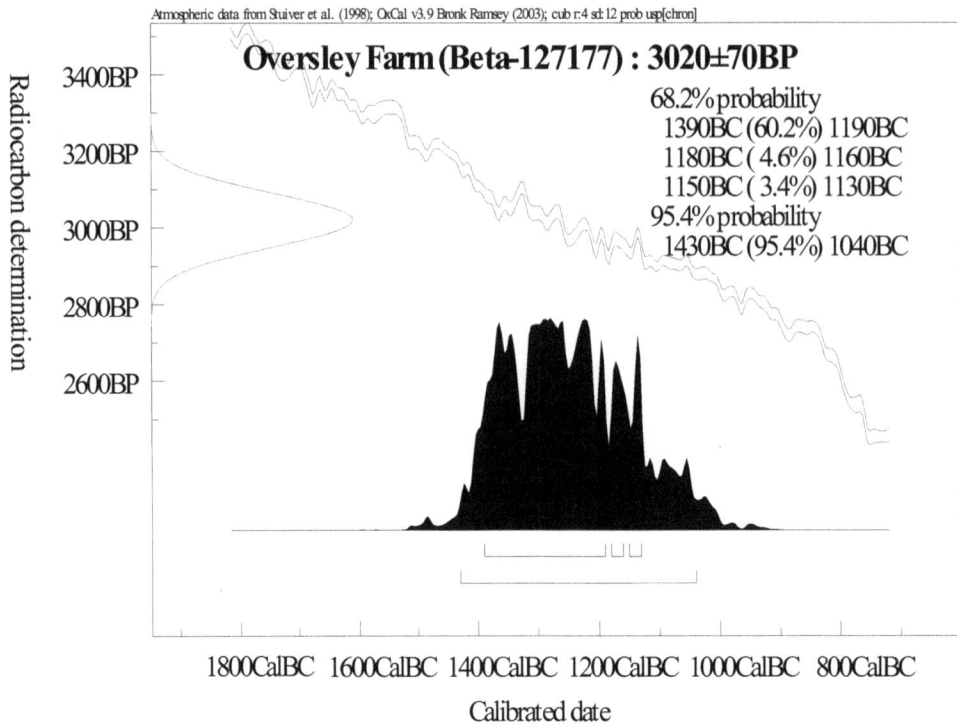

Atmospheric data from Stuiver et al. (1998); OxCal v3.9 Bronk Ramsey (2003); cub r:4 sd:12 prob usp[chron]

Oversley Farm (Beta-127177) : 3020±70BP

68.2% probability
1390BC (60.2%) 1190BC
1180BC (4.6%) 1160BC
1150BC (3.4%) 1130BC
95.4% probability
1430BC (95.4%) 1040BC

3400BP
3200BP
3000BP
2800BP
2600BP

Radiocarbon determination

1800CalBC 1600CalBC 1400CalBC 1200CalBC 1000CalBC 800CalBC

Calibrated date

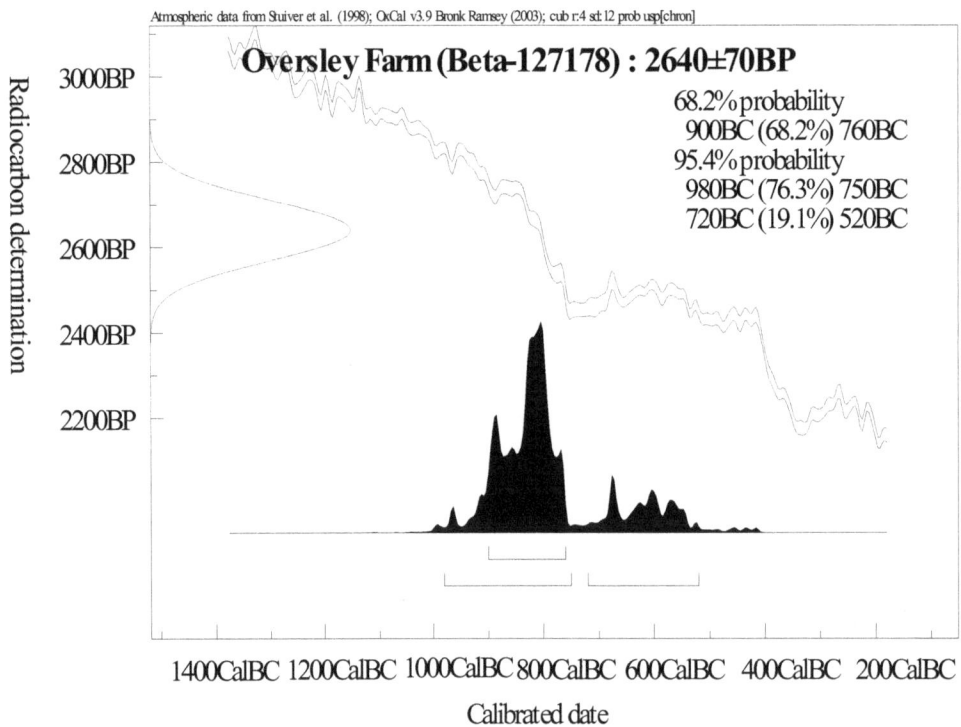

Atmospheric data from Stuiver et al. (1998); OxCal v3.9 Bronk Ramsey (2003); cub r:4 sd:12 prob usp[chron]

Oversley Farm (Beta-127178) : 2640±70BP

68.2% probability
900BC (68.2%) 760BC
95.4% probability
980BC (76.3%) 750BC
720BC (19.1%) 520BC

3000BP
2800BP
2600BP
2400BP
2200BP

Radiocarbon determination

1400CalBC 1200CalBC 1000CalBC 800CalBC 600CalBC 400CalBC 200CalBC

Calibrated date

94

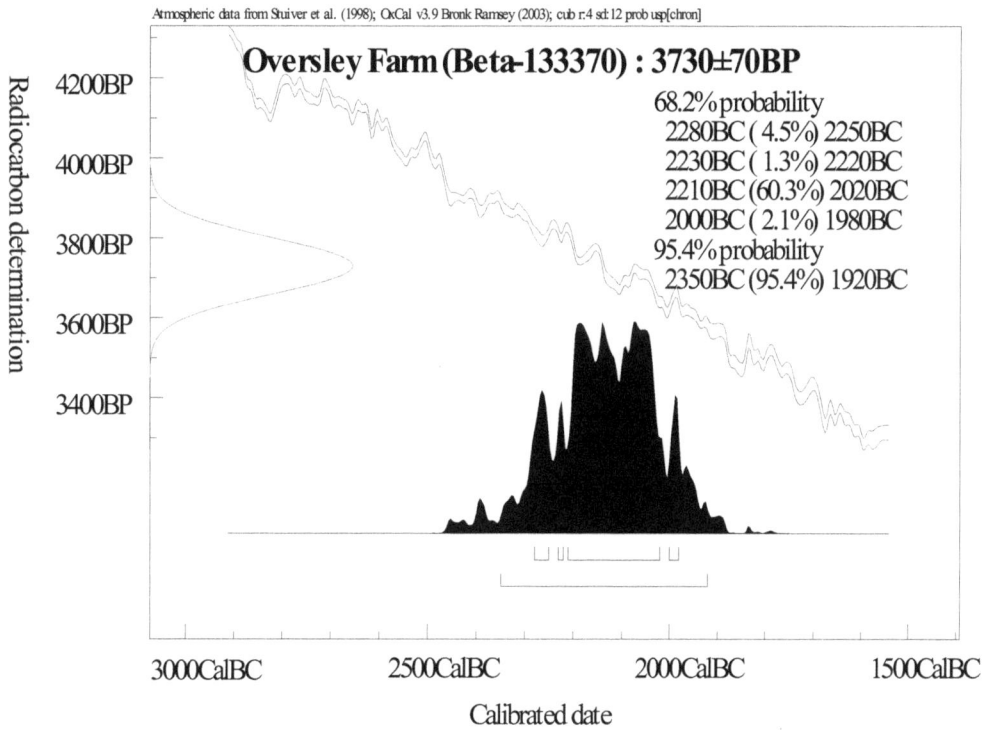

Atmospheric data from Stuiver et al. (1998); OxCal v3.9 Bronk Ramsey (2003); cub r:4 sd:12 prob usp[chron]

Oversley Farm (Beta-133370) : 3730±70BP

68.2% probability
2280BC (4.5%) 2250BC
2230BC (1.3%) 2220BC
2210BC (60.3%) 2020BC
2000BC (2.1%) 1980BC
95.4% probability
2350BC (95.4%) 1920BC

Radiocarbon determination

4200BP
4000BP
3800BP
3600BP
3400BP

3000CalBC   2500CalBC   2000CalBC   1500CalBC

Calibrated date

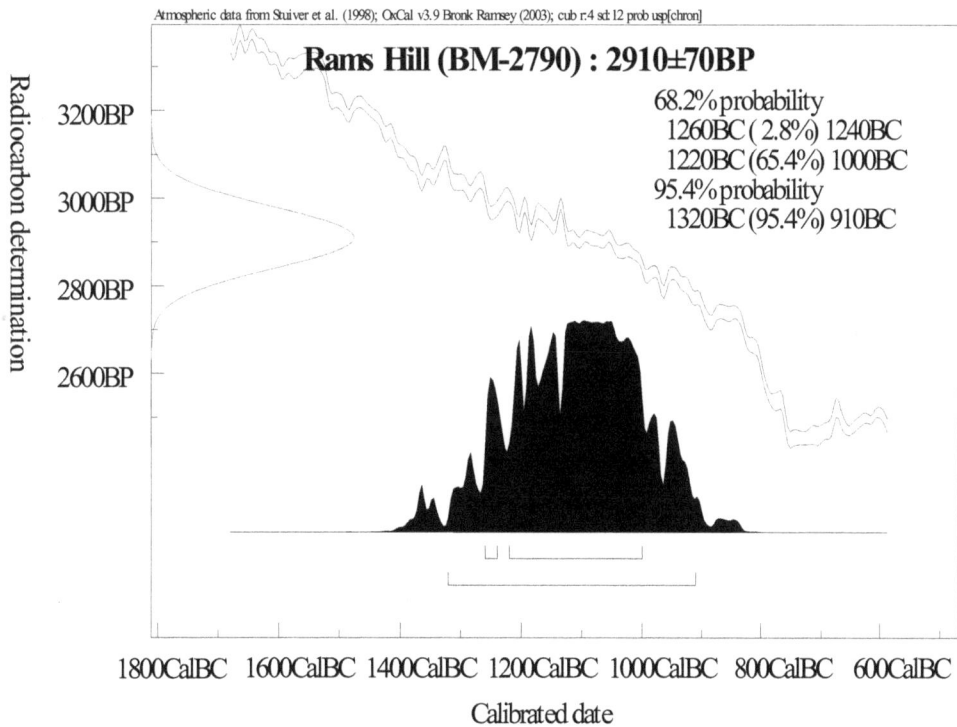

Atmospheric data from Stuiver et al. (1998); OxCal v3.9 Bronk Ramsey (2003); cub r:4 sd:12 prob usp[chron]

Rams Hill (BM-2790) : 2910±70BP

68.2% probability
1260BC (2.8%) 1240BC
1220BC (65.4%) 1000BC
95.4% probability
1320BC (95.4%) 910BC

Radiocarbon determination

3200BP
3000BP
2800BP
2600BP

1800CalBC 1600CalBC 1400CalBC 1200CalBC 1000CalBC 800CalBC 600CalBC

Calibrated date

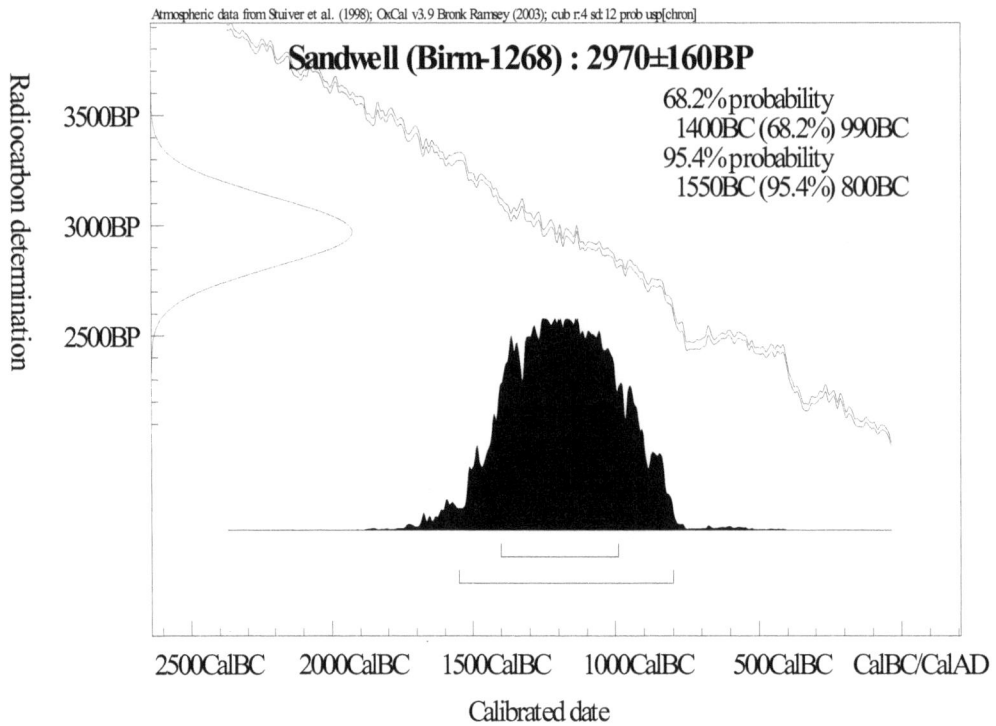

Atmospheric data from Stuiver et al. (1998); OxCal v3.9 Bronk Ramsey (2003); cub r:4 sd:12 prob usp[chron]

Sandwell (Birm-1268) : 2970±160BP

68.2%probability
1400BC (68.2%) 990BC
95.4%probability
1550BC (95.4%) 800BC

Radiocarbon determination

3500BP
3000BP
2500BP

2500CalBC   2000CalBC   1500CalBC   1000CalBC   500CalBC   CalBC/CalAD

Calibrated date

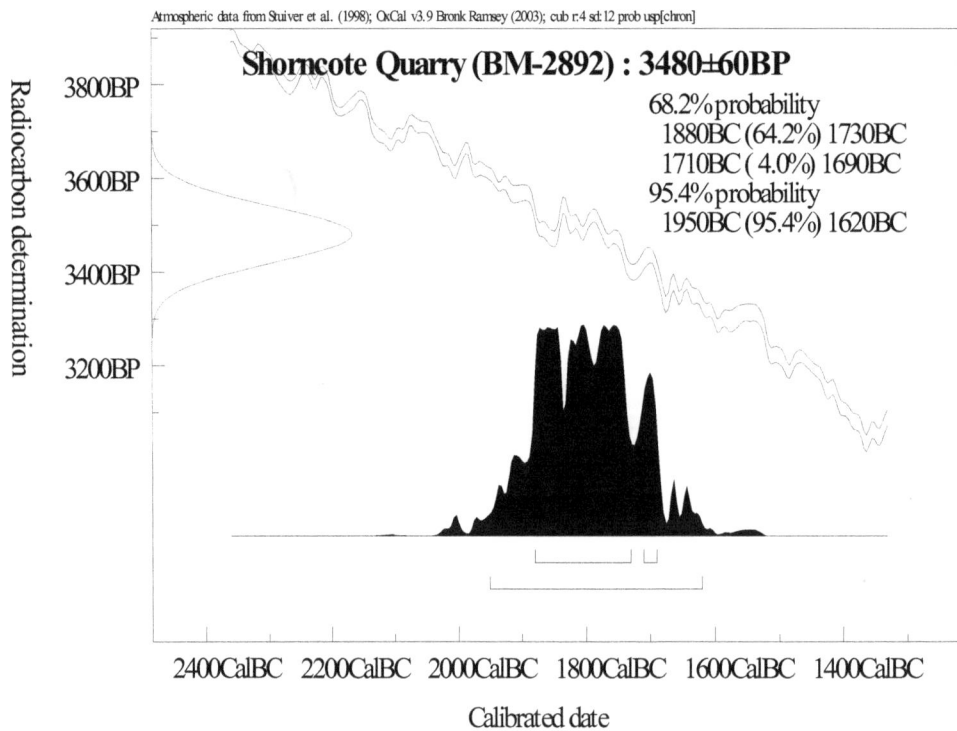

Atmospheric data from Stuiver et al. (1998); OxCal v3.9 Bronk Ramsey (2003); cub r:4 sd:12 prob usp[chron]

Shorncote Quarry (BM-2892) : 3480±60BP

68.2%probability
1880BC (64.2%) 1730BC
1710BC (4.0%) 1690BC
95.4%probability
1950BC (95.4%) 1620BC

Radiocarbon determination

3800BP
3600BP
3400BP
3200BP

2400CalBC   2200CalBC   2000CalBC   1800CalBC   1600CalBC   1400CalBC

Calibrated date

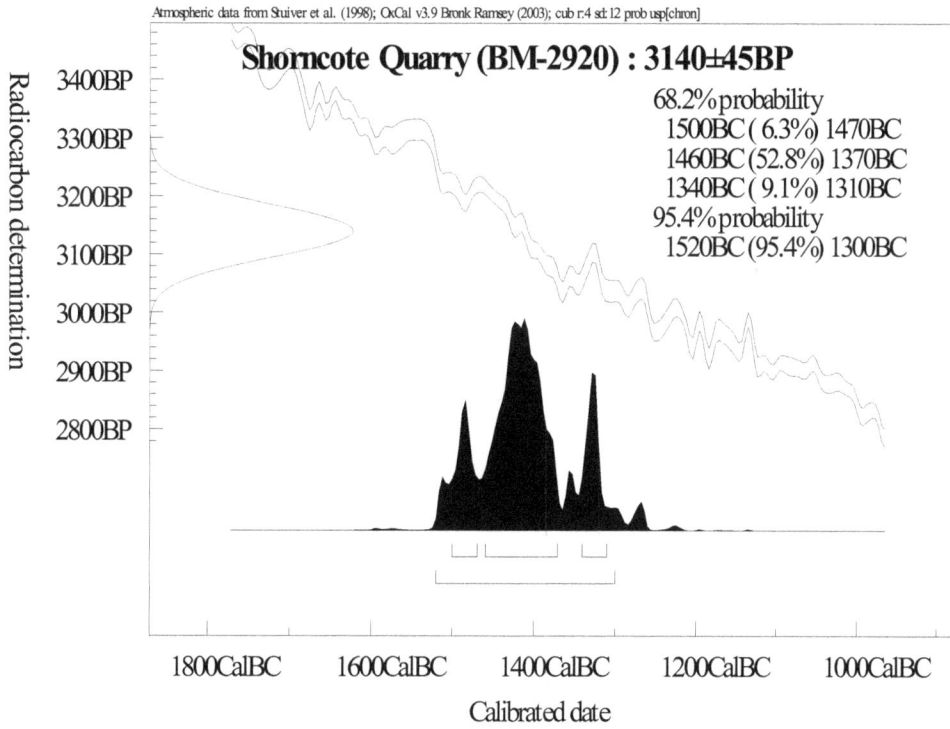

Atmospheric data from Stuiver et al. (1998); OxCal v3.9 Bronk Ramsey (2003); cub r:4 sd:12 prob usp[chron]

Shorncote Quarry (BM-2920) : 3140±45BP

68.2% probability
1500BC (6.3%) 1470BC
1460BC (52.8%) 1370BC
1340BC (9.1%) 1310BC
95.4% probability
1520BC (95.4%) 1300BC

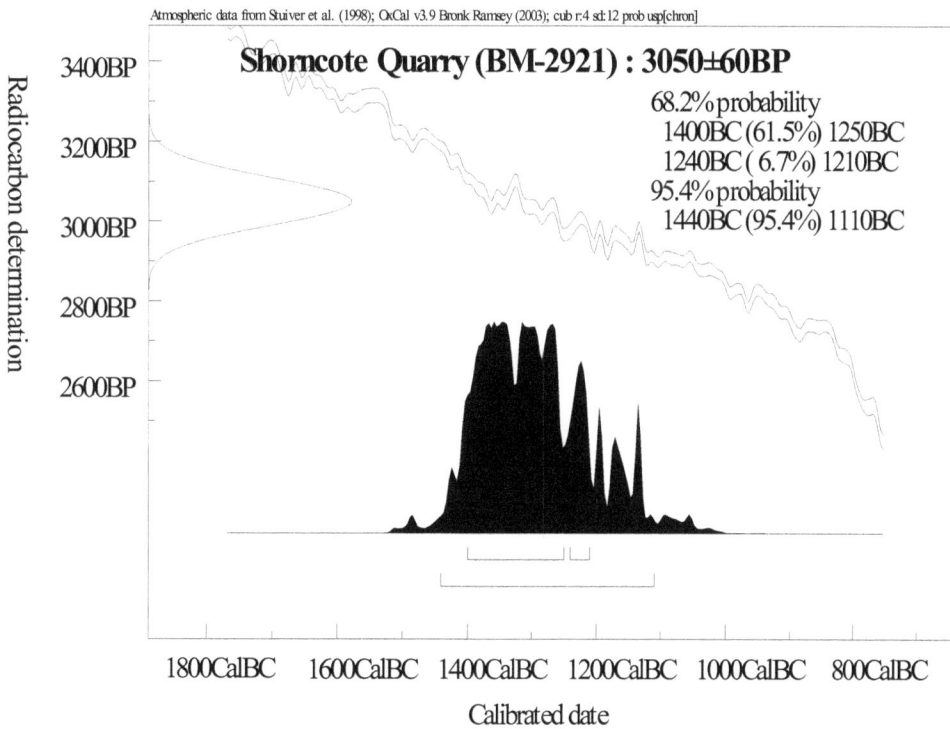

Atmospheric data from Stuiver et al. (1998); OxCal v3.9 Bronk Ramsey (2003); cub r:4 sd:12 prob usp[chron]

Shorncote Quarry (BM-2921) : 3050±60BP

68.2% probability
1400BC (61.5%) 1250BC
1240BC (6.7%) 1210BC
95.4% probability
1440BC (95.4%) 1110BC

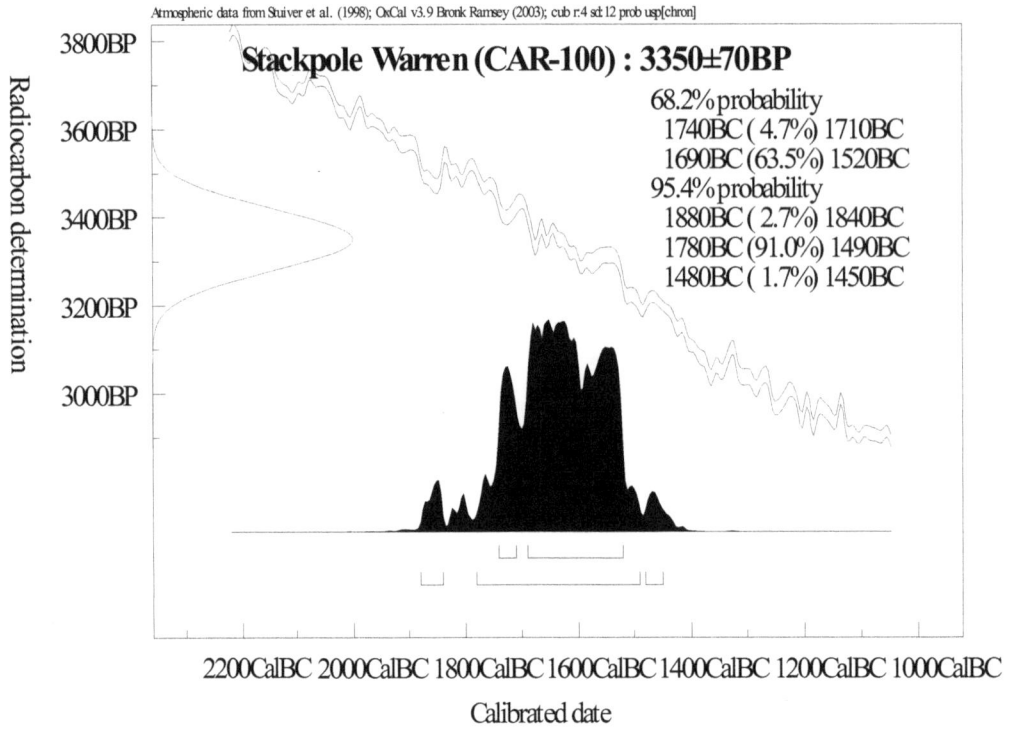

Atmospheric data from Stuiver et al. (1998); OxCal v3.9 Bronk Ramsey (2003); cub r:4 sd:12 prob usp[chron]

Stackpole Warren (CAR-100) : 3350±70BP

68.2% probability
1740BC (4.7%) 1710BC
1690BC (63.5%) 1520BC
95.4% probability
1880BC (2.7%) 1840BC
1780BC (91.0%) 1490BC
1480BC (1.7%) 1450BC

Radiocarbon determination

3800BP
3600BP
3400BP
3200BP
3000BP

2200CalBC 2000CalBC 1800CalBC 1600CalBC 1400CalBC 1200CalBC 1000CalBC

Calibrated date

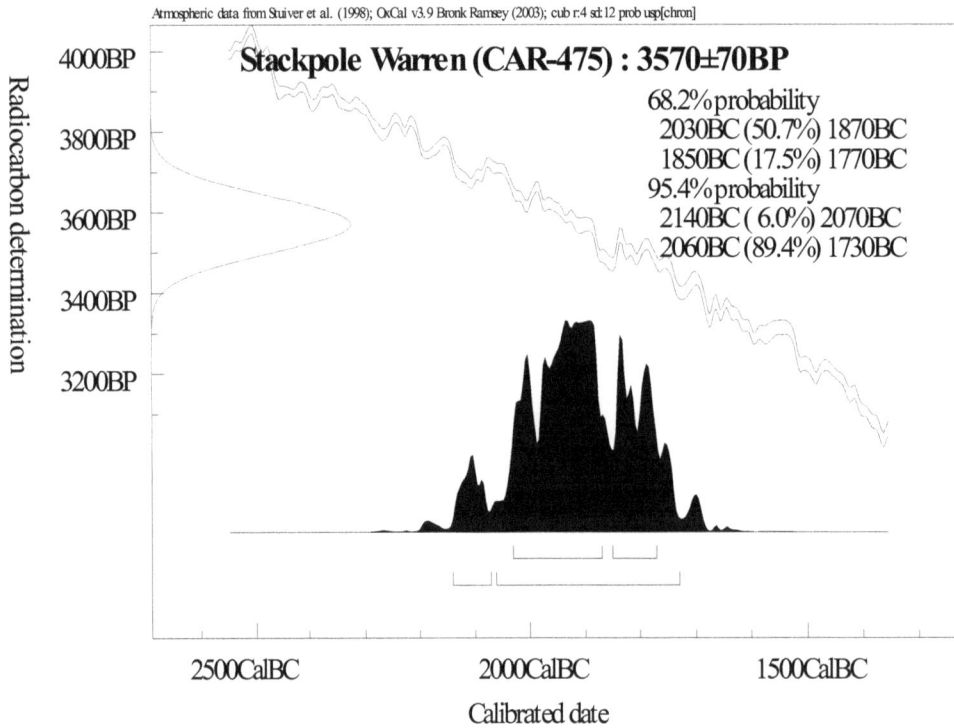

Atmospheric data from Stuiver et al. (1998); OxCal v3.9 Bronk Ramsey (2003); cub r:4 sd:12 prob usp[chron]

Stackpole Warren (CAR-475) : 3570±70BP

68.2% probability
2030BC (50.7%) 1870BC
1850BC (17.5%) 1770BC
95.4% probability
2140BC (6.0%) 2070BC
2060BC (89.4%) 1730BC

Radiocarbon determination

4000BP
3800BP
3600BP
3400BP
3200BP

2500CalBC 2000CalBC 1500CalBC

Calibrated date

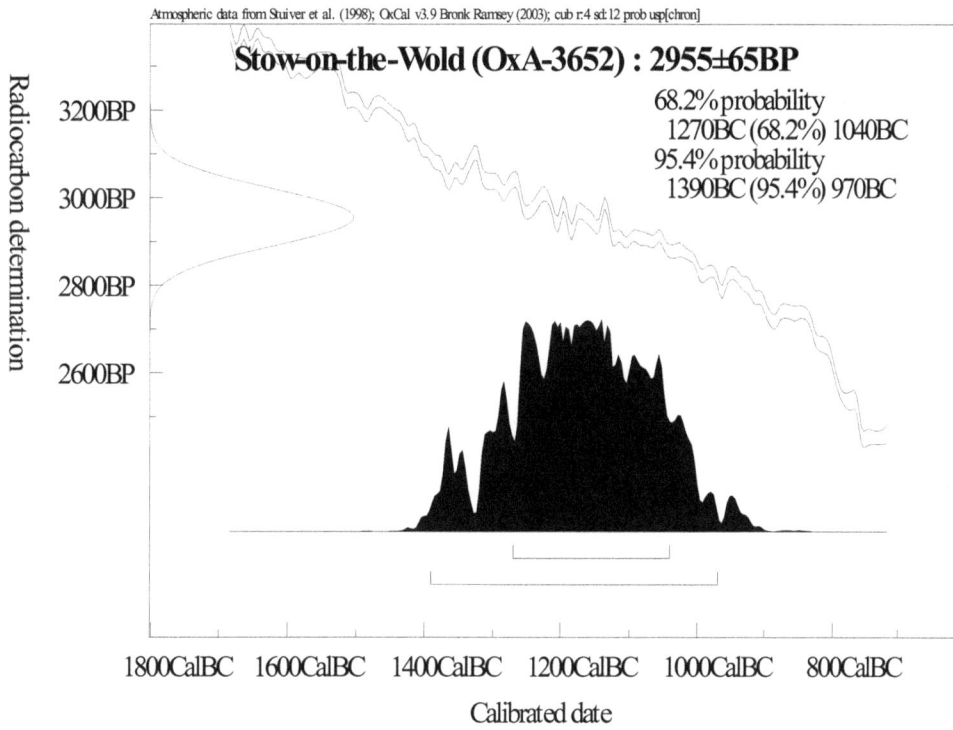

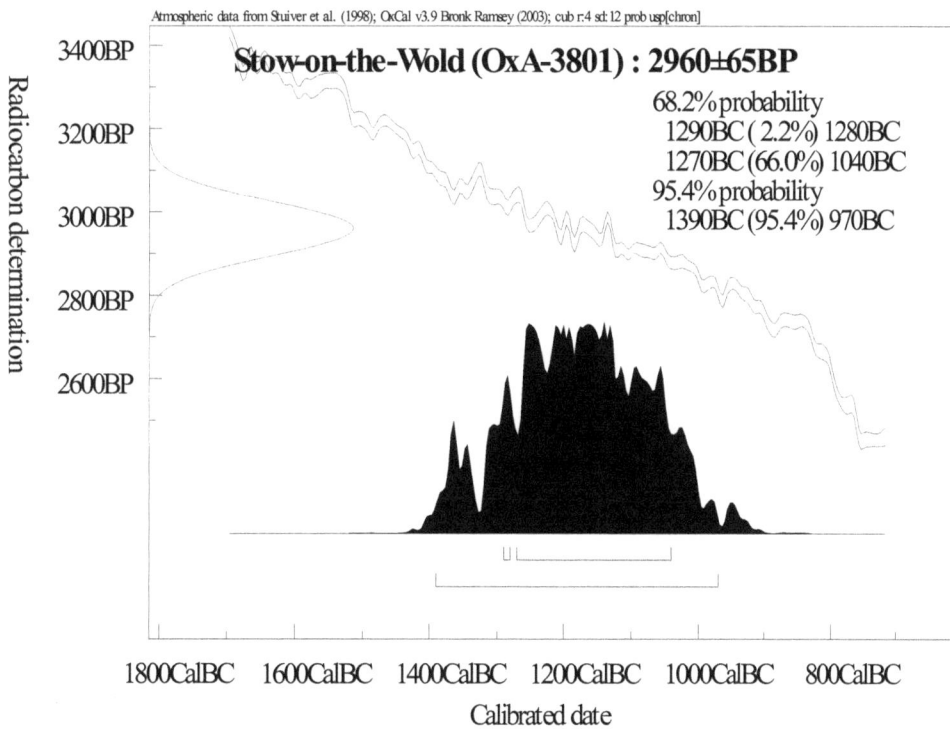

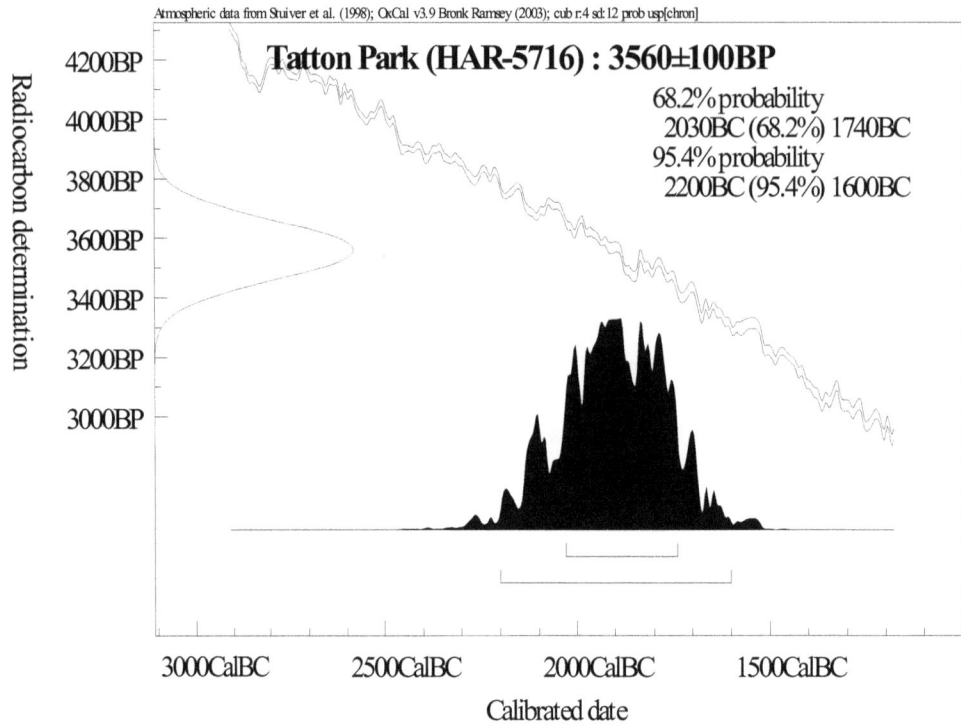

www.ingramcontent.com/pod-product-compliance
Lightning Source LLC
Chambersburg PA
CBHW061009030426
42334CB00033B/3421